ANNAPURNA
A WOMAN'S PLACE

ANNAPURNA

A WOMAN'S PLACE

ARLENE BLUM

FOREWORD BY
MAURICE HERZOG

Sierra Club Books
San Francisco

The Sierra Club, founded in 1892 by John Muir, has devoted itself to the study and protection of the earth's scenic and ecological resources—mountains, wetlands, woodlands, wild shores and rivers, deserts and plains. The publishing program of the Sierra Club offers books to the public as a nonprofit educational service in the hope that they may enlarge the public's understanding of the Club's basic concerns. The point of view expressed in each book, however, does not necessarily represent that of the Club. The Sierra Club has some fifty chapters coast to coast, in Canada, Hawaii, and Alaska. For information about how you may participate in its programs to preserve wilderness and the quality of life, please address inquiries to Sierra Club, 730 Polk Street, San Francisco, CA 94109.

Copyright © 1980 by Arlene Blum

Annapurna: A Woman's Place was first published in hardcover by Sierra Club Books in 1980. First softcover edition: 1983.

Library of Congress Cataloging in Publication Data

Blum, Arlene, 1945–
  Annapurna: a woman's place.

Bibliography: p. 246
  Includes index.
  1. Mountaineering—Nepal—Annapurna.   2. Women mountaineers—United States—Biography.   3. Annapurna—Description.   I. Title.
GV199.44.N462A563   796.5′22′095496   80–13288
ISBN 0–87156–236–7
    0–87156–806–3 (pbk.)

Sierra Club Books staff and freelance personnel for this book:
  Editor   Diana Landau
  Production   Eileen Max and Susan Ristow
  Book Design   Paula Schlosser
  Cover Design   Bonnie Smetts
  Proofreading   Rosemary Nightengale
  Maps   Dee Molenaar

Printed in the United States of America on acid-free paper containing 50% recycled fiber with 10% post-consumer waste
10   9   8   7

In memory of Vera Watson, Alison Chadwick-Onyszkiewicz, and Joan Firey

Contents

Foreword

Reading this book has stirred my deepest feelings. This is partly because of the dramatic memories that link me to Annapurna, of course. But I confess that the touching account of this adventure, in which two of the heroines reached the summit and two others lost their lives, moved me to tears.

The straightforward style, lively tone, and poignant details of Arlene Blum's book succeed wonderfully in making the reader a participant. For example, I couldn't help but laugh when, during the plane ride to Nepal, the last of the 15,000 T-shirts sold to finance the expedition was stretched—despite its tiny size—onto a colossal Sikh. The frequent posturing and lack of cooperation by the Sherpas filled me with indignation. I rejoiced with the team when the summit was reached. Finally, my throat tightened with anxiety and sorrow when the two climbers disappeared, and the others had to face the fact that they would never return.

When some of our contemporaries judge women to be incapable of exceptional achievement, I feel we must still be living in the Middle Ages. Why shouldn't women be chiefs of state, Nobel prize winners, heads of multinational corporations, legendary heroines? They have been in the past, and will be in the future. And I can't accept that part of their fame is due only to the fact that they are women.

The reasons given to prove women's inferiority are simply not credible. They are not facts, but prejudice—prejudice which has burdened mankind for thousands of years. To my way of thinking, we are dealing here with fundamental human rights. After all, we quite properly struggle to protect individual freedom from bigotry of all kinds and from all the old taboos that poison society. All the more reason, then, to oppose the most commonplace and perhaps the worst form of discrimination. Ensuring that women have the opportunity to attain the highest positions in our society must be the object of a revolution that is quiet, deep, and, above all, natural.

In this regard, I am happy to salute the accomplishment of Arlene and her companions. They too have conquered their Annapurna. I am convinced this success will lead to further triumphs by women in the fields of adventure, exploration, and discovery.

Any act of courage and sacrifice performed with passion, or in the service of a great cause, commands respect and admiration. But, however significant, its impact would be lost without a chronicle as authentic as this one. Readers will surely be as moved as I was. For what she has given all of us, I owe Arlene my sincere gratitude.

Maurice Herzog

(Translated from French by William Rodarmor)

Translator's note: Maurice Herzog is best known for his leadership of the French expedition which made the first ascent of Annapurna in 1950. A former Minister of Sports, he currently represents the Haute-Savoie district in France's Assemblée Nationale.

Preface

This book is a personal account of a public adventure. The 1978 American Women's Himalayan Expedition to Annapurna I could never have taken place without the support of hundreds, indeed, thousands, of people. I would like to thank them all, in particular the volunteers who worked so hard to give us the opportunity to attempt the climb, and the numerous companies and individuals who contributed equipment, food, and money. The National Geographic Society supported us from the beginning, when most people were skeptical about whether we would ever get to Nepal, let alone climb a mountain. Special thanks to the porters and Sherpas who worked for the expedition, to Mike Cheney, the staff of the Sherpa Cooperative, Douglas and Ernie Heck, and to the gracious Nepalese people who made us feel welcome and made it possible for us to reach our goal.

A number of editors and friends helped this book into being. The other twelve Annapurna team members made their diaries available and commented on the many drafts. The writing might never have been accomplished without the valuable advice and encouragement of my good friend Martha Coulton. Diana Landau, my editor at Sierra Club Books, Jessie Wood, Leslye Russell, and Jay Stewart worked on the entire manuscript. Marcy McGaugh accurately typed the many drafts, and my agent, Felicia Eth, provided wise counsel and encouragement. Mary Jean Haley, Linda Fletcher, Betsy White, Carolyn Strauss, Debbie Gage, and John Percival contributed to the earlier chapters. Ingeborg Prochazka helped research the bibliography using the excellent libraries of Nick Clinch and Dick Irvin. Mary Lynn Hanley, Steve Bezruchka, Diane and Edwin Bernbaum, Anna Ferroluzzi, Christine Harris, Karil Frohboese, Joel Bown, Ignacio Tinoco, and Susan Coons made many pertinent suggestions on the final draft. Lastly, I would like to thank John Henry Hall and Fred Ayres, who first taught me about the mountains and never at any time suggested that women are not supposed to climb high.

We did not organize the Annapurna expedition to prove that women could climb high mountains. We knew that before we began. But the publicized success of the venture brought that message to people all over the world.

For us it was a bittersweet victory, and its aftereffects have been complex. The deaths of our dear friends Vera Watson and Alison Chadwick-Onyszkiewicz have cast long shadows into our lives. Since separating as a team, each of us has had to deal in her own way with the adjustments of resuming a normal life after this extraordinarily intense experience. For me, the writing of this book has occupied eighteen months—a time spent focused on those three months in Nepal, trying to understand why we went there, what we experienced, and what we learned. Just as my comprehension is imperfect, so too is the telling. But I trust the result will provide some insight into how and why Annapurna became "a woman's place."

Arlene Blum
Berkeley, California
April, 1980

At this moment I am with no one
in my past   even the wind
is blowing somewhere else
Inside me I feel
something willing
I want to write it here

from "Climbing Aconcagua"
by Frances Mayes
(dedicated to Vera Watson)

Introduction

E arly in 1969 I applied to participate in a climbing expedition to Afghanistan. One of the members assured me that because I had more high-altitude experience than the other applicants, I was certain to be invited. For months I heard nothing; finally I received the following response from the expedition leader:

Re: Koh-i-Marchech (21,200')

Dear Miss Blum:

Not too easy a letter to write as your prior work in Peru demonstrates your ability to go high, and a source I trust has furnished a glowing account of your pleasant nature in the mountains.

But one woman and nine men would seem to me to be unpleasant high on the open ice, not only in excretory situations, but in the easy masculine companionship which is so vital a part of the joy of an expedition.

Sorry as hell.

That summer I went on a guided climb of Mount Waddington in British Columbia and was informed by our climbing guide that "there are no good women climbers. Women climbers either aren't good climbers, or they aren't real women."

Not long after that I received an advertisement for a commercial climb of Mount McKinley, on which "women are invited to join the party at base and advanced base to assist in the cooking chores. Special rates are available. They will not be admitted on the climbs, however." When I asked why not, I was informed that women are a liability in the high mountains: they are not strong enough to carry their share of the loads and lack the emotional stability to withstand the psychological stresses of a high-altitude climb.

And so I was introduced to the issue of whether women can or should climb high mountains. Other women climbers have told me of similar experiences. The subject of women's ability in the high mountains has elicited a wide variety of commentary from sources as disparate as Sir Edmund Hillary and the late Chairman Mao Tse-Tung. In 1975 seven Chinese women climbed above 8,000 meters on Mount Everest and one of them, Phanthog, a Tibetan, reached the summit. The chairman acknowledged this accomplishment with the statement:

> Times have changed, and today men and women are equal. Whatever men comrades can accomplish, women comrades can too. (*Another Ascent of the World's Highest Peak—Qomolangma*, 1975.)

Although Sir Edmund agrees that times have changed, the conclusion he draws is quite different:

> Wives have changed since the 1940s and 50s when I began going off on expeditions. In those days one expected a wife to stay at home caring for small children and in general keeping the home fires burning. Times have changed. I find increasingly when wives are around, I need to treat them with some circumspection if I happen to be proposing a new trip . . . the problems and dissensions in multinational expeditions pale into insignificance compared with those that can be brought about by a single woman in a party. (Sir Edmund Hillary, *From the Ocean to the Sky*, 1979.)

Some men seem to have no objections to all-woman expeditions but are strongly opposed to those in which both sexes participate. When Irene Miller, a member of our 1978 Annapurna expedition, joined Hillary's 1961 Makalu expedition at the base camp, one expedition member suggested a rather peculiar rationale for excluding her from the climbing: "If you want to climb with the expedition, you ought to be willing to sleep with all the men on the team."

Other objections to mixed expeditions have been raised, some more valid than others. In the past women have frequently been invited on expeditions because they were married to a team member rather than because of their climbing credentials. To include an unqualified woman as a climbing member of an expedition does a disservice to both the individual and the cause of women's climbing. Even if well-qualified, a lone woman on an expedition is usually subject to continual scrutiny and evaluation. This pressure can make a good performance more difficult for even the most competent climber and may even impel her to try too hard.

In addition to those who claim that women aren't good enough to participate in high-altitude mountaineering, there are others who argue that women are *too* good—the classic double bind. This contradiction is illustrated by the following comment from my friend Grant Barnes, a climber and former chairman of the American Alpine Club's Publications Committee:

> High-altitude climbing, with its awful one-in-ten death rate, may be the most dehumanizing of all noncontact sports, the most absurd of all recreational activities. One can understand the macho heroics of young and sometimes not-so-young men who

continue to push their personal limits till they are dead or disabled—their absurdity is socially and perhaps hormonally programmed. But women? In the name of all that is supposed to be superior about the sense of values and emotional maturity of women (love of life, avoidance of false heroics or false pride) you should not sacrifice life on the same altar of egoism that causes men to join the Marines, shoot buffalo, drive fast cars, fight over women.

The current controversy aside, the fact remains that thousands of women have climbed successfully with men and with other women over the past 150 years. The first woman mountaineer known to Western history was Marie Pardis, a Frenchwoman who climbed Mont Blanc in 1808. Her ascent is said to have been motivated by a desire for fame (and for more business at the refreshment stand she operated near the foot of the mountain); her only recorded comment on the climb is not encouraging: "Throw me in a crevasse and continue yourself." Apparently Marie was suffering from altitude sickness, but nevertheless she did reach the top of Mont Blanc—the first woman to do so.

An Englishwoman known only as Mrs. Cole made a number of Alpine tours including circuits of Monte Rosa and Mont Blanc in the mid-nineteenth century. She took a more positive view.

> Let me assure you that any lady blessed with moderate health and activity may accomplish tours [in the Alps] with great delight and few inconveniences. (Mrs. Cole, *A Lady's Tour Round Monte Rosa,* 1859.)

A brief look at some significant achievements by women in expeditionary climbing and high-altitude exploration makes it clear that their urge to explore remote regions and ascend high peaks is far from recent. In *On Top of the World: Five Women Explorers in Tibet,* Luree Miller profiles five of the many women who explored the high Himalaya between 1850 and 1920. One of them, Isabella Byrd, had been delicate and sickly for most of her life in England, but she underwent a metamorphosis as she traversed high passes in Kashmir. Miller writes:

> When she took the stage as a pioneer and traveler, she laughed at fatigue, she was indifferent to the terrors of danger, she was careless of what the day might bring forth in the matter of food . . .

The outstanding woman adventurer of her time was the Frenchwoman Alexandra David-Neel. Her series of journeys across the high Tibetan plateau from 1911 to 1944 have been characterized as the most remarkable ever made by any explorer in Tibet, man or woman. At the age of fifty-five she disguised herself as a Tibetan beggar woman and walked two thousand

Alexandra David-Neel in the Tibetan dress she wore during her remark-able journey from China via Tibet to India in 1926. Photo courtesy of Luree Miller and Archives de A. David-Neel.

miles across numerous high snowy passes to reach the forbidden city of Lhasa.

Fanny Bullock Workman and her husband, Dr. W. H. Work-man, of Massachusetts traveled and explored in the Himalaya between 1890 and 1915. They wrote six books about their adventures; in one of them, *Ice Worlds of the Himalaya,* Fanny offered her "personal experiences with rarified air for the benefit of women, who may not yet have ascended to altitudes above 16,000 feet but are thinking of attempting to do so." Fanny, an ardent suffragette, was once photographed on a high pass in the Himalaya carrying a newspaper bearing the headline "Votes for Women."

Another early woman climber and a rival of Mrs. Workman was Annie S. Peck, a New England professor. She began her climbing career with an ascent of the Matterhorn when she was forty-five. In 1908, at age fifty-eight, she made the first ascent of Huascaran South in the Peruvian Andes at 21,837 feet—she claimed it was the altitude record for any American. (The feud between Peck and Mrs. Workman centered on their conflicting claims to this record.) Peck described herself as "a firm believer in the equality of the sexes . . . any great achievement in any line of endeavor would be an advantage to my sex." (Annie S. Peck, *High Mountain Climbing in Peru and Bolivia,* 1912.)

In the years since World War II, women have made numerous significant climbs in the Andes and the Himalaya. One of the most remarkable of them was the late French climber Claude Kogan, "the first woman ever to lift up her voice in the sanctuaries of the Alpine Club." Until very recently the august British Alpine Club was an all-male institution, but in 1955 Kogan spoke to a packed house in London about her climbs on Salcantay, Alpamayo, Nun Kun, and Cho Oyu.

The British have historically led the way in many areas of mountaineering, so it is not surprising that this pioneering tradition should carry over to women's expeditionary climbing. From the 1950s onward, British women climbers have carried out many small, well-organized expeditions to previously unexplored regions of the Himalaya and written about them in an understated, characteristically British fashion. The bibliography at the end of this book will direct readers to these and other major works in the history of women's mountaineering.

In addition to the British and other small expeditions, women climbers throughout the world have made significant contributions to Alpine climbing and rockclimbing in the last hundred

Fanny Bullock Workman and her husband Dr. William H. Workman in Kashmir in 1897. Photo from the Workmans' book *In the Ice World of the Himalaya.*

years. However, until quite recently women have been notably absent on the world's highest mountains.

There are fourteen mountains in the world that soar above 8,000 meters (26,200 feet)—all located in the Himalaya. They have long been the prizes most coveted by mountaineers. Attempts to climb them began in the nineteenth century; in the first half of this century hundreds of men participated in dozens of expeditions to these lofty peaks. But even after Fanny Workman's auspicious example, only a handful of women took part in such climbs. Elizabeth Knowlton was a member of the joint German-American attempt on Nanga Parbat in 1932. In 1934 Hettie Dyhrenfurth took part in an expedition that explored and mapped the Baltoro Glacier region of the Karakoram Himalaya; she reached the top of Queen Mary Peak (24,370 feet), which gave her the world altitude record for women that had been so hotly contested by Annie Peck and Fanny Workman.

It was not until 1950 that an 8,000-meter peak was climbed by anyone. The epic ascent of Annapurna I by Maurice Herzog's French team was closely followed by successes on all the 8,000-meter giants over the next fourteen years—and all by men. During this period the only attempt on an 8,000-meter peak by a woman's team was the ill-fated 1959 International Women's Expedition to Cho Oyu in Nepal. Tragically, four climbers, including the leader, Claude Kogan, died on this attempt. By 1972, when the idea for our all-woman expedition to Annapurna was originally conceived, no woman from any country had yet reached the summit of an 8,000-meter peak.

Our expedition had its beginnings in August, 1972, on a mountain called Noshaq in the Wakhan Corridor, that unlikely piece of Afghanistan that separates Russia and China from Pakistan and India. Several European and American teams, including more than a dozen women climbers, were attempting Noshaq at that time. Late one afternoon I was laboring up to our high camp at 23,000 feet (7,200 meters) to get ready for a summit attempt the next day. Fog, wind, and occasional snow sprinkles whirled around me, and underfoot the slopes alternated between loose rock and powdery snow. A descending figure approaching rapidly out of the mist turned out to be the Polish climber Wanda Rutkiewicz returning from the summit. She greeted me warmly and said, "We have climbed to 7,500 meters. Now we must climb to 8,000 meters together, all women."

I was instantly taken by the idea. Later, at Noshaq base camp, Wanda, Alison Chadwick-Onyszkiewicz—a British member of the Polish expedition—and I decided to organize a Polish-American women's expedition to an 8,000-meter peak. We hoped to attempt Annapurna I (26,540 feet) in 1975, but we were unable to obtain a permit.

Meanwhile, in 1974, three members of a Japanese women's

expedition climbed Manaslu (26,750 feet), the long-awaited first ascent to 8,000 meters by women. And in 1975 a Polish expedition of women and men led by Wanda Rutkiewicz and including Alison Chadwick-Onyszkiewicz climbed Gasherbrum III, at that time the highest unclimbed peak in the world. On that same expedition, Anna Okopinska and Halina Krueger-Syrokomska ascended Gasherbrum II, the first time women had reached the top of an 8,000-meter peak unaccompanied by men. (The Japanese Manaslu climbers had been accompanied to the summit by a Sherpa.) In the same year, the Japanese climber Junko Tabei and the Tibetan woman Phanthog reached the top of Everest. (In his book *Everest*, the Italian superclimber Reinhold Messner describes Tabei in rather different terms than he uses for male climbers. She is "strongly built," he says, "with all the elegance one associates with Oriental women, but above all she is a very warm, sympathetic person, married and the mother of a daughter who was aged three at the time of Everest.")

In 1976 I was a member of the American Bicentennial Everest Expedition, which smoothly and safely put two climbers on the summit of Everest. This experience renewed my interest in an American women's expedition to an 8,000-meter peak and after the climb I stopped by the Foreign Ministry in Kathmandu to inquire about which peaks might be available in the next couple of years. The officials indicated that they would look favorably upon an application for Annapurna in 1978.

On my return home to the San Francisco Bay Area, I contacted several women climbers who responded enthusiastically to the proposal. With the nucleus of a team and the promise of a permit, the next step in making the expedition a reality was to secure the approval of our national climbing organization, the American Alpine Club (AAC). This was required by the Nepalese before they would grant the permit.

But the AAC hesitated and hedged for several months; the reasons they gave were vague, and I was dismayed. The other climbers and I knew that men's expeditions with less-experienced leaders and climbers were routinely approved. But the AAC had never previously approved an all-woman expedition and apparently was reluctant to do so.

This lack of support in the mountaineering establishment for women's climbing is not a new story. In its 1925 obituary of Fanny Workman, the venerable (British) *Alpine Journal* noted:

> She herself felt that she suffered from sex-antagonism and it is possible that some unconscious feeling, let us say of the novelty of a woman's intrusion into the domain of exploration so long reserved to men may in some quarters have existed . . . in time there tended to arise in certain high and serene circles an atmosphere, shall we say, of aloofness?

These "high and serene circles" did not seem to have changed much since 1925. "We've got to be more careful ap-proving a women's expedition," they had told Vera Watson, the expedition member who had done most of the negotiating with the club. "There would be a lot of bad publicity if things didn't go well."

We persevered, however, and finally—thanks primarily to Vera's unceasing efforts—the AAC relented and approved our application. The Nepalese announced to the press that we had a permit to attempt Annapurna I in the fall of 1978, and the American Women's Himalayan Expedition was official!

The name *Annapurna* can be translated as "the goddess rich in sustenance"—an appropriate objective for a women's expedition, we thought. But its other translation, "the harvest goddess," had more somber overtones, for the mountain had a formidable history. Of thirteen parties that had tried to reach the summit, only four had been successful, each putting a two-man team on the top. The price had been high: nine climbers had lost their lives on Annapurna's icy slopes. Nevertheless, we felt it was time women had the opportunity to attempt this classic Himalayan peak.

Although our expedition was conceived in an atmosphere of ambivalence about whether women could or should climb the highest mountains, Annapurna was for us primarily a personal challenge. Could we raise thousands of dollars, organize tons of food and gear, solve countless logistical problems, and adapt to the thin Himalayan air? If, in addition to all this, our experience helped to break down prejudice against women climbers, so much the better. Through the years I have felt both pain and occasional anger at the attitudes of many in the established climbing community towards me and other women climbers. But when the press asks me about discrimination by men—and they frequently do—my answers have always been deliberately vague. I would like to see attitudes change, and to that end I have tried to avoid strident statements. Our achievements in the mountains should speak for themselves.

Similarly, I am often drawn into debates about whether women or men have more endurance or some other physical or psychological edge in climbing. I don't believe that such comparisons are of any value. Individual differences are more important than sexual ones, and motivation counts most of all. Women do have the strength and endurance to climb the highest mountains, just as men do, and both men and women should have the chance.

The American Women's Himalayan Expedition gave ten women that chance—to face the challenge and earn the rewards. Maurice Herzog expresses this well in his account of the first ascent of Annapurna: "In attempting to do the hardest tasks, all our resources are called upon, and the power and greatness of man*kind* [my emphasis] are defined."

Beginnings 1

Flying west across the Pacific, I watched the setting sun cast a golden light on the shimmering sea far below, and felt more relaxed than I had in many months. It was August of 1978, and nine members of the American Women's Himalayan Expedition were on their way from San Francisco to Nepal and Annapurna I. To get this far we had selected a qualified team —ten climbers, two filmmakers, and a base camp manager; had succeeded in raising eighty thousand dollars; and had purchased, packed, and shipped eight thousand pounds of food and gear. Even with these tasks completed, we were still a long way from the top of the mountain.

The question everyone asks mountain climbers is "Why?". And when they learn about the lengthy and difficult preparation involved, they ask it even more insistently. For us, the answer was much more than "because it is there." We all had experienced the exhilaration, the joy, and the warm camraderie of the heights, and now we were on our way to an ultimate objective for a climber—the world's tenth highest peak. But as women, we faced a challenge even greater than the mountain. We had to believe in ourselves enough to make the attempt in spite of social convention and two hundred years of climbing history in which women were usually relegated to the sidelines.

I had taken part in a previous all-woman expedition—an ascent of Mount McKinley in 1970—and it had been my most satisfying climb so far. Before that trip we had been told that woman were not physically strong enough to carry heavy loads, that we didn't have the leadership experience and emotional stability necessary to climb the highest mountains. But the McKinley climb turned out to be a wonderfully lighthearted adventure. We felt as though we were climbing our mountain "without the grownups," and we successfully handled some difficult problems. When the six of us stood on that Arctic summit on July 6, 1970, my belief that women could climb the highest mountains was confirmed.

Annapurna offered the opportunity for further confirmation. In the twenty-eight years since the first ascent, no woman

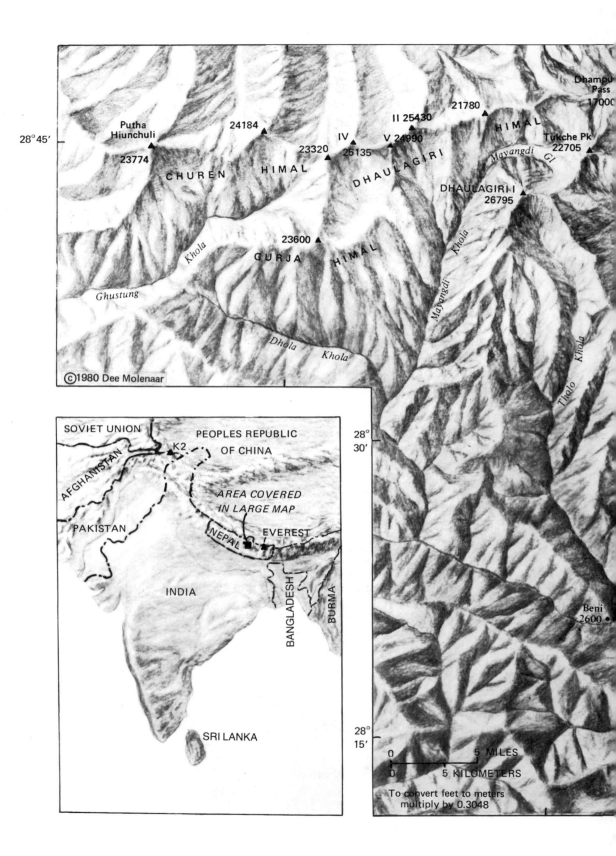

28°45'

Dhampu
Pass
17000

Putha
Hiunchuli
23774

24184

21780

II 25430

HIMAL

Tukche Pk
22705

CHUREN   HIMAL

23320

IV
25135

V 24990

DHAULAGIRI

Mayangdi Gl

DHAULAGIRI I
26795

23600

GURJA   HIMAL

Mayangdi
Khola

Khola

Mayangdi
Khola

Ghustung

Kohla

Dhola   *Khola*

Thalo   Khola

©1980 Dee Molenaar

28°
30'

SOVIET UNION

PEOPLES REPUBLIC
OF CHINA

AFGHANISTAN

K2

AREA COVERED
IN LARGE MAP

PAKISTAN

NEPAL

EVEREST

INDIA

BANGLADESH

BURMA

Beni
2600

28°
15'

0   5 MILES

0   5 KILOMETERS

SRI LANKA

To convert feet to meters
multiply by 0.3048

83° 45'   84° 00'

Muktinath
12460

Thorong La
17650

Gandaki

Jomosom
8900

Kali

Marpha
8760

Tilicho Pass
16730

Tukche
8485

Tilicho
Lake

Nilgiri North
23166 ▲

Tilicho
23405 ▲

Larjung
8400

Manangbhot
11650

Khangsar Khola

oya
00

Jungle
Camp
11100

Pass
Camp
14000

Special
Porter
Camp
14650

Base Camp
14500

Grand Barrier

Annapurna GI

Matsyandhi

Khola

Ghasa
6700

Khola

I
II
III
IV
V

Roc Noir
24557

Glacier
Dome
23191

Gangapurna
24457

III
24786 ▲

Gandaki

Miristi

ANNAPURNA I
26504 ▲

Fang
25090 ▲

Fluted Pk
21801

S. Annapurna GI

A N N A P U R N A

Dana
4600

Taropani
4000

Annapurna South
23684 ▲

H I M A L

IV
24688 ▲

II
26041 ▲

Hiunchuli
21133

Machapuchre
22848 ▲

Kali

Khola

Modi Khola

Mardi Khola

Seti

Khola

Ghorapani
9300

Khola

Tirkedunga
5175

Madi

Birethanti
3600

Chandrakot
5250

Khare
5700

Suikhet

Lumle
5300

Hyangja
(Tibetan Camp)
3325

Kholo

Naudanda
4675

Khola

Madi

Pokhara
2900

Phewa Tal

*The Annapurna-Dhaulagiri region of the Nepal Himalaya. The broken
line traces the expedition's trek from Pokhara to Annapurna Base
Camp; the smaller, dotted line shows the route up the mountain itself,
with campsites numbered.*

Vera Watson. Vera Komarkova.   *Irene Miller*. Marie Ashton.

had even tried to climb it. Our expedition would give ten women the chance to attempt one of the world's highest and most challenging peaks, as well as the experience necessary to plan future Himalayan climbs. If we succeeded, we would be the first Americans to climb Annapurna and the first American women to reach eight thousand meters (26,200 feet).

Our preparations for the climb had begun to weld the team members—thirteen very different individuals—into a strong and cohesive unit. As I looked around at the other women on the plane, inheritors of the tradition of Alexandra David-Neel and Annie S. Peck, I felt confident that whether or not we reached the top of the mountain, we were going to make a good effort and enjoy ourselves in the process.

Vera Watson was the proper lady of the group. Outwardly feminine, even fluttery; inside she was strong, efficient, and close to fearless—a complex woman with a romantic spirit and a determined will. A computer scientist and the first woman ever to make a solo ascent of Aconcagua in Argentina, the tallest mountain in the Western Hemisphere, she was now at forty-six realizing a long-standing ambition to climb in the high Himalaya. Vera looked slim and elegant in her beige traveling suit and Dior glasses, but typically, she was discontented with herself. "I shouldn't be eating these, I'm so fat," she said as she offered me her airplane almonds.

Irene Miller was already writing a letter to her family. A physicist at IBM, she was the only mother on the expedition with children still at home. She had confided to me that she was extremely concerned about the dangers of Annapurna—not only the risk to herself, but the potential loss to her children. Irene was very close to her two teenage daughters and, indeed, though she was forty-two, she could have been mistaken for her elder daughter, Carolyn. Irene had taken part in several expeditions since the birth of her daughters, but most of her significant climbing—including first ascents in Peru and the Tetons—had been done more than sixteen years earlier.

Vera, Irene, and I, who were close friends and lived near each other in the San Francisco Bay Area, had shared much of the responsibility for the overall organization of the expedition. Our first task had been to choose a qualified team. Back in 1973, when Wanda Rutkiewicz, the British climber Alison Chadwick-Onyszkiewicz, and I were trying to organize a 1975 Polish–American women's expedition to Annapurna, I had invited Irene and two other women climbers, Piro Kramar and Joan Firey, from among the very few I knew at that time. The permit from the Nepalese government to climb the mountain had not come through for 1975, so we all temporarily turned our attention elsewhere.

When Vera, Irene, and I began early in 1977 to plan for the current expedition, Piro, Joan, and Alison were obvious choices for the team. Now, as we flew westward in the twilight, Joan and Alison were already in Nepal making arrangements for local food and supplies. Coincidentally, Wanda was there, too, as a member of an international expedition that would be climbing Mount Everest while we were on Annapurna.

Piro Kramar, sitting in the seat behind me, was writing in her diary. Piro, forty, an ophthalmologist from Seattle, was our expedition doctor. Glancing at her diary, I could not make out any familiar words.

"What's that you're writing?" I asked.

"I'm practicing my Hungarian," she answered.

"I guess I won't be able to use excerpts for the expedition book." I was disappointed. A diary is by nature a private document, a diary in Hungarian doubly so. This was characteristic

Irene Miller, Wanda Rutkiewicz, and Arlene Blum wearing the expedition T-shirt. Joan Firey.

Piro Kramar. Christy Tews.

of Piro, who guarded her privacy to the point of seeming emotionally detached. She stayed aloof from squabbles, was slow to make judgments, and was inclined to keep to herself.

Piro had done most of her climbing with only one or two friends, often Joan Firey, in the Washington Cascades. She had doubts about being away from home for so long and about climbing with such a large group. Yet here she was on an expedition that would take three months and require close cooperation among dozens of people.

The rest of the team had heard about the expedition through the climbers' grapevine and the general press. When the Nepalese finally gave us our permit to attempt Annapurna in the fall of 1978, our plans were well publicized. Hundreds of women asked to join us, ranging from some of the world's best technical climbers to two Berkeley masseuses who wanted to come along to massage our tired muscles.

Finding climbers with the right mental and physical qualifications was extremely important. The first American Women's Himalayan Expedition naturally would seem a most exciting and desirable venture. But for many climbers the initial glamor of expeditionary climbing soon fades, and the actual experience—altitude, grinding hard work, damp, cold, tedium, bureaucratic hassles, the possibility of illness or injury—can be wearisome, disappointing, even devastating. During the long, severe storms frequently encountered in the Himalaya, climbers sometimes become apathetic and quit eating and drinking, which quickly leads to debilitation. The determination needed to keep melting snow for water and cooking can ultimately be more valuable than the skill to climb steep ice. Mental toughness and physical endurance, rather than muscular strength, are the essential qualities of successful high-altitude climbers. Just as important is the ability to enjoy this peculiar form of recreation despite its inevitable hardships.

Prior high-altitude climbing experience was also desirable, for there exists in some people an "altitude barrier" above which they cannot stay healthy. The reasons for this phenomenon are not well understood yet. Such a problem plagued the woman who led the 1970 all-woman McKinley climb. Up to fourteen thousand feet she could climb the most severe slopes carrying very heavy loads, but beyond that elevation she was relatively weak and suffered intensely from the altitude. For Annapurna, we tried to invite women who had successfully climbed above twenty thousand feet before. In most cases, however, this did not mean Himalayan experience; few women had had that opportunity.

Applicants with the requisite credentials and enthusiasm were invited to participate in one of our many practice climbs in the High Sierra. After we had been climbing together, both the prospective member and the rest of the team had a better sense of whether or not she belonged on the expedition. The selection process worked well, and even women who ultimately did not join the team made new friends and found new climbing partners. There were no seriously hurt feelings or bruised egos.

The other team members we chose were Margi Rusmore and Elizabeth Klobusicky-Mailaender, who would meet us in Nepal, and Vera Komarkova and Annie Whitehouse, who were among the group on the plane.

Just now Vera Komarkova was dozing next to Irene. (We called her Vera K., and Vera Watson became Vera W.) She and Irene had become good friends while climbing together in the Brooks Range of Alaska, and Irene had persuaded me to invite Vera K. on the expedition. Together they had begged, borrowed, and bought our three thousand pounds of equipment, from hardware to helmets, sleeping bags to socks, and gloves to garbage bags.

In her thirty-five years, Vera K. had emigrated from her native Czechoslovakia to the United States; spent an entire year walking across Europe and North America to the Mexico City Olympics; obtained a Ph.D. from the University of Colorado, studying Arctic and high-altitude plant ecology; and made some of the hardest wall climbs ever done by a woman, including an epic twenty-day ascent of the vertical, windblasted face of Mount Dickey in Alaska. Irene had described Vera K. to me as a real powerhouse, strong and energetic; others who had climbed with her had been put off by her overriding individualism. I found her the most enigmatic character in the group. I didn't know whether I would eventually rejoice or regret that we had invited her, and I wondered why she never took off her tinted glasses.

Annie Whitehouse, sitting next to me, was smiling her wonderful smile and working busily on her diary—drawing cartoons, I noticed. Ordinarily Annie would never have been invited to the Himalaya. She was only twenty-one, generally considered too young, and she was the wrong sex. But this sturdy young woman had determination, endurance, a tolerant disposition, and a fine sense of humor; we believed she would make a first-class expedition climber.

For most of the women invited, all serious climbers, a Himalayan expedition was a long-cherished but unlikely dream. Many members, particularly the older ones, felt that this trip was probably their only chance to climb in the high Himalaya. Piro, Irene, and Vera W. were in their forties, and Joan Firey would celebrate her fiftieth birthday on the mountain. Occasionally Irene or Vera W. would protest half-seriously that they were too old for Himalayan climbing. The conventional wisdom is that expedition climbers are at their prime in their thirties. But this does not allow for the experience, tolerance, and steadiness that often come with age and which more than compensate for a small decrease in physical strength.

Christy Tews, our base camp manager, a solid thirty-eight-year-old woman from the Midwest, possessed those qualities

Vera Komarkova. Arlene Blum.

Annie Whitehouse. Irene Miller.

Christy Tews. Irene Miller.

but lacked the mountaineering experience to be a climbing member of the team. She had worked as hard as anyone to get us this far, and at the moment she was doing a good business selling expedition T-shirts to the other passengers on the plane. The profits from these remarkable T-shirts had helped make the expedition possible.

When we received our permit, we had no idea how we were going to raise the eighty thousand dollars we would need for the climb. None of us had extensive private resources or even secretaries to help with the endless details of fund raising. But we did have something much more important: numerous supporters who believed in what we were doing and offered their skills and their time. Because the climbers themselves were too busy with other preparations, such as buying and organizing food and gear, friends and volunteers undertook the enormous task of raising money. My house in Berkeley was usually overflowing with volunteers and enthusiasm—the phone ringing constantly, the air electric with excitement.

Fund-raising ideas varied: balls, banquets, bumper stickers, and bay cruises; posters, placards, parties; signet rings, celebrity cocktail parties, races, tennis tournaments and treks were all proposed at various times. A suggestion that we design and sell an expedition T-shirt seemed promising. At one hilarious meeting, we looked at about twenty possible designs—sketches of Annapurna, of a woman climber with her hair sweeping into the shape of a mountain, of climbing equipment, climbers on top of mountains, mountains on top of climbers. Finally, on the very bottom of the pile, I came to the most delightfully perfect design imaginable. I hugged it to my chest and burst into laughter. This was it. I passed the stack of designs to Irene, and when she came to the last one, she too began to laugh. The reaction around the entire circle of climbers and volunteers was the same, and the decision was unanimous. The design was a distinctive outline of a mountain with a daring slogan: "A Woman's Place Is On Top . . . Annapurna."

Originally we ordered several dozen shirts to sell to our friends, but the demand for the shirts soon became overwhelming and left us completely disorganized. Hundreds of T-shirts were stacked all over my house, and I dealt with myriad bewildering inquiries from people wanting different colors or styles ("I'm sorry, it doesn't come in a chartreuse Qiana jumpsuit"), while the snows of Annapurna seemed to recede farther and farther. But soon Christy, together with Lynn Lee, who had designed the shirts, Sylvia Paul, who had thought up the slogan, and Sandy Formoso, who handled the bookkeeping, had the business running smoothly. The company we ordered the T-shirts from had told us our price was too high, that the shirts would not sell. But they did—fifteen thousand of them—and paid for most of our expenses. The slogan "A Woman's Place Is On Top," provided inspiration for countless jokes and became the expedition's motto.

In addition to the T-shirt business, Mary Lynn Hanley organized treks to Annapurna to benefit the expedition, and other volunteers solicited donations of food and equipment, helped us pack, and—most important of all—kept our enthusiasm and energy high. Without their hard work, we would never have reached Nepal. So the climb had a special meaning for the volunteers and for the thousands of people who had bought T-shirts and contributed money. Their caring helped propel us towards Annapurna and strengthened our determination. At the same time, it increased the pressure we felt to succeed.

Christy sold her last T-shirt—a medium-size blue one that was slightly worn—to an extra-large Sikh, who struggled into it within the confines of his plane seat. Apparently he was pleased with his purchase, for a few minutes later the stewardess offered us headphones and cocktails, "compliments of Mr. Singh."

Our two-woman film crew recorded the scene. Dyanna Taylor, camera, and Marie Ashton, sound, were young filmmakers with impressive experience and credentials. We didn't know until the last minute if we would be able to afford to make our own film, and Dyanna and Marie had dropped their other commitments on short notice to join us. In less than a month they had managed an extraordinary variety of preparations, from taking climbing lessons and conditioning with heavy packs in the Berkeley hills, to finding cameras and sound equipment that would work well at low temperatures.

The team had been divided about what sort of film would be best. Some favored the traditional approach, focusing on precipitous slopes and windblown summits. Others of us

Marie Ashton. Margi Rusmore.   *Dyanna Taylor.* Vera Watson.

believed that a unique film could be made showing how we as
women faced the hardest physical and mental challenges. We
felt that such a film would best be made by a two-woman crew
who could unobtrusively record our dealings with the mountain
and with each other. Commercial television networks had
wanted to send large film crews of men who would climb with
us and film us on the steepest slopes. When we decided to hire
two women without climbing experience, one network officer
told us that this approach was unlikely to yield anything better
than home movies, and that we should not bother bringing the
film to show them afterwards. He was wrong. Dyanna and
Marie climbed above Camp II to 19,000 feet to shoot superb
high-mountain footage, and their excellent hourlong documen-
tary about the Annapurna climb was aired on ABC-TV.

As our plane flew on and on, crossing the dateline and time
zones, the sun rose and set—or did it? Airports came and went.
Time and space were changing so rapidly, I felt as if I could get
off the plane anywhere in the past, present, or future—Athens
during the Peloponnesian War, Mars, or back home in Berkeley.

I thought back to the scene at the San Francisco airport as
we had been leaving. Hundreds of friends, family, loved ones,
and members of the press had come to see us off. Leaving my
boyfriend, John Percival, when the flight was called was very
hard. Although I had worked for this moment for so many
years, I just wanted to keep hugging him and not to get on the
plane.

When I reluctantly let go of John and joined the other
women boarding the plane, I had the sensation of being pulled
from one pole of a magnet to its opposite. As soon as I entered
the plane, John, my world in Berkeley, my work as a biochemist

were suddenly far away. I was now the expedition leader, responsible for guiding ten women safely to the top of Annapurna I.

Leaving was hard for the others, too. Irene looked particularly solemn. I knew that her younger daughter, Teresa, had been worried about her mother. It's not that usual for women to leave husbands, lovers, children for three months while they climb a dangerous mountain, and Annapurna has a bad reputation for avalanches.

I dozed uncomfortably and dreamed of John Henry Hall, the friend who had first taken me to the mountains. We had met during the great October storm of 1962, when I was a freshman at Reed College in Oregon. A hurricane with incredible winds, thunder, and lightning had hit Portland, knocking down wires and trees. When a call went out for people to help clear fallen trees, I volunteered and found myself working with a sturdy, handsome young man. His passion was climbing mountains, and as we chopped down tree branches and cleared away the debris of the storm, he told me about the white icy heights. Soon we began to study together, spending long evenings over chemistry problems, solving differential equations, arguing about Kant. I was seduced by the ice blue of his eyes and the blue ice of the glaciers he described, and on our first trip to the mountains together, I fell in love with them and him at the same time. When I first climbed on a glacier, it was like coming home to a place of beauty, splendor, and peace—a place where I felt I belonged and to which I would return again and again.

At that time the mountains were totally benign for me, full of joy and wonder, the best place to know people and to be happy. Climbing made me feel strong and at peace. Although I had some close calls during my early years in the mountains, I was unaware of the danger because my confidence in the goodness of the mountains was so great.

My naive trust ended abruptly. In August, 1971, I read in the morning newspaper that John Henry Hall and three other friends had been crushed by an avalanche on Mount St. Elias in the Yukon Territory. Since then I'd had a recurring dream of being frozen into the ice by a huge avalanche. Now again on the plane I dreamed of death, of an enormous avalanche sweeping down and engulfing all of us.

I woke up in despair. Since the tragedy on Mount St. Elias, I had lost many other friends in the mountains, and at times during the last months I asked myself why I was organizing this trip. The unhappy statistics are that one out of ten Himalayan climbers does not return. But that has not prevented hundreds of men from climbing in this most beautiful and challenging arena. It was time for women to get that chance too.

Once my avalanche dream faded, I was calm and confident about our preparations as we flew westward in the twilight toward Nepal. For me the climb had already begun during those two arduous years of preparation. I had learned, for instance, that the stamina needed to stay alert during interminable meetings was as essential to climbing Annapurna as the ability to carry heavy loads up icy slopes. In climbing, we each face private battles as well as the mountain itself. My own struggle was with indecision: I'd had to become more decisive in order to make the meetings work and to stay on top of the encyclopedia of details.

My scientific training contributes to a natural tendency to see all sides of an issue. I tend to agonize about the full range of possibilities and, even after I've made a decision, to worry interminably about whether it was the right one. In Nepal decisions would have to be rapid and firm, for on a high mountain, indecision can be lethal. I could envision factions forming, with convincing arguments bombarding me on all sides. I would have to listen carefully, make up my mind, then—hardest of all—stop thinking about the decision. I would have to accept the risk that sometimes I would be wrong.

"On the left side of the plane are the Nepal Himalaya." The pilot's voice pulled me from my thoughts and drew my eyes to the window of the jet. I could only see the foothills; Annapurna and the other high peaks were veiled in billowing white monsoon clouds. But I knew they were there and wondered what conditions we would find on those distant slopes.

Our plan was to hike into base camp during the monsoon rains so as to be ready to climb in September when the rains ended. We hoped there would then be a short "window" of good climbing weather before the days grew short and cold and the winter jet stream winds dropped down on the highest summits, making climbing almost impossible. But if we reached base camp too early and had to sit there for weeks waiting for the monsoon to end, we could use up all our food and wear down our morale.

I had talked to dozens of people who had climbed in the Himalaya. Based on their experience and mine, I had finally chosen August 6 as our departure date. Still I worried: would there be problems with customs in Kathmandu or landslides along the way that would delay our arrival in base camp; how about porter strikes, unseasonable monsoons, an epidemic of dysentery, or war? The possibilities, however likely or unlikely, were endless, and I couldn't stop thinking about whether I had chosen the right date.

"Fasten your seat belts in preparation for landing in Kathmandu, Nepal, where the time is 8:30 A.M." Almost instantly, my worries were replaced by excitement.

We had left San Francisco about twenty-four hours earlier on a Sunday afternoon, but in Kathmandu it was Tuesday morning. I moved my watch ahead eleven hours and forty minutes, remembering that the rules are different here. Indian time is half an hour out of phase with the time of other countries.

A temple complex in Kathmandu. Vera Komarkova.

India was supposed to be divided into two time zones, but the Indians chose to use the average time throughout the country. The Nepalese, for their part, wanted to show their independence from India and set their time ten minutes ahead of India's.

"Incredible! Almost an Irish green!" Vera W. exclaimed. I looked out to see a distinctly non-Irish countryside: steep terraced hillsides dotted with thatch-roofed huts beneath a canopy of monsoon clouds. The hills gave way to a broad emerald valley, and at its center was Kathmandu, bejeweled with countless shrines, stupas, and towers. As we landed, the cows were cleared from the runway.

Imperturbable Kathmandu 2

Our jeep threaded its way among the rickshaws, wandering cows, holy men, and women in saris that filled the Kathmandu streets. The air was warm, an aromatic blend of the smoke from thousands of cooking fires, the sweet odor of incense and spices, and the acrid reek of urine, feces, and decaying vegetable matter. Nepalese music drifted from the teahouses and mixed with the blare of taxi horns, the tinkle of bicycle bells, and the multilingual bargaining of shoppers and street vendors.

The jeep was driven by Mike Cheney, our representative in Nepal. Cheney, an elfish-looking Englishman with a hooked nose, and a delightful dry sense of humor, manages the Sherpa Cooperative, a trekking business. Its profits are divided among the Sherpas employed there. Today Cheney wore the flared khaki shorts, nearly as full as a skirt, often seen on Gurkha officers and a somewhat incongruous-looking rust-colored "Woman's Place Is On Top" T-shirt. I appreciated the support implied by Cheney's wearing the shirt.

"You girls sure shook up the Nepalese," he chuckled. "I was astounded when Christy took off her T-shirt."

Cheney was referring to an incident at the Kathmandu airport. Christy had made friends on the plane with Kurt Diemberger, a noted Austrian climber who happened to be on the same flight with us on his way to Everest.

"I really would like a T-shirt like yours," he told her as they got off the plane. "Do you have any for sale?"

"No, I sold all my extra shirts. I only have the one I'm wearing."

"If you give me your T-shirt, I'll give you the fine French one I'm wearing in return," he smiled beguilingly.

So at the bottom of the plane steps, right on the runway, Christy and Diemberger turned to face each other, took off their T-shirts, and traded—to the cheers of our group and the wide-mouthed astonishment of the Nepalese. The blue French T-shirt came to Christy's knees, and a bit of the Austrian's stomach poked out from beneath his new "A Woman's Place Is On Top" T-shirt.

Kurt Diemberger and Christy exchange T-shirts at Kathmandu airport.
Arlene Blum.

Still laughing, we turned to face the waiting Nepalese press—
several Nepalese men in Western attire and one American
woman. Mountaineering is often major news in the kingdom of
Nepal and is well covered by AP, UPI, and Reuters correspon-
dents. The inevitable questions: why all women, why Annapurna, will you have women Sherpas, why do you want to climb
Annapurna? It went on for twenty minutes, the questions the
same as those we had been asked when leaving San Francisco.

"Your advance team has matters well in hand," Cheney
filled me in as we drove through the familiar crowded streets.
"Joan has bought about 4,000 pounds of local food, and she,
Liz, and Alison have been working with your Sherpas to pack it
all. Customs may be a major problem though."

The customs office had already opened, rifled, and confis-
cated the boxes we had packed and sealed so carefully, with
hopes that they would survive the long, wet march to base camp
intact. I asked Cheney why customs was being so tough with us.

"An American climber was caught last spring trying to
smuggle in three thousand watches, so now they're suspicious of
all Americans," Mike explained.

I couldn't help laughing and wondering how anyone could
hope to hide three thousand watches. And Liz Klobusicky who
had met us at the airport, chuckled and reassured me about
customs. She looked cool and calm in her green Nepalese pants
and shirt with her long brown hair pulled back into pigtails.

It was hard to imagine that this softspoken, thirty-three-
year-old woman had scaled some of the most severe ice faces
in the Alps. Slender yet strong, Liz sometimes looked fashion-
model elegant; at other times her well-muscled leanness seemed
almost masculine. She had been born in Hungary but had grown
up in Spokane, Washington and obtained a Ph.D. in German
at the University of Colorado. Now she taught English in
Tübingen, Germany, where she lived with her German-Irish husband, Nicko. Living in Europe had given Liz the opportunity
to make many severe ice climbs, and she was our most experienced technical ice climber. I counted on her to help lead on
the hard steep ice we would encounter. Now, however, she was
dealing well with another sort of challenge.

"It took patience, but I got most of our gear out of customs
already. You know how slow things are here, but they always
work out eventually." Liz had already been in Kathmandu for a
week. "These past days without the whole expedition have been
fantastic—I've been slowly exploring Kathmandu. I'm even a
little sorry you're all here now. I guess the real work is going to
begin."

Indeed it was. After two years of preparation in the States,
we still had to rescue our remaining gear from customs; repack
and reseal all 150 boxes; select, equip, and insure our Nepalese
staff; buy and pack several thousand pounds of local food;
arrange for a possible helicopter rescue; and comply with a host

of local regulations before we actually obtained our permit. The list was endless but familiar. As much as I enjoyed negotiating all these matters with the Nepalese, I knew things must be done as expediently as possible. The longer we stayed here, the more money we would spend, and the more likely it was that one of us would succumb to the local bacteria.

We turned off the main street into a narrow alley and stopped in front of the modern Siddhartha Hotel, where Joan Firey and Alison Chadwick waved us in enthusiastically.

Joan Firey, forty-nine, an artist, physical therapist, and seasoned mountaineer, was a tall, handsome woman with short silvery hair. In spite of the raucous, unfamiliar surroundings, Joan radiated certainty. Whatever doubts or fears she had, she held in. I wondered if she were even aware of them.

Joan was a very determined woman. She had climbed countless peaks and explored many wilderness areas in the northwestern United States and Canada while raising three children. She also had definite ideas about the best way to do things, usually the opposite of mine. During the frustrating months of preparation, there were times when I had wished she was not going with us. But now, as usual when I was actually with Joan, I was charmed by her assuredness and her engaging personality. Joan had no doubt that we would succeed in climbing Annapurna.

I also felt slightly uncomfortable with Alison Chadwick, thirty-six, the British member of our team. Alison was an artist in Leeds, where she lived with her Polish husband, Janusz Onyszkiewicz. Even though Alison and I had first met on Noshaq in 1972 and she had spent several days with me in Berkeley last spring, Alison was still a stranger to me. She seemed to know just how a proper expedition leader should

Liz Klobusicky-Mailaender. Arlene Blum.

Joan Firey. Irene Miller.   *Alison Chadwick-Onyszkiewicz.* Vera Komarkova.

behave, and I'm not strong on propriety. Her British reserve and formality accentuated my own uncertainties and left me feeling anxious to please but very awkward. Alison had climbed higher than any of the rest of us, and I respected her experience and knowledge. I wanted approval from her that I never seemed to get. Perhaps it was because we were such very different women.

Alison felt we not only had to reach the top of Annapurna, we had to do it in style. She was a purist and did not like the group decision to employ Sherpas and to have oxygen available for the summit day. My style is that of a pragmatist.

Liz Klobusicky, on the other hand, was becoming very close friends with Alison already. In addition to both living in Europe and being superb technical climbers, Liz and Alison were both married to renowned alpinists, with whom they usually climbed. But they obviously welcomed this chance to take full responsibility for a climb themselves.

We all greeted each other warmly and began to exchange stories of the various trials we'd encountered traveling to Kathmandu. When I mentioned money worries with customs impounding our gear, Alison at once suggested that we eliminate the five Sherpas we'd planned to hire to help carry our loads.

"They may turn out to be a bloody nuisance," Alison warned. "This is a women's climb, after all. We don't really need Sherpas. We should do it on our own."

Joan, who had been working closely and well with the Sherpas for the last five days, protested. "The Sherpas have been great during the packing. They're helpful and hardworking— we can't fire them now."

"They'll make the climbing faster and safer," I emphasized. "If anyone's injured, the Sherpas can carry them down."

Most Himalayan expeditions have employed Sherpas. Although a small proportion of such ascents now are being made without them, I wanted the increased safety of Sherpa support for our effort. Last spring when Alison had visited the States, she and I had many similar talks about this issue. I only wished there were some way to satisfy her purist ethic without decreasing the safety of the climb.

Liz chimed in. "I think we should hire ten Sherpas, not five. Any money spent to make the climb safer is fine. But otherwise I agree with Alison—we've got to do this climb within our budget and not spend money on unnecessary frills." We had barely enough funds for budgeted expenses, and everyone was worried that we would run out of money.

During the discussion Christy stomped in, looking hot and uncomfortable. "This place is impossible. I set up my camp stove to boil water for drinking, but I couldn't get any water from the tap. Then I tried to call the desk to complain, but the phone didn't work. And the heat and humidity make me remember why I left Iowa."

"Relax, Christy. You're in Asia. Everything will work out eventually," Annie smiled. "It's strange, but I already feel more at home here than anywhere I've ever been before. I'd like to stay here a long time. Nepal is paradise."

Paradise or impossible, we were all in Kathmandu at last.

The next morning the tropical sun was turning the early morning fog to steam as Irene and I rode our rented bikes to the austere gray stone building that housed the Sherpa Cooperative. A dozen Sherpas were cheerfully working in the muddy front yard resealing our boxes. Inside an airless room on the first floor, Alison was packing with meticulous care, fitting each item in perfectly and making sure each box weighed precisely 66 pounds, the maximum weight for a porter's load. She looked anxiously over at Vera K., who was throwing crampons from one box to the next with great energy.

"We should carry in just what we'll need and no more. I keep telling Vera K. we have too much hardware, too many pairs of crampons. It's a bloody waste to carry all that to Base Camp," Alison looked to me for support.

"No, we should take everything to Base Camp and then decide what we need," Vera K. said. "You never know. We could always lose things and need more."

Meanwhile Vera W. looked worried. "Vera K., you've got to keep track of what you're putting in each box. If the lists aren't correct, we'll have a total mess."

"Oh, of course I'm keeping track," said Vera K., who was throwing mittens and socks into boxes with abandon.

Irene and I gratefully escaped the heat and confusion of the packing room for Mike Cheney's breezy upstairs office. Mike immediately complimented us on our organization, and I was

Bicycle rickshaw in front of the Sherpa Coop. Irene Miller.

pleased because he had worked with dozens of other expeditions.

"Money's a big problem," I told him. "We're running short. Is any of the advance money Irene sent you left?"

"Sorry. It's all gone."

He handed me the ledger and I scanned the neat figures. "Two hundred dollars for the get-together tonight? That's ridiculous! There are only twenty of us getting together. In a restaurant here you can get a huge meal for less than two dollars a person."

"Well, a few others are invited. Besides, restaurants buy in bulk and can afford to charge less. Cooking at home is more expensive here than eating in a restaurant."

"Sorry, Mike, we'll spend one hundred dollars for the party. Even that's too much."

"You won't be able to have fruit salad with rum, then."

"Fruit salad with rum? For a hundred dollars?"

"I've heard you girls have strong supporters back home. You can always get more money from the States."

I was dismayed that Mike Cheney thought we had an inexhaustible supply of money back home. Our Nepalese staff would be only too willing to believe that and perhaps be encouraged to try for higher wages than we could afford.

He continued, "Establishing good relations with your staff

from the beginning is very important. You'll meet your Sherpas and Sherpanis tonight."

"Oh, fantastic!" I said. "You did manage to find some women Sherpas who want to learn to climb."

"Not exactly." Mike was hesitant.

In the United States the expedition had tried to employ women whenever possible. It seemed reasonable to extend this policy to Nepal and hire some Sherpa women to climb and carry loads on the mountain.

Loads are traditionally carried to the mountain by ordinary porters—Sherpanis or low-caste Nepalese—but the climbing and carrying on the mountain itself is the domain of the male Sherpa. The Sherpas are a tribal people of Tibetan origin who live in eastern Nepal, frequently above 10,000 feet elevation. Physiologically they are extraordinarily well adapted to high altitudes. They are known for their innate mountaineering skill which visiting Western climbers have helped to develop, their strength, and also for their loyalty and sense of fun.

I had always enjoyed climbing with Sherpas and had looked forward to climbing with some women Sherpas and giving these women a chance at the prestigious and relatively high-paying job of a high-altitude porter. But Mike Cheney had been skeptical. He had written me several letters warning that things were different here. If we insisted on hiring Sherpanis for high altitude work, the Sherpas would disapprove, and we would be heading for *big trouble*. I found this hard to believe at the time, as Sherpa women are usually quite independent. They own half of the couple's property, and they can and do initiate divorce; indeed the society is traditionally polyandrous. So we had insisted. And now it appeared Mike had managed to hire some Sherpanis.

"Was there time for the Sherpanis to have climbing and English lessons?" I asked. This had been the plan.

"I'm afraid not." Mike was embarrassed. "Your sirdar hired two of his women relatives. They're not the strongest, the most intelligent nor attractive Sherpanis I've ever met. They're supposed to help with laundry and washing up, and having them around will be good for Sherpa morale."

"Oh, no, Mike. That's exactly the opposite of what we want. Remember, when I was here last year, I asked you to find two Sherpanis who had worked as low-altitude porters and wanted to learn to climb?" I was distressed to learn that these particular Sherpanis had never carried loads and had no interest in learning to climb.

"It's the sirdar's prerogative to hire his relatives," Cheney shrugged. "And he said that these two women cannot climb above Base Camp—you'll have to hire two more male Sherpas to carry loads on the mountain."

After some discussion I gave in, realizing the impossibility of changing the system. "Okay, Mike, hire the two Sherpas. But if we take them, we won't be able to pay and feed the two Sherpanis. How about giving them six weeks wages and dismissing them? Explain how sorry we are that we can't afford to take them with us."

Mike shook his head. "I'll try, but the Sherpanis would be very disappointed not to come along at all. Since they've already been hired, you're obligated at least to take them along to Base Camp as ordinary porters."

I agreed reluctantly. Staff inflation is a common problem for expeditions in this country of high unemployment, but I was afraid dismissing the Sherpanis might cause problems later.

On my way out, I stopped off at the packing room to tell the others about the Sherpanis and our money problems.

"That's just terrible," Vera K. sympathized. "But maybe we should have the two-hundred-dollar party. Rum *is* good in fruit salad."

Alison was more concerned about the Sherpanis. "It would be repugnant to have them along as our servants. That's exactly what we don't want women to be."

"They look so sad." Vera W. pointed to the two dejected-looking Sherpanis sitting on the steps. Mike had apparently told them the news. "It wasn't their fault they were hired, and they do want to come along. I think we should at least let them come to Base Camp so they won't feel so bad. I'm sure we can find something useful for them to do."

"I'm sorry I ever tried to invite the Sherpanis," I sighed. "We can't afford both them and the two extra male Sherpas Lopsang wants. But since we're going to pay them six weeks wages anyhow, I suppose we can let them come along to Base Camp as ordinary porters." I was later to regret giving in on this point.

That evening we gathered at Cheney's house for the party where we were to meet our Sherpa staff.

Purna, a Sherpa who had been Mike Cheney's cook for twenty years, greeted us at the door of the large stone house. "Namaste, memsahibs." He brought his hands together in front of him and bowed in the traditional manner. Christy looked at me.

"*Namaste* means 'I respect the God in you,' " I whispered to her. "*Memsahib* literally means 'woman master.' It's left over from the days of the British raj."

Christy raised her hands together. "Namaste, Purna."

"Namaste, Purna," Irene smiled. "I first met you in 1961, when I was here with Hillary's Makalu Expedition."

"Nineteen sixty-one. You must be very old lady then." Irene's face fell.

"Old lady very strong. Will get to top of Annapurna first," Purna laughed. Irene looked dubious.

Purna proudly wore a blue "Women's Place Is On Top" T-shirt we had given him. "Please, bara memsahib [*bara* denoted my role as leader]—you sell me more T-shirts?" Purna was a shrewd businessman, and the T-shirts were a current status item in Kathmandu.

"These T-shirts are very expensive," I warned him, knowing they cost six days wages for a local porter.

"How many rupees, memsahib?"

"One hundred rupees," I told him, embarrassed.

"Down-filled T-shirt?" he laughed and showed us into Mike's austere living room. The other members and various Sherpas were sitting on straw mats on the floor, where they were served rice and dal, a spicy lentil stew, from huge vats. The meal was good, though surprisingly simple for the price tag. But people were having a good time, even without the rum. Annie was happily eating the rice and dal with her fingers. "This is good." She licked her fingers.

Vera W. was less enthusiastic. "Can I have a fork?" she asked. "I haven't gotten used to eating with my fingers yet."

After we had eaten, Mike Cheney introduced the Sherpas to us. "First, this is Lopsang, your sirdar, or head Sherpa." A fine-boned man of nearly forty bowed respectfully to us. An ex-officer in the Indian Army, Lopsang had been sirdar on many trekking trips and small expeditions, but this would be his first expedition to an 8,000-meter peak as sirdar. Cheney had selected him for his good English, organizational ability, and climbing experience. He would be the primary liaison between expedition members and Sherpas.

"Your high-altitude porters, Mingma Tsering, Chewang Rinjing, Lakpa Norbu, Ang Pemba, and Wangel." Five sturdy younger men bowed and grinned. They wore bell-bottomed pants and Western shirts. I remembered Chewang from Everest in 1976. I had been impressed with his strength, good humor, and ice-climbing ability. The other Sherpas were new to me.

"Your kitchen staff. Pasang Temba, Yeshi Tenzing, and Pemba." Three more smiling Sherpas bowed.

"Your kitchen helpers, Pasang Yangine Sherpani and Ang Dai Sherpani." The two Sherpa women, in their traditional black Tibetan jumpers, striped aprons, and pantaloons bowed shyly. But how had they become our kitchen helpers? I had agreed only that they could work as porters. I must have looked surprised, because Vera W. whispered an explanation to me.

"They were so sad at not getting to stay at Base Camp, Cheney persuaded me to pay their salary myself. They can stay and help in the kitchen."

"Oh, no, we can't afford to feed them. Besides, it's degrading," I objected.

Our party was now double in size. We had carefully selected the members for their compatibility and experience. I hoped the Sherpas had been chosen with equal care, but I had some doubts. I knew Mingma was Lopsang's brother-in-law, and Wangel was his close friend. I had insisted on Chewang

Lopsang Tsering, our sirdar. Christy Tews.

from Everest and on Lakpa, who had been on the Dutch Annapurna expedition last year. Lopsang had reluctantly acquiesced
to my choices, warning me that they were not "his men" and
might not obey him.

Chewang wore a hat with a woman's power badge embroidered on it. When I inquired about its origin, he told me a
trekking group had given it to him. Chewang had been on
Annapurna three times before, so I asked him how he felt about
going back there once again.

"Very big mountain, very dangerous. Almost dying there in
avalanche with Japanese five years ago. Four Japanese, one
Sherpa dying. Yes, memsahib, I like Annapurna. Very much."

I doubted I would want to go back to a mountain if I'd
almost died there. "Sounds dangerous," I said.

"We put up prayer flags to mountain gods at Base Camp.
Then mountain gods happy. Avalanche not dangerous. Everything okay."

I hoped he was right.

Jet lag hit suddenly, and I yawned widely and stumbled
back to the Siddhartha where I passed out at 9:30 P.M. But I was
wide awake again at three in the morning, making plans for the
next day.

Normally when I'm in Asia I adapt to the local sense of
time. "When does the bus come?"

"Just wait. The bus will come." On previous trips I would
wait happily for hours, even days, drinking tea and chatting
with the local people. The bus would always come, and waiting
three days for a bus was a welcome contrast to life in the States,
where every moment was full, with the phone ringing, dozens of

people to talk to, things to do—all planned and programmed in advance.

But this time I already had a two-page list of people to see and things to be done. I was forced to bring my Western lifestyle to Asia, but it was worth it if we climbed the mountain. I thought of more and more things to do as I dozed back into a troubled sleep.

The next morning Liz, Alison, and Joan were giving out gear to the Sherpas as I parked my bike in front of the Sherpa Cooperative. Sherpas are paid relatively little in cash for the demanding, dangerous work they do as high-altitude porters. Their major payment is several thousand dollars worth of clothing and high-altitude climbing gear, and their success on an expedition is measured not only by the prestige of the summit, but also by how much gear and money they obtain.

For now our Sherpas seemed very pleased with what we were giving them. Joan had drawn a picture of Annapurna on their white sunhats and had written "American Women's Himalayan Expedition" underneath. The Sherpas strutted proudly around town wearing these hats and their expedition T-shirts.

Inside, Mike Cheney introduced me to a Nepalese man who wore blue jeans, tennis shoes, and a cowboy shirt. He was Dambar Singh Gurung, a thoughtful and well-educated lieutenant in the King's Guard. As our liaison officer, he would accompany us to solve any problems with the Nepalese and to make sure that we obeyed the mountaineering regulations of His Majesty's government.

"Namaste, Mr. Gurung," I bowed respectfully.

"Namaste, bara memsahib. Now you must go with me to obtain a permit for the expedition," he said slowly in correct English.

We taxied rapidly across town and up into the hills, where we stopped in front of an old palace. Passing a rose garden, we entered a dark, musty office full of files. After shaking a great many hands, we were ushered in to see the undersecretary of tourism and his assistant. Like many rooms in Nepal, this office was decorated with pictures of His Majesty Birendra Bir Bikramshah Dev and Her Majesty Aishwarye Rayja Laxmi Devi, the king and queen of Nepal. The royal family looked down on us benignly through their tinted glasses.

The few Nepalese men in this room had the authority to decide who could or could not climb the world's highest mountains. Every year the tourist office receives hundreds of applications for permits to climb mountains like Everest and Annapurna. Only two expeditions are given permits for each peak per year; one for the premonsoon season from March to June, the other for the postmonsoon season of August to November.

In February, 1977, when we had applied for a permit to climb Annapurna in the fall of 1978, we were told there were

Dambar Singh Gurung, our liaison officer.
Irene Miller.

three other expeditions who wanted that date. But somehow our application was given precedence. Who knows why? Perhaps they thought it appropriate for an all-woman team to attempt Annapurna, a harvest goddess.

Mr. Sharma, the undersecretary, explained the lengthy expedition regulations. "The most important thing is that expedition news be sent straight to the Tourist Ministry. You must not talk to reporters. All information must come from His Majesty's government," he informed me sternly.

A striking young girl, wearing an orange sari with a matching tika mark on her forehead, came in and stared shyly at me. She whispered in Nepali to the undersecretary.

"She says she wanted to see a woman expedition leader. She expected you to look like a man," he explained. "Surprised. You are beautiful."

I was speechless and acknowledged the compliment with a smile.

Mr. Sharma continued. "Particularly when any climber gets to the top, you must send a runner at once to cable that he—I mean she of course—has succeeded." He laughed self-consciously.

I promised to abide by all the regulations and was presented with a simple certificate proclaiming in both Nepali and English that we were now official. We could now legally go off to spend eighty thousand dollars and risk our lives to try to stand on top of Annapurna.

Feeling ebullient with the permit tucked into my purse, I bounced into Joan's spartan room at the Himalayan View Hotel. She had chosen not to stay at the more expensive Siddhartha. But I thought a couple of extra dollars a day for air conditioning and Western comfort was worthwhile; it should help us to stay healthy. Once again Joan and I had different approaches.

"How's the shopping going?" I asked.

"Pasang cook has taken over. He's doing a marvelous job. Here's a list of what's been bought."

In the States, Joan and I had had endless disagreements about the necessity for luxury foods. She believed that the food, indeed all aspects of the climb, should be as frugal as possible. But I felt her romantic view of the simple life in the mountains would not work on a Himalayan expedition. I scanned the food list with growing uneasiness. "The rice and dal seemed adequate. But the amounts of meat, dried fruits, nuts, jam, and peanut butter don't seem quite, uh, sufficient," I said, trying to restrain my impatience at this rerun of an old dispute.

"We can't afford to buy any more," Joan said defensively. "People can't be too picky. They can eat dal and rice."

"But we won't be able to climb unless we keep eating and stay healthy. Many Westerners get tired of dal and rice and quit eating—I've seen it happen. Luxury foods are worth the money. Besides I'm sure these foods were included in the budget we made back in the States." I could hear my voice cracking with strain.

"It's too late now. Before I buy anything else, I would need to poll the members about what they like, and there's no time to talk to everyone and then buy more food. We'll have to make do with what we have." She was sure she was right. Letting go of any remaining tact, I ordered, "Buy that food today, Joan. I'm not going to see this expedition fail because we don't have the food we need." I stomped off, my adrenalin level high.

My education as an expedition leader was continuing. Although my upbringing and experience had taught me to be moderate and soothing, I was learning the hard way that these traits are not always compatible with effective leadership. Although I didn't yet sound like an authentic army general, I was moving in that direction. The trick was to move just far enough. Could I somehow have gotten Joan to buy the food without being so authoritarian? The expedition needed a strong leader but not a dictator.

Trying to calm myself, I decided to play tourist and turned down a narrow alley of small shops and vendors whose carts were piled high with deep fried pastries. I tried to ignore the temptation, remembering the many times I had eaten such food and become violently ill. Usually while retching I would promise myself never to eat street food again and then succumb to its lure as soon as I had recovered. But this time I was firm in my resolution. Annapurna was too important to be lost for a *Salmonella* samosa.

At a tailor shop I pointed to a pair of wonderful pants that tied at the ankle, ballooned out at the legs, then tied again with a

drawstring at the waist. "Can you make me two pair overnight?"

"Yes, memsahib." The tailor did not look up from his
work. "You choose the colors." I selected deep red and purple
from the rainbow of Nepalese cottons available. Self-
consciously, the tailor measured me. "Memsahib very tall, very
much material. Pants cost thirty-five rupees each [about three
dollars]. Please pay now."

I paid and wandered down to the bazaar to look for some
tampons. Johnson & Johnson, the makers of OB tampons, had
been the only corporation to make a large cash contribution to
our expedition, and I had assumed that they had also supplied
us with tampons. But apparently we had neglected to ask for
any, and although we had brought 8,000 pounds of the usual
expedition supplies to Nepal, this vital item wasn't among them.
I went all through the bazaar from chemist to chemist explaining
with some difficulty what I wanted, but tampons did not seem
to be for sale in Kathmandu.

In front of the Everest Pie Shop I ran into Liz who said she
had brought an extra supply. Then she suggested a cup of tea
at the pie shop, which catered to the hippies who flocked to
Kathmandu. On the way to our table we passed a delectable
array of sweets.

"I'd like tea and two macaroons," I told the waiter, a
Nepalese youth wearing a denim vest with a fierce Tibetan dragon embroidered across the back.

"Memsahib want special macaroons?"

"Just two plain macaroons, please."

"Sorry, memsahib. Only have special macaroons today."

"Why special?"

"Hashish macaroon." He grinned.

"Chocolate cake, please." I laughed. "A hashish macaroon
would finish me for days."

I followed the dark chocolate cake with a large piece of
creamy fudge pie. At last I could eat sweets with a clear conscience. Fattening now was a good idea as we would certainly
lose weight during the climb.

While we ate Liz told me of her trials at customs. "What a
pain! But you should have seen Margi. She got some of our
things out yesterday without paying any duty."

"How'd she manage that?"

"She just plain insisted. The Nepalese were simply overwhelmed by this delicate-looking young blond woman shrieking, 'Those are my suitcases and I want them now!' Her voice
shook the building."

Margi had arrived the day before, full of energy after a brief
vacation in Greece.

I laughed. "I wish Margi could have rescued all our stuff
like that."

We were about to leave when Annie Whitehouse and Margi

Margi Rusmore. Arlene Blum.

Rusmore, hot and tired but happy, joined us.

"Margi and I managed to buy most of the local stuff to-day," Annie told us. "We had to go to twenty different stores to get it all. What a job!"

Annie, twenty-one, and Margi, twenty, were our youngest but in no way least competent members. Both had attended Ravenswood, an experimental public high school in Palo Alto, California, where they had "majored" in mountain climbing. I'd first met Margi in 1975 when she came to me for advice about a post-high school expedition to Mount McKinley in Alaska. She and Annie reached the summit on that trip—at seventeen and eighteen, then the youngest women to do so. Margi had come along on our Labor Day practice climb in the Sierra Nevada and had impressed us with her competence and cheerful disposition. Then she persuaded us to invite her friend Annie. Margi was now a geology student at the University of California, Santa Cruz, and Annie was a nursing student at the University of Wyoming. Both had taken time off from school to help with the packing and shipping of food and equipment. It was a massive job, which they had handled well. Now they seemed to be doing equally well with the local supplies.

"It took us hours to bargain for all the stuff," Annie told us. "But Yeshi, the cookboy, made it all fun. I really like him." As Annie went on telling us about Yeshi and his wonderful deep brown eyes, her own became dreamy, and I began to worry.

"As soon as I met him, I felt really comfortable with him, as if I'd known him for years."

"You know the expedition rule," I said stiffly. "No romances during the climb." I did not want to interfere in other's personal lives, but a love affair could be disastrous for group unity and member-Sherpa relations. Annie looked surprised.

"Well, people are people and romance just complicates things. Our first loyalties must be to each other. We're here to climb a mountain and that's going to take all our energy."

"Of course," Annie sighed.

I hoped Annie would understand the importance of what I had just said and not rebel. She was mature, thoughtful, and hard working, but she did not always believe in following rules.

Leaving Annie and Liz in the pie shop, I wandered back to the hotel in the dusk. Tibetans, Newars, and many of the other tribal clans—Gurungs, Limbus, Rais, and Tamangs—thronged the streets. I made my way carefully among Buddhist monks in saffron habits, holy sadhus wearing white sarongs, Hindu women in bright print saris, pigs, holy cows, carts laden with all manner of foods, and taxis honking their horns. Looking up from this kaleidoscope of color and movement, I suddenly saw the tops of the mountains amidst the clouds, deep violet in the setting sun. I caught my breath.

Irene and Piro knocked on our door at 5:30 the next morning. "All ready for our bike ride?"

"Sure." Christy and I sleepily joined them. Everything seemed set for our departure to Pokhara the next morning, so I felt I could take a couple of hours off.

The city was just coming awake as we rode in thick fog out to the rim road circling Kathmandu. The sun rose, cutting through the fog and casting golden rays across green fields. Swooping down a hill on my bike, I felt the wind around me as if I were flying. At the bottom of the hill Irene stopped and peered intently through her binoculars.

"Look." She handed me the binoculars. "You can see three egrets—a cattle egret, an intermediate egret, and a pond egret." I looked but couldn't distinguish one distant bird from another.

A curious group of children gathered nearby and stared. They took turns peering through the binoculars.

"What time?" asked a small boy, proudly showing off his English.

"Seven o'clock." I pointed to my watch. "We'd better get back. There's lots to do at the Sherpa Co-op this morning."

We rode back, pedaling as fast as we could. "I can sure use this exercise after a week in airplanes and offices," I called over to Irene.

"Yeah, after working out every day for a year, it's a shame to get out of shape now," she agreed as we whizzed past a rice paddy.

I thought of our training over the past year. I always try to spend an hour a day outside exercising anyway, but recently I had worked extra hard.

Our fitness had been tested nearly a year ago at the Institute of Environmental Stress located at the University of California, Santa Barbara. The strength and endurance of the entire team was found to be well above average. Particularly interesting was the fact that, although we ranged in age from twenty to forty-nine, there was no decrease in fitness with age apparent in our group—testimony to the value of regular exercise in maintaining fitness. At least a half hour a day of aerobic exercise had been recommended for each of us to maintain and improve our condition, and each had her own approach. I had walked up a steep hill near my house with 60 pounds of bricks in my pack or had run five to ten hilly miles each day. Margi and Annie had biked long distances. Irene had played soccer, run, and also carried heavy packs.

Arm strength is vital for carrying loads up steep faces on fixed lines, and women have a relatively poor arm-strength-to-weight ratio. Almost all of us had started lifting weights, and we were pleased at how rapidly our upper body strength increased. But most important, we had all done as much climbing and mountaineering together as we could—amidst the demands of the expedition's organizational work and of our normal lives.

"Anyhow, the trek up and down to Base Camp should get us back in shape," I said as we pedaled past two hundred members of the Nepalese Army out for a morning jog.

Irene looked doubtful. "I sure hope we can actually leave Kathmandu tomorrow."

"I can't see why not," I said. The food and gear had been bought and packed; Joan and Alison were already in Pokhara arranging for our porters; our staff had been selected, insured, and equipped; all the formalities had been completed. I was full of optimism as I pedaled over to the Sherpa Co-op, where Mike greeted me with the news that we had to pay the Sherpas food and lodging allowances for the time we were in Kathmandu as well as the air fare from their homes.

My optimism evaporated. "But that's not in the budget, Mike," I protested. "You were supposed to itemize *all* in-country expenses."

"I was sure you knew about it. It's the custom."

I sighed and did some quick mental arithmetic. "A thousand dollars extra we don't have."

The phone rang. It was Joan in Pokhara. She needed to know immediately how many loads there were. I raced down to the packing room to find out, but everyone had gone, leaving no word about the number of loads. I hurried back to an impatient Joan. "I need to know how many porters right away."

Just then Douglas Heck, the American ambassador, arrived to pick up the bottles he had kindly offered to fill with purified drinking water. I didn't know where they were.

Piro appeared. "What food should I buy for the bus ride tomorrow?" Liz rushed in wanting to know where to buy seam sealant. Annie needed money to pay for food, and they were all talking at once.

I felt overwhelmed for a moment, and then remembered we were in Asia. "I'm going out for some tea. Anybody want to come along?"

That evening Mike Cheney came over to the Siddhartha to give us a sendoff talk on trekking protocol. We all crowded into one of the larger rooms.

"First of all, girls," Cheney said, "I must commend you. So far you've been one of the best organized expeditions we've seen. You've been working awfully hard; now you ought to relax and enjoy the first week of the approach march as much as possible. Let the Sherpas take care of things. They expect to give you tea in the morning, do the cooking, select campsites, and set up the tents.

"And don't worry about the porters. They've been doing this for generations, and they have worked out their own system. But do try to get to know the porters as people, and keep an eye on their loads. When you're walking beside them, don't ignore them. Let them know you're the same party as they are."

"But we can't talk with them," Vera W. objected.

"There are all sorts of ways you can communicate. When they're sitting down for a rest, sit down with them and offer them a cigarette. If they make a sign like they're striking a match, that means they want a light.

"It's especially important for you to build good relations with the porters because the last four days to Annapurna Base Camp are particularly rugged. Try to reassure the porters you're going to look after them. If you get a good set of porters, it's just possible you may go straightaway to Base Camp.

"Even though trekking during the monsoon has a bad reputation, I think it's the best time. The flowers and green countryside are spectacular. Just keep an eye out for leeches."

"Where are the leeches?" Vera W. looked worried.

"Wherever the cattle graze, especially along the paths on which they're taken out of the villages each morning and brought back in the evening. The leeches are quite intelligent. There are many more around at five o'clock in the evening than at midday. They seem to know when the cattle are due to come by.

"In fact, when you look closely at the grass and bushes alongside the paths, you can actually see leeches stretching out from them, just waiting for something to pass by. Don't go into the undergrowth because that's where the leeches will certainly be lurking."

I tried to reassure the others, who looked somewhat disgusted. "Leeches aren't so bad. They don't carry disease, and their bites seldom get infected."

Mike continued. "The other annoying thing about walking

through the hills in the monsoon is that farmers invariably use the paths as irrigation ditches. Even when it's not raining, the main trail is usually a running stream because someone is using it to take water from one field to another."

"Are there any local customs we should know about, Mike?" Margi asked.

"Well, it's considered very rude to step over someone's legs, so be sure not to do it. And don't sit with your legs across the trail. And last, but it seems to me the most important thing for your group, is to be a good expedition. Lots of expeditions aren't, even if they manage to get to the top. You've got to stay together as a team all the way through.

"You all know that altitude affects people's tempers and attitudes. So at the high camps some of your sister climbers will be so bloody irritating you'll just want to wring their necks. But once you get down to Base Camp, it will all be forgotten.

"You've got a lot of people rooting for you. The press here will be watching you. We don't want two girls coming back saying, 'Oh, we couldn't get on with them.' You should come back as one happy group, just as you're setting out. And with the same number of people, of course."

I looked around the room at the attentive faces of our team and said a silent prayer that this would indeed be the case.

3 The Trek

August 15–21

We cheered loudly as our overladen bus lurched forward. We were finally on our way to Pokhara, and from there we would begin walking to Base Camp. Boxes were piled three high on top of the bus, and the inside was crammed with mem-sahibs, Sherpas, and an assortment of potatoes, cabbages, anonymous packages, and small Nepalese boys who seemed to have come along for the spectacle. Our driver—a swarthy Sikh with a magenta turban, fuzzy black beard, and ballooning paunch—kept glancing licentiously at Dyanna on his left, rather than keeping his eyes on the road ahead. Seven hot, dusty hours, four tea stops, three checkpoints, and two flat tires later, we had covered only half the distance to Pokhara, which is advertised as a five-hour trip.

As we waited for the latest flat tire to be repaired, Vera W. cast longing glances at the Japanese sedans speeding by, and

Annie wandered aimlessly down the dusty road. Suddenly she spotted wild *Cannabis* growing in the drainage ditch three feet to her left. Glancing over her shoulder to make sure she wasn't being watched—most difficult in Nepal—she enthusiastically began picking the tender, sticky tops. Piro and Irene noticed Annie busy in the ditch and came over to see what she was up to. Irene's face broke into a grin, while Piro seemed puzzled about the significance of these roadside weeds. Soon we were all laughing and watching Annie.

"It's a doper's paradise," was proper Vera W.'s analysis.

At twilight we reached Pokhara and gratefully stumbled out of the bus. This was to be our last ride for months. We had just motored 80 miles in ten hours, but our next 80 miles would take ten days of walking. The 15 miles between Base Camp and the summit would take at least six weeks.

We greeted Joan and Alison who told us everything was ready for an early morning departure on the following day. Meanwhile, local porters swarmed all over the bus, throwing our none-too-sturdy boxes off the top with little care for how or where they landed. Lopsang handed me a bill for forty-five rupees for the services of these porters.

"Lopsang, we can't afford to pay so many extra bills. Members and Sherpas should unload boxes themselves." I felt obligated to protest in order to help dam the flood of unexpected expenses.

"All Americans very rich. Can pay," he said.

"Memsahibs are not so rich. We can't afford these things."

"All expeditions say they cannot afford, but America is a rich country. Plenty money," Lopsang was certain.

"No, we are not rich. This time we'll pay, but next time no." I slowly counted out the forty-five rupees.

At dinner, Lopsang watched as most of the members ordered beer at fifteen rupees a bottle—a day's wages for a local porter. I blushed as I imagined him thinking, memsahibs have little money for porters—much for beer.

The next morning was gray, but as the fog dissipated, the mountains appeared like a painted backdrop behind our camp. The peaks seemed two-dimensional, colored white, gray, and black; and foothills led to higher peaks lost in the clouds. It was a welcome reminder that there were indeed calm, cool mountains up there somewhere. All was chaos and heat down here. Liz described the scene in her diary:

> The sight of the two-hundred barefoot people thronging outside the gate, like hungry hordes waiting for their rations, made me feel sick. They're herded in one at a time, the Sherpas shouting orders at them like taskmasters. Each gets a headstrap, a sheet of plastic for the rain, a 66-pound package, a number, a fingerprint instead of a signature, and a small advance in pay and then the next one is herded in. Watching them get loaded down with our

Liz and Christy organizing our 200 loads, Pokhara. Vera Komarkova.

tons of superfluous crap is turning my stomach. There are women and children who don't look strong enough to carry 30 pounds. The common excuses are "They're carrying lighter weights than usual and getting paid more . . . There wouldn't have been donations of eighty thousand dollars for a hospital, and we're giving them ten days work, after all." It doesn't seem justifiable for something so absurd as climbing a dangerous mountain.

After our two-hundred loads had been given out to two-hundred porters, dozens of others were left without employment. Some had walked several days from their homes in hopes of getting work, and I saw the pain in their eyes as the Sherpas turned them away. Like Liz, I had always felt uncomfortable about porters carrying my gear, but after several trips to Nepal, I knew that the rural people were eager for the job, which brought them much more money than working their farms.

Nepal has few roads, and numerous rivers cut across its terrain. Many trails include bridges that cannot be crossed by pack animals, so commodities are transported into the hills on people's backs. The increasing development of Nepal is not necessarily bettering the life of the ordinary porter yet. Road-building means that the porters are replaced by trucks. Deprived of their livelihood, many are forced to move to the city, where they frequently end up in the destitute ranks of the urban unemployed.

By the time our caravan of 230 people—porters, Sherpas, memsahibs—finally left Pokhara, it was midday and steaming hot. We filed through the Pokhara bazaar and the dusty suburbs, then out onto a trail leading eventually to Mustang and Tibet. This ancient path, between one and three feet wide, is one of the major trade arteries in the kingdom, as important as Interstate 80 is in the United States. The number of caravans has decreased since the Chinese closed the Tibetan border nineteen years ago, but the trail was still full of Nepalese going from one village to the next and porters laden with all manner of goods, from brass bedsteads to coops full of live chickens.

Two sweltering hours from Pokhara we reached our evening's campsite—a Tibetan refugee camp on a bluff above the Yangdi Khola. Pasang had set an elaborate tea table, with a red and white checked tablecloth and a vase of flowers. We sat peacefully admiring the view of green terraced hillsides as a gentle breeze dried our sweat. After their tea, the Sherpas pitched our brand-new red and green tents. Meanwhile the villagers had gathered around our camp. Dark, politely curious eyes stared at us—these American memsahibs in shorts and fancy hats, sipping tea at an elegant table.

The contrast between our material affluence and the ragged throng watching us made me uncomfortable. But I knew that although we have our money and our possessions—things the Nepalese may want—they have things we are lacking. An American woman married to a Nepalese once told me, "I want my children to grow up in Asia where they will have a strong sense of family and a connection with the past."

"Mithai, mithai." A child stretched out her hand for sweets. Many tourists had traveled this way before.

After tea, I went off to record the day's events by talking into the tape recorder, which I was using to keep a diary. I sat in the shade of a large peepul tree, said to be the kind of tree under which the Buddha attained enlightenment. As the wind blew the thick monsoon clouds in, an enormous hawk soared by so close that I could see its eyes staring at me. The Nepalese children were staring too. How strange—this lady was talking to herself! But soon they were singing into the tape recorder and laughing with delight as I played their voices back to them.

While sitting there, I suddenly felt nauseated—as though I would burst with severe gas pains that extended from the bottom of my feet to the top of my head. With some difficulty, I escaped my entourage and squatted behind a bush. The pain dissipated as quickly as it had come, leaving me drained and weak—a too-familiar experience for me in Asia. Now that we were on the trail cooking our own food, I assumed I would recover soon.

Every day before dinner Piro and Annie held a clinic, and I went there to consult with them on the state of my intestines. They were treating the assorted complaints of a long line of patients—porters and local people. This makeshift clinic was quite a change for Piro, who is a specialist in ophthalmic surgery and hadn't treated such diverse illnesses since medical school. During the last year Piro had practiced setting bones and pulling teeth to get ready for expedition doctoring. "Just don't get appendicitis," she had cautioned us.

Piro had come to the United States from Hungary as a child; she hadn't started climbing until after she had graduated from medical school and was a resident in the Northwest. There she became an expert rockclimber, met Joan Firey, and took up Alpine climbing. Piro was slender, almost frail looking, but she had a toughness that I suspected would make her one of our strongest climbers. She lived alone in Seattle and was devoted to her home and to her privacy. Christy described Piro as fiercely independent, and in some ways she managed to live alone even on the expedition, avoiding meetings and never taking sides during a disagreement. Despite her separateness—maybe sometimes because of it—everyone liked and respected Piro.

Piro had finally worked her way through the many patients, and we went into the mess tent for a sumptuous dinner of fresh cucumbers, noodle soup, carrots and turnips, rice, chicken, cabbage salad, strawberry jello, tea and coffee.

As we ate, Piro told us about her first surgery. "Wangel got hit by a falling rock today. Not only did he get a cut on his head, he bit his tongue hard at the same time. Dyanna and I set up for surgery in a nearby yard, between the pecking hens and wandering goats. I was kneeling in the barnyard, stitching along smoothly, when I decided to change knees and managed to drop some barnyard material on my instruments. But Wangel seems to be doing okay."

We listened to Piro and to the rain, which was beating down on the tent like hailstones. Inside, we felt warm and close.

Trekking in Nepal is a most pleasant and civilized way to spend one's time. Our days usually began at half-past five in the morning with a cup of tea handed into the tent by our smiling cookboy, who was squatting under an umbrella outside. Drinking the tea very carefully so as not to spill any on our sleeping bags, we would gently wake up. Then we would pack and eat breakfast rapidly, aiming to be on the trail by half-past six. The day would be spent strolling through exquisite Nepalese countryside. Members usually walked in pairs and would meet at teahouses from time to time during the day. On a typical day, we would cover ten miles during five to eight hours of walking.

The porters and Sherpas stopped frequently to smoke, eat, and drink, too; but some of them walked faster than we did and would reach the evening's campsite first, so that our tents would be set up and tea ready when we arrived.

On the second morning Liz, another early riser, and I left camp before breakfast. I soon found myself telling her my wor-

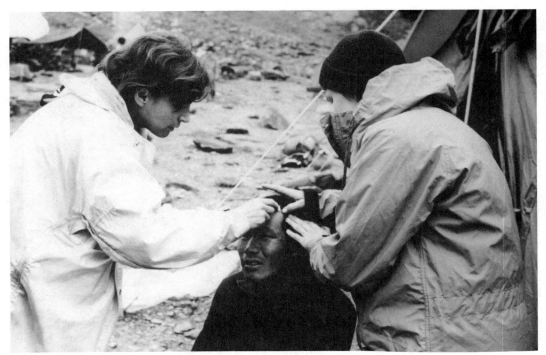

Piro, assisted by Dyanna, stitches up the cut on Wangel's forehead.
Arlene Blum.

ries about whether there was enough food.

"Why don't you stop worrying and leave the food to Joan?" she suggested. "It's her job."

"I wish I could," I replied. "But there are lots more people eating with us than we had originally planned on, and I can't persuade Joan that there's a problem."

"Actually, I've been more worried about the tension between you two than about running out of food," Liz said. "You've got to settle your differences."

As usual, Liz had picked out the important issue. Expedition stresses can bring out the extremes in people, but Liz maintained a moderate position. She was a strong voice on safety matters, and I agreed with her point of view on most climbing issues. Although she was one of our strongest and most experienced ice climbers, she had no intention of risking her life unnecessarily to climb Annapurna. Nor her teaching job: when we had arrived in Kathmandu, she had told me she had to be back at work by mid-October and might have to leave before we reached the summit. I hoped we could make our summit attempt before she had to leave; we needed her strength and stability.

"Don't worry," she continued, "I'll work with Joan to inventory the food. It's pretty hard for me to imagine that we don't have enough of everything. Watching the porters sweating up the hills loaded with all our junk makes me feel sick."

As the path went up a steep hill, Liz and I caught up with a

Porters ascending steps on the way to Ghorapani. Vera Komarkova.

row of laboring porters. They carried their loads in baskets suspended by tumplines from their foreheads. According to His Majesty's government regulations, the expedition was to pay each porter $1.75 and two cigarettes per day for the arduous work of carrying a 66-pound load over these steep, rough trails. A few porters carried two loads—a total of 132 pounds—an amazing burden for a slight man.

We stopped to rest, and Mr. Gurung, our liaison officer, came up carrying about 30 pounds in a brand-new red backpack. It was democratic of him to carry this load, as liaison officers traditionally don't carry anything at all. Liz told Mr. Gurung about her guilty conscience every time she saw a barefoot porter struggling up the steep hillside.

"Oh, memsahib, don't worry," he said. "This is a very good job. Porters are very happy. Other work they earn much less money. Fourteen rupees a day. We pay twenty-one. Expedition work is best. They go off with friends, dance and drink at night, leaving their families at home to work on the farm."

Liz listened closely to Mr. Gurung but wasn't convinced. "Let's do whatever we can to make it easier for them," she urged me.

I agreed with Liz, both for the porters' benefit and our own. Only if porter morale was high did we stand much chance of getting our loads directly into Base Camp.

After dinner that night I proposed a meeting to discuss potential problems with porters and food and how we were getting along as a group. Piro immediately disappeared, Margi groaned loudly, and Vera K. yawned. I gave up.

I hoped this evident lack of enthusiasm wouldn't be repeated every time I called for a group discussion. Before leaving the States, the team had met several times with Karin Carrington, a clinical psychologist. Initially when she had offered to work with us on group dynamics, I told her we needed gear and food more than therapy. But several members, in particular, Joan and Vera W., had persuaded me that such a meeting could be valuable.

Usually not mentioned in the traditional expedition account is the fact that large climbs are frequently not happy experiences for some of the participants. The stress and oxygen deprivation of high-altitude climbing can lead to depression and to hostility between climbers. There had been general doubt amongst the climbing community about whether women could pull off this climb and even greater doubt about whether a group of women could continue to get along under high-altitude conditions.

The first meeting with Karin had taken place one day in May, after a hard day's packing. Gradually, we had begun to share some of our fears and expectations. The conversation, which was vague at first, sharpened until Joan admitted that she did not fully trust my leadership and wanted to be climbing leader herself.

It was an uncomfortable moment for me, but it led to a worthwhile discussion of the issue of leadership. The other climbers said they respected Joan's judgment and experience but still wanted me as leader. And they wanted me to be a strong, decisive leader, but they also expected to contribute to major decisions. I was pleased at the expression of confidence in my ability but somewhat confused by their mandate. What does it mean to be the "strong leader" of ten tough-minded women who all want to contribute to each decision?

We met with Karin several more times and left for Nepal resolved to keep discussing our differences and to avoid building up resentments. So far morale was high even though nobody wanted to have group meetings to discuss it.

Our physical health was not holding up quite so well, however. One evening the cook confused Betadine—an iodine-containing brown liquid that we diluted to disinfect our wash water—with the soy sauce. We sprinkled the thick brown liquid on our spicy fried rice and within hours a diarrhea epidemic swept the camp. A cold was also making the rounds. Still, colds and diarrhea on the trek were not disastrous, as long as we recovered by the time we reached Base Camp.

The next day the trail wound through paddy fields and frequently became an irrigation canal as Cheney had warned. At first we balanced from stone to stone to keep our feet dry, but soon we gave up and sloshed along ankle deep. The cool water was soothing to our blistered feet. Sweat dripped off my forehead, and my back was soaked wherever it touched my pack.

When I took my pack off, the metal frame was so hot it scorched my fingers.

The sun burned away the mist just as we reached the bustling village of Chandrikot. Annie ran up to me in a state of high excitement. "The mountains! They're finally clear. Come tell me which one is Annapurna I."

She pulled me to the edge of the village, where we could see the panorama of the Annapurna Range. Annapurna is the name of an Indian harvest goddess. The name roughly translated means "full of sustenance." There are five mountains bearing the same name: Annapurna South, dominating our view; Annapurna III, a smaller peak a few miles to the east; Annapurnas II and IV, a separate massif reaching 26,000 feet, about 10 miles to the northeast; and Annapurna I, the highest of the Annapurnas and our goal.

The Annapurnas are so spread out and so varied in appearance that their greatest similarity is the name. I had made a quick trip to Nepal a year earlier to carry out a reconnaisance of Annapurna I and Annapurna II with a friend who had a permit for the latter peak, also for the fall of 1978. I was amazed to discover it took about a week's walk across a 17,700-foot pass to go from Annapurna I Base Camp to Annapurna II.

"That's the south face of Annapurna I peeking out behind Annapurna South." I pointed to a small white triangle, impossibly far away.

The summit, floating more than four vertical miles above us in the clouds, was so remote that our desire to stand there seemed arrogant. I thought of those mortals who had angered the gods with their presumption and been struck down. We must make our peace with the gods—and with ourselves—before we could reach the top.

From Chandrikot the path dropped 2,000 feet down a steep rock trail to the crystal blue Modi Khola, crossed it, and continued straight up the other side. Most rivers in Nepal flow from Tibet to India, north to south across this small kingdom. For now our route was west, continually up and over ridges, down to rivers, across bridges then back up. And what a remarkable assortment of bridges took us across these rivers!

The classic Himalayan suspension bridge is made of two parallel strands of chain-link, braided rope or vine, often several hundred feet long, hung high across the stream about three feet apart. Ten-foot lengths of rope or vine connect the two strands forming a trough in which boards are placed. You grasp the two heavy strands and walk carefully across the boards. There is invariably a broken board and a sway to the bridge when you reach the center, leaving you to step dizzily from rope to rope as the foaming river beckons from below.

As Nepal has become a popular target for foreign aid, these old bridges have been largely replaced by an international col-

Crossing a bamboo bridge just beyond Pokhara. Arlene Blum.

lection. China, India, Britain, and New Zealand have all contributed solid wood and metal structures. Presumably more substantial than the classic vine and hemp models, these new
bridges fall victim to the fury of the spring floods too.

A thousand sweltering feet above the Birethanti wooden
bridge a clump of peepul trees offered relief from the sun. When
we reached them, Annie and I gratefully took off our packs and
joined a tiger-striped cat stretched out in the shade.

Some Gurung women walked by, talking loudly. They reminded me of the buxom Midwestern matrons from my child-
hood on their way to the supermarket, except that they were
wearing flowing robes of purple and gold and large gold rings
in their noses. One of them came up to me and boldly
reached down to feel my calf. She said, "Memsahib very big."
At five feet ten inches, I am taller than most of the Nepalese,
who seem to find my size extraordinary in a woman.

Two of our women porters walked by talking happily.
About ten of our porters were women, who worked smoothly
along with the male porters and carried the same heavy loads up
and down the steep trails without complaint. What a contrast to

the Sherpanis, who had porters carrying their personal gear and needed help on slippery parts of the trail. They tried to make themselves useful by helping with the laundry and packing and unpacking our baggage, but they primarily succeeded in making us uncomfortable. I wondered whether we could train a couple of the strong women porters to help us carry loads up the mountain.

All too soon, it was time for Annie and me to put our heavy packs onto our still-damp backs and leave the shade of the peepul tree. But we soon came to a teahouse where a tame monkey begged coins and picked lice from the scalp of an old woman. Alison and Vera W. were already there, and as often was the case Alison was surrounded by a group of children playing some private game. As we watched them play, Vera W. remarked that Alison would be a good mother. Over tea, I complimented Alison on her way with children.

"I'd really like to have my own some day," Alison sighed. "I'm waiting for things to settle down."

"Me too," I agreed. But I was thirty-three and Alison thirty-six; we both knew too well that things would have to settle

One of our women porters carrying a heavy load. Irene Miller.

down soon. We were facing the age barrier that would force us to make a choice between a family and other things. The thirties are said to be the optimum age for high-altitude climbing, but that's also the time when most women are raising families. Several women with young children had been invited on this expedition, but after much deliberation they had decided not to go. All the women here were childless or had older children.

The next day stone steps, worn smooth by the feet of countless porters over hundreds of years, led abruptly from hot moist fields at 3,500 feet through rain forest to the chill windswept Ghorapani Pass at 9,300 feet. In just a few hours walk, we could see climate and vegetation changes equivalent to those encountered when traveling from Mexico to Alaska.

The rain forest was a spooky place. Ancient knotted trees dripped with mosses, lichens, and leeches. Sweat on my face mixed with droplets in the air and joined puddles on the ground. Wild orchids—purple, blue, and white—grew out of rotting vegetable matter. Vera K. was off the trail happily stuffing orchids, rhododendrons, and countless unknown plants into her collecting bag.

Alison playing with Nepalese children near Khare. Arlene Blum.

Inching my way across a slippery downed tree trunk that
bridged a stream, I realized something was missing. Where was
my big black umbrella? Umbrellas—used to protect the traveler
against rain and sun and as a walking stick—are essential in
Nepal. I must have forgotten it back at a rest stop. I dropped my
pack and began to run down the trail. There was a smiling
porter walking up and carrying a big black umbrella. I thanked
him profusely for returning it.

Torrents of icy rain made us cold, wet, and miserable by the
time we reached our campsite at Ghorapani—a soggy field full
of leeches. Lopsang was standing under an umbrella barking
directions at the porters to keep our loads dry. His job was
complex and he did it well, working about fourteen hours a day
managing the porters, Sherpas, memsahibs, bookkeeping, and
bargaining. For all his skill and hard work, the climbing regulations decreed his salary to be about three dollars a day.

Lopsang told me that five porters had deserted in the cold
rain, and that he was trying to hire five others. Looking at the
shivering, unhappy porters, I asked, "Do you think many of the
others will desert before we reach Base Camp?"

Lopsang assigns loads to the porters in Pokhara. Arlene Blum.

He shrugged. "On Japanese Churen Himal expedition last spring, 330 porters. Big problem."

"What do you mean?"

"Two days before base camp we had to cross pass with snow." He indicated snow up to his waist. "Most porters run away. Only sixteen porters stay. Five Sherpas, ten members, sixteen porters must carry 330 loads to base camp. For one month we carried loads over the snowy pass. Over and over same route. Very hard work. Then all tired. No summit."

I thought of the high pass we would have to cross two days beyond Choya. During last December's reconnaissance it had been snow covered. Would our porters run away, too, forcing us to waste all the good weather relaying loads to Base Camp?

I forgot these larger worries when I looked at the ground and noticed an army of leeches moving towards me. Three were already attached to my ankle. I pulled them off with some disgust and retreated to the tent where half a dozen more had already taken up residence.

Irene returned from the bushes shaken. While she had squatted, four slimy leeches had crawled onto her bottom. She managed to pull them off before they could attach and begin to suck her blood, so no damage had been done—except possibly to Irene's psyche. "Squat high if you have to squat," was her advice to us.

I had to go off to the bushes, too, and noticed with alarm that as soon as I squatted the leeches started towards me. I couldn't help admiring their sinuous locomotion. A half-inch leech would stretch to a length of nearly two inches, wave around until it sensed a warm object, plant its waving end on the ground, contract and repeat the graceful stretching motion with its other end. I was reminded of a Slinky, the coiled wire toy that climbs down stairs. Undoubtedly my appreciation would have been enhanced had I not been the leeches' prey. The best strategy, I decided, was to squat quickly in an open area.

After dinner I accepted Mr. Gurung's invitation to visit the local hotel. The porters were dancing and drinking rakshi (a sharp-tasting liquor distilled from fermented rice) in front of a blazing fire. The dancers moved sensually to the rhythm of a drummer; their rapid hip movement reminded me of the veiled dancing boys of Afghanistan.

An assortment of other travelers watched the dancers from around the fire. A large Sikh, his fingers greasy with remnants of rice and dal, enthusiastically waved and clapped in time to the music. Our Sherpas crowded in to watch and join the dance, except Mingma and Lakpa, who were out in the rain guarding the loads.

As I passed them on the way to my tent, I wished them good night and thanked them for their efforts.

"Only three more nights out," Mingma responded. " After Choya no people. Loads safe."

Putting on our soggy tennis shoes and damp clothes each morning was unpleasant, and most of us were subdued at breakfast. We usually ate our porridge, tea, and chapatis (Nepalese tortillas) in silence. Margi was more talkative.

"God, I'm sick of porridge, especially lumpy porridge," she began.

Silence.

"At least there's strawberry jam." Margi grabbed the jam tin from in front of Vera W. who was just about to put some on her chapati.

Everyone groaned inwardly. Margi had a large presence, and her breakfast manners were getting on our nerves. She was in charge of making all the lunches; today she carried on that this would delay her, and she wanted to leave early. After fifteen minutes of complaining, Margi got to work and efficiently packed thirteen lunches in a few minutes.

As she handed me my lunch, I asked her to walk with me, saying that I wanted to get her opinion on food calculations. Though the youngest of the climbers, Margi had an acute mind and a good sense of organization. She had been keeping track of our fast-diminishing stores of rice, and she shared my concern that we would run out of food. Before we discussed logistics, though, I thought a few personal comments were in order. If Margie was annoying people down here, her complaining could be intolerable high on the mountain.

"You know, Margi, you do as much work as anybody else and help me a lot with planning, but you complain so much that you don't get credit for all your hard work."

She looked surprised, thought a minute, and finally agreed. "Yeah, maybe I do." She paused and said, "Thanks for telling me—I'll try to cool it. And please tell me again if there's stuff about me that bothers you later on." I was pleased by her lack of defensiveness. She was secure enough to accept my criticism and to realize that it was meant in her own best interest.

Soon we emerged from the forest, and the Kali Gandaki River came into view. I turned to Margi. "That water comes from the Annapurna Glacier and from Mustang, a piece of Nepal that extends north into Tibet."

We crossed a modern suspension bridge above the churning torrent. On the other side our trail joined the route north from India followed by Maurice Herzog and his team when they made the extraordinary first ascent of Annapurna in 1950. At that time the few maps of the area were inaccurate, and the French spent weeks trying to penetrate the "Grand Barrier" of icy peaks rising to 25,000 feet and surrounding Annapurna I. In April, they pioneered the difficult route we would follow from Choya above the precipitous Miristi Khola Gorge into the Base Camp on the north side of Annapurna. After they finally found the peak, they climbed it rapidly by the Sickle Glacier route, and on June 3 Herzog and Louis Lachenal reached the summit.

Annie and Vera K. crossing a bridge over the Kali Gandaki on the way to Tatopani. Marie Ashton.

The monsoon had broken just as they began their harrowing descent. Herzog's hands and toes became severely frostbitten after he lost his gloves right below the summit. Delirious with pain, he was carried on porters' backs down to base camp and then all the way to India on steep, muddy trails in the monsoon. He crossed the steaming Indian plains by railway, the expedition doctor removing his gangrenous fingers and toes and throwing them off the train as they went.

Since that epic first ascent, Annapurna had been attempted twelve more times with three successful ascents. In 1970, the British-Nepalese Army Expedition, led by Henry Day, made the second ascent of Herzog's route. Writing to me about the avalanche danger on this route, Day said, "I do not believe the Sickle is a justifiable route—now that I am the father of two."

At the same time another British expedition led by Chris Bonington climbed the peak by a new route on the precipitous south face—the most difficult climbing done at such altitudes up to that time.

In 1976 a Dutch team, led by A. A. Verrijn-Stuart, avoided the dangers of the Sickle by climbing a steep ice rib to the east.

Our plan was either to repeat the Dutch route or to try another new variation even farther east.

Margi and I walked just beyond the village of Tatopani, which is noted for its hot springs. We joined Alison for a bath at a hot pool on the edge of town. When we got back to the hotel where we were spending the night, the whole back courtyard was spread with newspapers and hundreds of drying plants. Vera K. had a grant to study the vegetation of the Nepalese countryside and was trying to collect and identify most species of plants that grew in the area. A mammoth task, but she was enjoying it.

Meanwhile, Lopsang, Liz, and Vera W. were off trying to buy rice for the porters. It was hard for our Sherpa cook—or even the members—to grasp the enormous quantities of rice we would need to get to Base Camp. Margi and I had made the calculations that morning. The porters would spend six days going from Choya to Base Camp and back. Beyond Choya there were no villages to provide food and lodging. Porters carry 60 pounds and eat at least two pounds of rice per day: in six days, two hundred porters would eat at least 2,400 pounds of rice. Forty more porters would be needed to carry this amount of rice. These porters would, in turn, eat another 480 pounds of rice, and eight more porters would be needed to carry the rice to feed the porters who carried rice for the original porters—the ones who carried our boxes. These eight porters would eat 96 pounds of rice . . .

Lopsang could find only five additional porters, so we bought 300 pounds of rice. "Very much rice," he assured me. It was not nearly enough, but we could not buy more rice if there was no one to carry it.

August 21 was our last day on good trails. At about noon we camped on the outwash plain of the Pangbu Khola, just beyond the village of Choya. While most of the team went off to take baths, Liz, Lopsang, and I went into Choya to shop for more porter food. Rice was not available, so we tried to buy about 1,500 pounds of tsampa (flour ground from roasted barley). In order to get it we had to go from house to house, buying as much as we could at each. We would sit on the floor of a smoky room around an open fire, where the mother would be cooking potatoes as the children peeled them. Frogs hung from the ceiling, being smoked over the fire, and a hole in the roof served as a chimney.

The father would squat by the fire and negotiate a price. The mother would loudly protest that too many of her rations were being bargained away or that the price was too low. After the bargaining, the father would drag out the gunny sacks of tsampa and begin a complex measuring ritual—pour out of one bag onto a tray and scoop by handfuls into a measuring cup. Meanwhile, the woman would chant, almost as though praying, the Nepali numbers "*ek-ek-ek . . .*" until the measure was poured; then "*dui-dui-dui . . . tin-tin-tin . . .*" until the sackfuls were measured. This same procedure was repeated at the next house.

Liz and I went to house after house, but when we got back to camp exhausted, we still hadn't collected nearly enough tsampa. Joan offered to buy the rest the next day.

At twilight, the clouds separated briefly, exposing an icy ridge leading to the top of Annapurna. As I drifted off to sleep, I heard the Sherpas singing with the villagers—the last villagers we would be with for two months.

The French Pass 4

August 22–27

"*Om mani padme hum, om mani padme hum.*" Mingma had been praying in the next tent since before dawn. Today we would begin the most difficult part of our ten-day journey to Annapurna North Base Camp.

I remembered this part of the route from my reconnaissance trip the previous year. The first day is a four-thousand-foot thrash through dense vertical forest on a slippery mud trail to "jungle camp." The next day the forest diminishes and equally steep grassy slopes lead to the French Pass at 14,500 feet, first crossed by Maurice Herzog's party in 1950. Then a lengthy exposed traverse above the immense canyon of the Miristi Khola leads to the third camp. The leader of the Dutch expedition had written me that they had lost four loads last year on this traverse. (What had happened to the porters carrying the loads wasn't made clear.) On the final day the route descends precipitously several thousand feet to the river and then goes up again for several thousand feet to the site of Base Camp at the foot of the Annapurna North Glacier.

Outside my tent I saw Lopsang surrounded by a throng of gesticulating porters. He came over when he saw me awake.

"Namaste, bara memsahib. These porters are afraid. They do not want to go to Base Camp. They want to run home."

Looking at their bare feet and the ragged shorts and shirts that most were wearing, I sympathized. If there were an unseasonable snowstorm on the French Pass, their clothing would be woefully inadequate.

"Ask the porters to carry one load today up to jungle

camp," I suggested to Lopsang. "If they're still afraid, they can go home tomorrow."

If most of the porters were to leave, we could wind up spending all the good weather after the monsoon ferrying loads rather than climbing, just as the Churen Himal expedition had done. Lopsang did persuade the porters to carry their loads at least one more day, though they left inhabited terrain with some reluctance. Irene and I waited to make sure that all the loads were taken and then followed behind the last of our porters. We walked along talking as the terrain became steeper and steeper.

"After hearing about your trip here last year, I'm anxious about losing my nerve before I ever get to Base Camp," she confessed. "I'm afraid of the steep slopes near the French Pass."

"Come on. I said that the way to Base Camp would be hard for people who had never done cross-country hiking. But you won't have any trouble with it, I promise."

We followed the narrow track down between cliffs to the banks of the Tangdung Khola, where we stopped for lunch. This was the only area on today's trek both flat and large enough for a comfortable lunch stop. It was also the last convenient source of water for two days.

Beyond the river, the trail abruptly switchbacked up a nearly vertical rock slab covered with mud, slimy leaves, and an occasional root to grasp for balance; then it entered the rain forest. Rhododendron bushes, gnarled trees, and unfamiliar yellow, white, and blue flowers grew densely along the extremely steep slope to many feet above our heads. A narrow muddy path led straight up through the impassable vegetation. Our boots and tennis shoes slipped and slid in the steep ooze; the toes of the barefoot porters seemed to provide better traction. By the time I reached jungle camp, my face was running with sweat, and my arms and legs burned from repeated encounters with stinging nettles. Still, I was elated at finally climbing above the last villages.

Last year I'd named this camp Dhaulagiri View Camp for the panorama it offered of the Dhaulagiri Range across the way. Dhaulagiri I, at 26,795 feet the highest peak of the group, is only 15 miles from Annapurna I. The Kali Gandaki Valley cuts between the two mountains at an altitude of only 9,000 feet— one of the most spectacular elevation changes to be found anywhere in the world. Today the camp boasted neither view— because of a heavy cloud cover—nor water, despite the moisture in the air. We had to walk half an hour down to a small spring for water.

Food for the porters was by now the critical problem. Yesterday we had only managed to buy 300 of the 2,000 pounds of food we needed. Joan had stayed behind to buy the rest, but at about four o'clock in the afternoon she came up to jungle camp with the meager results of her tsampa buying. "It's a local holiday. Nobody would make tsampa today."

A line of porters descends a steep trail on the way to jungle camp.
Vera Watson.

After totaling our rice and tsampa supplies, I was aghast. We had nearly two hundred hungry porters and only 400 pounds of food—enough for one more day. I pulled a three-legged stool over to the cook fire where Lopsang was eating tsampa with relish, dipping his fingers knuckle deep into the brown, pasty stuff, rolling it into a ball, then eating it.

"We cannot go on without more food. After one more day all the porter food will be finished. Porters will go home and leave six Sherpas and ten members to carry two hundred loads to Base Camp. We won't be able to climb Annapurna."

Expedition members breakfasting in Choya while the Nepalese look on curiously. Arlene Blum.

At last Lopsang grasped the seriousness of the situation. As long as we'd had several hundred pounds of rice, he had kept saying, "Very much rice," not realizing the huge amounts we actually needed. If the porters stayed here the next day, they would eat up all their food without getting any of the loads closer to Base Camp. I quickly formed a plan. The 400 pounds of rice was barely enough to get fifty porters to Base Camp. They could go on while a few porters would go back to Choya for more rice. The rest could carry loads to the French Pass and then come back down here to sleep. Lopsang agreed it was worth trying, so Irene advanced the head naike (a naike is the leader of a group of about fifty porters) 3,000 rupees to buy rice and tsampa in Choya. Night was falling when he and his porters began to slide down the muddy trail.

The next morning was pandemonium. Food and loads had to be organized for Alison, Annie, and the fifty porters who were going straight through to Base Camp. Hardware and fixed line had to be taken out of boxes so that hand lines could be placed for protection on the more treacherous sections. The 100 porters who were to ferry loads to the French Pass and return needed these loads too. Rain was pouring down, and 150 porters were milling around trying to grab a load—any load—and start on their way at the same time as we tried to organize the 200 heavy boxes and baskets.

Vera W. and Liz were handing out four days' rations to the porters going all the way to Base Camp. But the other porters also wanted four days' rations and had to be persuaded that they would get more food that night. As the porters left, Irene checked off their identification numbers, while Joan passed out the cigarettes, made a copy of the list of contents, and helped Irene read the box numbers. A crowd of porters waited impatiently, and I saw several of them try to avoid the checkpoint.

"That's too many jobs for one person. I'll get somebody to help you," I offered.

But Joan silently continued doing all three jobs.

"You copy the list," I told her sharply. "Margi, come here and give out cigarettes. Christy, help read the numbers off the boxes."

The system finally worked smoothly—there are things to be said for army generals. But my stomach was knotted with stress. Annie had told me Lopsang was having stomach problems too, and his blood pressure was very high. I went over to his tent to see how he was feeling.

"Namaste, Lopsang. How are you?"

"Ah, bara memsahib. Namaste. Stomach very bad. Thank you."

So Westerners weren't the only ones to suffer from stress. Apparently the problems of leadership, the complexities of keeping track of Sherpas, porters, memsahibs, rice, and a thousand details were lodging themselves in both of our stomachs.

"In America, rich businessmen have many worries and must make many decisions. They get a bad stomachache called an ulcer. Maybe a sirdar is like a rich businessman. Work very hard."

Lopsang laughed loudly, delighted by the comparison.

I anxiously waited all day for the porter food to arrive. To my relief, at three in the afternoon the head naike came up from Choya smiling broadly and followed by porters carrying huge loads of tsampa and rice. It looked like enough. But we still had to weigh each load to make sure, and I thought to myself that today could be called the Day of the Pathi. A pathi equals three person-days of tsampa, or four person-days of rice. (Twelve pathis of tsampa weigh 48 pounds. Eight pathis of rice weigh 56 pounds.) The naike had bought 100 pathis of tsampa and 60 pathis of rice. A muri is twenty pathis. So actually he bought three muris of rice and five muris of tsampa—barely enough to get us to Base Camp. Despite all these muris and pathis, more of the porters were leaving. They wanted to go down where it was warm and dry.

Two porters heading up a grassy slope near the French Pass; Dhaulagiri in the background. Arlene Blum.

In the morning, as we climbed the steep trail from our camp up toward the French Pass, Dhaulagiri poked through the clouds, looking close enough to touch. The muddy path was overgrown with a magnificent profusion of brightly colored flowers. I've always been intrigued by the possibility of cloud-walking, and today it looked as though I could push off from the path, jump onto a cloud, and just stroll across to the summit of Dhaulagiri.

Joan was right behind me as I moved slowly up the grassy slopes beyond jungle camp. She had carried out an inventory which showed that in seven days of trekking we had consumed over half the rice and other staples that were supposed to last for three months. This meant we would have to send out for more local food at inflated prices.

"You've got to keep better track of the amounts of food," I told her with some impatience. "If we run out, we won't be able to climb the mountain."

"Well, I assumed Pasang cook could do it. I had no way of knowing we'd be feeding so many extra people." Joan sounded hurt. "And besides, I've never been good at complicated calculations."

How many times had I heard women lament their incompetence at mathematics more complex than simple arithmetic. Our conditioning holds us back in many hidden ways, not least among which is the dictum that "Girls can't do math." Fear of math keeps women from many careers, and now it was even threatening our climb.

I turned back to Joan with more sympathy for her problems in calculating amounts of food.

"I'll ask someone else to take charge of local food supplies if you don't feel comfortable doing it," I said.

"That's fine." But she did not look happy.

I let Joan go by and walked on alone, thinking about her. She was an extraordinary woman. Her three children were born within six years of each other, and she kept climbing the whole time. She told me she had ski-toured up to 9,000 feet on Mount Rainier when she was eight months pregnant. Carla, her first child, was taken to the Sawtooth Range when she was three weeks old. ("I didn't want to miss the annual Fourth of July outing.") Back in those days of bottle feeding, Joan had breast-fed her children so she could take them climbing more easily. "But I felt slightly apprehensive climbing and carrying a baby. So I'd lead the peak, and my husband would follow with those little feet dangling in the air."

I had climbed several times with Joan in the rugged North Cascades and had great respect for her toughness, self-sufficiency, and route-finding ability. If I hadn't been the leader, I was sure we would have become better friends.

I suppose Joan got to me because in some ways she was what I wanted to be—a natural leader, charismatic, decisive. We disagreed, it seemed, over virtually every issue that arose, and we both feared that factions might form around each of us and destroy the unity of the team. Before leaving for Nepal, we had discussed our conflict at length. She finally promised to support my decisions, yet the feelings between us had remained tense. Here on the trek it was crucial to do something about the food, but our past history had made me reluctant to step in until absolutely necessary. I worried that I had not handled the problem smoothly; Joan had looked hurt.

I walked alone the rest of the morning until I joined a group of porters for lunch. As we shared our food, they chattered away cheerfully enough, seemingly unaware of the cold mist descending on us. Would they still be this content tonight, sleeping on the exposed French Pass? Just below the pass I noticed the huts of shepherds who had brought their flocks up for the summer. This gave me an idea of how to raise porter morale. As soon as I got to camp I found Lopsang. "Tonight porters will be cold and hungry. We must give them some warm clothing and buy a sheep for them to eat."

Lopsang looked dubious about lavishing good clothing and meat on low-caste porters. "Cannot give clothing to porters unless all get the same. Do not have a hundred same," he objected.

We had brought along enough wool pants, shirts, sweaters, and hats to outfit thirty porters completely. Now that we had fewer than one hundred porters we would be able to partially outfit each one.

"Better to give each porter either a shirt or sweater or pants than nothing," I said.

"Okay, bara memsahib." Lopsang looked unconvinced. "Sherpas also need meat."

"Of course. Sherpas and members can take two legs of the sheep. Give porters the rest."

A large sheep with magnificent curved horns was dragged struggling to our camp. After a lengthy discussion of the unfortunate creature's merits, a price was agreed upon and the sheep led off to its fate.

Next I found Vera W. and asked her if she would be willing to take over buying the local food.

"Sure," she agreed. "But what about Joan?"

"Joan says she's not good at calculations," I said. "I'm afraid we'll run out of food unless the amounts are carefully monitored."

We went over to tell Pasang cook of the change. He immediately said, "Memsahib, show me how divide," pointing to the bloody carcass of the sheep. Vera W. suddenly looked uncertain about her new job, but I left her gamely discussing the sheep's anatomy with Pasang.

Meanwhile, Joan and Irene were giving out the clothing to the porters. I wished we could equip them all completely, but they seemed quite pleased as they marched around showing off their new gear. One porter wore a pair of wool pants belted under his armpits; another, a sweater down to his knees; a third sported bright red knicker socks, gloves, and cap along with his threadbare shorts, T-shirt, and plastic sandals.

The rain beat down on the tents steadily that night, but the morning was calm. Vera W. went outside early and exclaimed, "Oh, my God! You can see Annapurna—the west side, the Fang. You can see Dhaulagiri, the glacier. You can see Nilgiri."

The heavy rain had washed the dust particles from the air, leaving the icy peaks clearly visible for the first time. The pass was brilliant with flowers opening in the early morning sun, their petals spotted with shimmering droplets of water. We walked west along the ridge, knee deep in flowers; the steep Himalayan gorges dropped off vertically for thousands of feet on either side of us.

The Himalaya are a young mountain range, still thrusting higher and higher under the pressure of the collision of the Asian and Indian continental plates. Tanya Atwater, a geophysicist who is a friend, had once explained it to me. "India is running headlong into China, pushing the Himalaya upward. China is moving east into the Pacific to get out of the way, which causes faulting and numerous earthquakes in China."

While we were walking toward Annapurna, Tanya was leading an oceanographic expedition to study the rift that was formed in the middle of the Atlantic Ocean by the pulling apart of the African and the American continents. She and a woman graduate student were going one and a half miles below sea level in a submarine to carry out their research—the first time a woman was to lead such a complex diving expedition. Tanya and her student were wearing shirts that said "A Woman's Place Is On The Bottom." So this summer, we hoped women would be reaching both the "top" and the "bottom."

Vera K. was in her element in this steep terrain punctuated by gentle flowering meadows. "I've seen this species of moss in Alaska," she said excitedly as I passed her kneeling and peering intently at some uninspiring-looking vegetation. "But I didn't know it occurs in Asia too. Maybe I can write a paper about it." I looked at the plant with renewed interest.

Irene, whom I caught up with next, was not having such a good day.

"I'm the only one here who is not a good climber. I think I should drop out," she worried aloud as I sat down beside her on a rock looking out at the steep slopes.

I tried, as usual, to reassure her. "That's ridiculous, Irene. You're one of the strongest people here and one of the hardest workers besides. You've done a fantastic job on the bookkeeping and equipment and paying all the porters. Besides you're the only other member who's been in Nepal before. What you need is more self-confidence."

Irene had been to Nepal in 1961 with her former husband, who was a member of Sir Edmund Hillary's Makalu Expedition. Hillary did not want women in his base camp. Several wives, who had come to Nepal to make the walk to base camp, were hurried up to 19,000 feet in a few days and then sent back to Kathmandu. Not surprisingly, this rapid ascent led to altitude problems, and the expedition book only commented that women could not adapt well to high altitude.

Later in the expedition, Irene volunteered to help one of the climbers, Barry Bishop, with the meteorological work. She was twenty-six then and in the prime of her strength, having done extremely difficult climbs in Peru, Wyoming, and California. Irene was eager to set a world altitude record for women. When Hillary became aware of this, he told Barry Bishop that he himself would be off the expedition if she set foot above 19,000 feet. So Irene was restricted to helping Barry with his work below that altitude.

"At that time no one thought this was an unusual way to treat a woman," she told me. "Since then I've had two vertebrae fused in my back. Between that, working full time, and taking care of my family, I'm not such a good climber anymore. Besides I'm forty-three now. It's too late for me to climb high. I could have done it when I was twenty-six."

"You never know until you try," I said. You've been really strong so far. You might just make it to the top."

As we talked, the inevitable mist crept up on the gorges, and soon we could only see a few feet in any direction. The dropoff was right next to our narrow track, and a porter carrying a double load of 132 pounds slipped and twisted his ankle. Fortunately, Piro was right there to bandage it. We tried to take part of his load, but he insisted on keeping it all.

Farther along, a knee-deep, roaring stream that was littered with boulders blocked our progress. Last December it had been a calm trickle, but this was the monsoon season. I put my boots in my pack, rolled up my jeans, grabbed a rope that had been left by a previous party and stuck my foot into the icy water, searching for a solid place to put my weight. I crossed with some

Porter crosses a stream on the traverse from the French Pass to Special Porter Camp. Arlene Blum.

Three of the special porters. Liz Klobusicky.

difficulty and then stayed to help the porters. Several ran nimbly across, scorning the hand line, but others had an awkward time with their heavy loads. Margi went back across and spent an hour ankle deep in the icy water, helping the porters cross.

The traverse seemed interminable—into a gully, out around a rocky corner, over and over. Finally tents appeared out of the mist. There were our ten "special porters"—who had gone ahead to build a bridge over the Miristi Khola. (We named the spot Special Porter Camp.) These so-called special porters were hard-working but inexperienced young Sherpas who had been hired to help us carry loads to Camps I and II. On this trip they were learning the skills that would enable them to become more highly paid high-altitude porters later.

Joan arrived last, moving very slowly. During the course of the day she'd developed severe pains in her chest and a fever of 102 degrees. Piro diagnosed pleurisy and prescribed several weeks of rest, but we were only one day from Base Camp, and Joan stoically insisted on finishing the trek with the rest of us.

The next day we descended 3,000 feet straight down to the Miristi Khola. After passing vertical meadows of flowers and traversing around steep cliffs, we crossed some familiar rock slabs. On my reconnaissance trip a year earlier, also in heavy mist, I had stepped on one of these same rock slabs covered with ice and sat down hard. Glancing over my left shoulder, I saw that I was on the edge of a 150-foot vertical cliff. All I could think of was how embarrassing it would be if the expedition leader did not survive the reconnaissance.

Finally we reached the thorn bushes lining the banks of the Miristi Khola. The Miristi Khola Gorge is an awesome place, the vertical rock walls split by the roaring wild river. At Tatopani, six days earlier, we had seen the outflow of the river 9,000 feet below. The route we had taken from Tatopani to Choya was roundabout—moving away from the river, up and over the French Pass, and back down. Nevertheless, it had been the easiest way; between here and Tatopani the Miristi Khola rushed through impassable canyons and gorges.

The path through the thorn bushes led to our custom-made bridge, a bundle of logs and grass extending between two large boulders on either side of a narrow portion of the foaming river. The special porters had done a good job on the bridge, but at a high price: a week's wages apiece to ten men for what amounted to one day's work.

As I cautiously crossed above the foaming river, I reflected on the attitude of some of the Nepalese. They ask, "Why shouldn't rich Americans who come here to climb pay well for the privilege?" Why not indeed? If they were clever enough to persuade us to spend hundreds of dollars for a bridge, I supposed they deserved the money.

Vera Watson and I were sitting on the riverbank eating lunch when we heard an insistent ringing back on the other side of the water. "Oh, it's Pinchon's bell," Vera W. said. Pinchon was a large furry puppy with huge paws; he belonged to a shepherd who had just signed on as a porter. "Here doggy! Here Pinchon! He can't cross." Vera was agitated. She was about to go back for the puppy when he came across, treading carefully on the unstable bridge. He bounded over to be rewarded with half of Vera's lunch.

"Oh, you poor little puppy," Vera cooed. "Has your master left you behind?" Vera had been feeding and fussing about Pinchon since his master had joined us.

"Why are you so worried about this puppy when there are all these hungry porters around?" I wondered, pointing to some cold-looking porters on their way back down after leaving their loads at Base Camp.

"The porters are too big a problem for me to cope with," she admitted. "Besides, I've fallen in love with Pinchon. He reminds me of a dog I had when I was a child in China."

Vera W. had been born in China in a community of Russian émigrés; she had moved to Brazil, Canada, and finally settled in the United States in 1962. Her early ambition was to be an actress, but shortly after coming to the United States, she took a job as a computer programmer at IBM in upstate New York. She learned to rockclimb in the nearby Shawangunks and rapidly became a skilled climber noted for her style and grace on difficult rock. In addition to her solo ascent of Aconcagua, Vera had climbed Mount Robson in Canada; challenging peaks in Afghanistan, Pakistan, and Bolivia; and had made several first ascents on the Kenai Peninsula in Alaska. She put passion, artistry, and good taste into her climbing as she did into everything else. A snack after a meeting at her house might consist of shrimp and avocado salad, two kinds of quiche, cream of lobster soup, stir-fried chicken with pine nuts, Grand Marnier soufflé, red raspberries and cream—and Vera's disclaimers. "Oh, I'm a terrible cook. The soup's too salty. I've ruined the chicken," she would say.

I had always suspected that Vera was raised in an environment where women weren't supposed to appear competent. She disguised her ability under a self-deprecating manner, but had it not been for her determined efforts, the American Alpine Club might not have approved our expedition, and we might never have gotten to Nepal. Vera had also done a superb job of organizing a group of volunteers to raise money for the climb. She had designed an imaginative fund-raising brochure, written magazine articles and hundreds of letters, and provided a large share of the energy and enthusiasm for initiating the entire venture. But when anyone praised her excellent work, she would say, "Oh, no. I'm not doing an important job like the rest of you. Fund raising isn't that important." Everyone, of course, would reassure her. I never knew whether deep down she actually knew what a good job she was doing.

Here in Nepal, Vera W. had been unhappy that she didn't have a major area of responsibility for the climb. Now she had taken over an important job—the low-altitude food—but she was still full of doubts.

"I'm worried about whether I can really make the food work out," she told me as we found our way from cairn to cairn in the drizzle. "And I'm also very concerned about Joan's health."

As we walked, the narrow canyon suddenly opened up to a flat plain with a large glacial lake in the center. At the far end of the lake, the headwaters of the Miristi Khola burst like a geyser from the heart of the glacier. We stopped to look, and a curious procession resembling a scene from Ingmar Bergman's *Seventh Seal* materialized out of the mist. Irene, in the lead, was carrying a porter load suspended by a tumpline from her forehead in the traditional Nepalese manner. Two porters followed her. They marched solemnly by us without pausing and disappeared into the fog. Vera W. and I were again impressed by Irene's strength. Irene later told me that although the load was bearable, it made her neck tired. Small wonder: the Nepalese begin carrying loads like this as children.

"Yesterday I was walking with Mr. Gurung. He thinks Irene and I—the older members—have a good chance for the top," Vera W. told me as we moved on. "He said such a nice thing to me—that he hopes to be able to send a report to the Ministry of Tourism saying 'Vera Watson got to the summit of the north face of Annapurna I.' So kind of him. What a nice young man."

She also confided that her dream was to make the first

The memorial stone at Base Camp. Arlene Blum.

ascent of the middle peak of Annapurna with her good friend
Alison. The mountain actually has three summits: the highest,
to the west, was our chief goal; the east summit had been
reached by the Spanish in 1974, and the center peak had never
been climbed. This made it a tempting objective.

"First let's put all our energy into climbing the main peak.
That will be hard enough—maybe impossible if everyone goes
off doing different things," I cautioned her. "But after someone
gets to the main summit, the center peak is a good possibility."

The moraine stretched on and on. Just when we despaired
of ever reaching Base Camp, the cluster of orange and green
tents appeared through the mist—our home for the next two
months. The advance party had pitched the tents on a flat section of the moraine, and a nearby stream promised the chance of
a welcome bath if the sun were ever to shine again. At the edge
of the site we passed a memorial stone bearing the names of the
seven climbers who had died on this side of Annapurna.

Base Camp was cold and dark, but our welcome was warm.
Pasang greeted us with the traditional hot tea, and Annie and
Alison told us about their journey here. Meanwhile, the porters
who had accompanied us were dropping their loads and hurriedly disappearing down the moraine, leaving us with Annapurna.

Base Camp and Camp I 5

Afterter a night of torrential monsoon rain, the early morning was calm and clear. I stretched luxuriously and unbuttoned my sweater as the first rays of the sun struck the hillside where I was perched, 300 feet above our Base Camp. I had climbed here at dawn to get a clear view of Annapurna; I wanted to sit quietly and look at the mountain before the turmoil of the day began.

Two and a half miles almost straight above Base Camp, the icy tip of the mountain seemed impossibly remote. Looking left from the main summit, I saw the lower center and eastern summits of Annapurna as well as the other peaks of the Grand

Base Camp at 14,500 feet, with the summit of Annapurna two-and-a-half vertical miles straight above. Liz Klobusicky.

Barrier. The only break in this imposing wall of jagged mountains encircling Annapurna I was the deep Miristi Khola Gorge that we had traversed above.

Base Camp was pitched on a flat moraine next to the Annapurna North Glacier—an awesome and wild icefield. The glacier, extending 2,000 feet up the north side of the peak, was continually creaking and groaning; occasionally a giant ice tower would collapse with a mighty roar. It was the classic "impassable" glacier with a dense maze of crevasses cutting through it that constantly changed as the glacier slowly moved down the mountain. I was relieved that our route did not lie up this glacier. To the left of the glacier, a series of rock slabs could be ascended to reach the level area at the top of the glacier where we planned to locate our first camp.

I knew that climbing the difficult slopes ahead was only a part of the challenge of Annapurna. The success of the expedition, and indeed our very survival in this harsh world of rock and ice, depended on our equipment, our food, and our planning. So far we had managed to transport 12,000 pounds of supplies to Base Camp with only the loss of one tent pole—quite a feat, considering that most of our boxes had been packed in Palo Alto, California, shipped by sea to Bangkok, then by air to Kathmandu, by bus to Pokhara, and finally carried for twelve days through the monsoon rains.

To climb the peak we would have to design and construct a logistical pyramid of food and equipment. The way in which our gear was distributed amongst the base camp and the five camps we would eventually place on the mountain was critical to our success. Very large amounts of food and gear would be needed at the various lower camps to sustain the climbers who would move up to stock the higher camps. This "siege" approach is used by most large Himalayan expeditions.

It would be vital to have the right items at the right camps at precisely the right time. A very slight error in logistics can have enormous consequences. For example, the 1976 American Bicentennial Everest Expedition used both gasoline stoves and propane-cartridge stoves. At Camp IV during the second summit attempt, we had several cartridge stoves but no cartridges and a great deal of gasoline but no gasoline stoves. After months of planning and hard work, that small error could have ended the entire climb, for without a way to cook food and melt snow for water, the climbers would have been forced to abandon their summit attempt. In that case, an extraordinarily strong Sherpa ran from Camp II at 21,500 feet to Camp IV at 24,500 feet in three hours to bring up a gasoline stove.

On the Everest trip we had employed forty Sherpas to help carry loads for ten climbers; on this trip, with a similar number of climbers, we had only hired six Sherpas and four special porters to help with the heavy work of load carrying. So, much of our job here would be similar to that of pack mules: we would make our laborious way between camps—heavily laden, slowly and repeatedly, day after day. All of us would climb the lower parts of the mountain many times before the summit could be attempted.

This massive movement of people and supplies contrasted with the small "go-light" expedition I have always preferred for peaks somewhat lower than Annapurna. Beginning in the 1930s, the legendary British mountaineers and writers Eric Shipton and Bill Tilman charted much previously unexplored terrain in the Himalaya and climbed many peaks simply and economically. Today climbers are adapting their Alpine style of climbing in the Himalaya to the highest peaks: two climbers will make an ascent in a matter of a few days, eschewing fixed camps and carrying all their food and supplies with them as they move up the mountain. The benefits of this streamlined approach are greatly simplified logistics and staff, food, and equipment needs; the cost is far higher risks. If the weather deteriorates, or if one of the climbers becomes ill or injured, the Alpine-style ascent offers very limited resources with which to wait out the storm or evacuate a disabled climber.

In planning our tactics for Annapurna, we considered the Alpine approach but decided it would be more prudent to emulate the traditional siege tactic of large expeditions before trying anything more dangerous or demanding. But even meticulous planning and diligent hard work are not enough to ensure success. On the world's highest peaks, storms can sweep gear, camps, and climbers away; or avalanches can bury them in an instant. We were very small, and our hold on existence was fragile in the shadow of this enormous mountain and the forces it could unleash.

The sun's rays moved down the hillside, striking the camp and illuminating the bright nylon of the ten red sleeping tents and the large green mess and storage tents. People were beginning to stir, and it was time for me to go back down and assign the day's chores. I knew that everyone was eager to begin climbing the mountain, but first we would all have to spend several days organizing our six tons of food and equipment. Each of the climbers had an area of responsibility. Vera W., Annie, and Joan were in charge of food; Liz, Alison, and Margi, climbing equipment; Vera K., cameras and two-way radios; Irene, porters and money; and Piro, oxygen and medical supplies. My job was to construct an efficient logistical scheme and then make sure that it was carried out by members and Sherpas. Insisting that the tedious work of sorting get done before the more enjoyable climbing might not be well received but was part of my responsibility as leader.

I felt isolated up there between the mountain and the Base Camp—and not just in the physical sense. When people ask me why I climb, I frequently tell them that climbing gives me a chance to be with people without artifice or distraction—to know both my companions and myself better. Much of the motivation for my joining previous expeditions had been to form new friendships and to strengthen old ones. However, as the leader I sometimes had to subdue my natural inclination to make myself well-liked. On this climb, my primary goal would have to be the overall success of the expedition, not friendship.

I continued to gaze at the peak towering above me. The Harvest Goddess had a disquieting history. I said a quiet prayer. "Dear Lord, please protect us. Please don't let avalanches fall on us. More than anything else I've ever wanted, I pray that we return from this mountain together, alive and in harmony."

My running shoes gave me little traction as I slid back down the slope among the knee-deep flowers just opening in the early morning sunlight—leafy purple blossoms, tiny red ones, big white and yellow ones. Once again, I reminded myself to ask Vera K. for their names. Then the steep flowered slope gave way to level gray gravel with patches of green grass and edelweiss, and I was back in Base Camp.

Lopsang rushed up to me as I passed the stone shelter that served as our kitchen. "One bad problem, bara memsahib," he said, beginning his usual morning litany. "Special porters very

Annie and Piro sort the medical supplies. Arlene Blum.

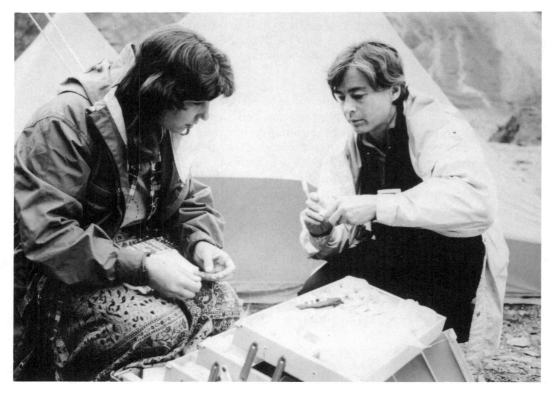

angry. Think not paid enough for building bridge. Say they will throw bridge back in river."

This was the primitive log bridge we had already paid too much for. Just as I was sorting the matter out, Liz diverted me, asking if she and Alison could go up and establish Camp I that morning. I took a deep breath and set about making myself unpopular.

"Mañana, Liz." I pointed to the chaotic piles of equipment and food scattered all over the camp. "We've got to get this stuff sorted out first."

After assigning the day's chores, I ate my breakfast hurriedly, wanting to take my first bath in a week before the daily fog came up from the Miristi Khola Gorge. After about 10:30, Base Camp was too chilly and gloomy for bathing. By any but Himalayan standards, our bathing arrangements were spartan. I went over to the foot-deep icy stream beyond the kitchen area. Feeling courageous, I immersed myself in the glacial water. The shock was so paralyzing I could scarcely breathe, but even so, the water felt delicious to my dirt-scaled skin. Soon, I stretched out on a warm rock to dry in the sun with my hair clean and my mood lifted.

The Sherpas and porters went about their tasks, not seeming to notice me or other expedition members who were bathing. When I first came to Asia in 1972, I was uncertain about the conventions that governed modesty. But I soon learned that in countries where many people bathe in streams and squat behind bushes, even foreign women attract little attention when they do the same.

Porters were busy digging the two trenches that would take us a step up in luxury from squatting behind bushes. Before I went back to my tent to work on the logistics plan, I walked over to admire our new facilities. About a foot beyond the ladies', the slope dropped vertically for hundreds of feet to the glacier below. While I stood there considering what a misstep during a night visit might cause, an avalanche chute across the glacier suddenly discharged an enormous bombardment of ice and rocks. I tensed, until I realized our camp was not in range. Still, Annapurna seemed to be providing us with diversion no matter what we were doing.

Back in my tent, cuddled in down with Vivaldi playing on the tape recorder, I began one of my most important jobs: reworking the supply pyramid. First I calculated what gear would have to be carried to the very highest of our six camps for three climbers to make a summit attempt. My estimate came to 180 pounds of food, oxygen, fuel, and personal gear. Members and Sherpas can carry loads of about 30 pounds at these altitudes. That meant at least six trips would have to be made between Camp IV and Camp V.

Working backwards, I started figuring how much gear would be needed at Camp IV to provide supplies for those six

Arlene consults with Christy and Irene about logistics at Base.
Vera Komarkova.

trips to Camp V, and so forth. For each successful trip, I
assumed that there would be one or two days of bad weather or
illness that would prevent a productive carry. My final calculations were that we would have to carry more than 2,000 pounds
of gear to Camp II in order to make it possible to get 180 pounds
of gear to Camp VI—the amount needed for one summit attempt.

It was all a little like "The House That Jack Built." I made
copies of the detailed plan to pass around as I wanted a double
check on my own calculations and to hear any other ideas about
improving the supply plan. The rest of the members also had to
know the plan's details, so that if I got sick or were injured, the
climb could continue with a minimum of disruption.

As I approached the supply tent where Vera W. and Annie
were inventorying the food, I heard giggles. Vera W. was taking
a ladylike bite of a mint cake, and Annie had a chocolate
smudge on her lips and was looking very pleased with herself.
Clearly they were taking the chore of taste testing and quality
control seriously. I pitched in to help them decide what kind of
candy bar tasted the best. Apparently Vera W. and Annie had
the food problem well under control. And Joan, who had been
ill with pleurisy and pneumonia, was recovering and beginning
to help with the food again.

Radio equipment was another matter. We had brought
two-way radios along—vital for communication between the
camps on the mountain. Each radio weighed about two pounds,

and a clear line of sight was required between the users. We had used four radios on the trek, and two of them had already broken. Vera K. was attempting to fix them, and I went over to see how she was doing. As I gingerly climbed inside her tent to look at the faulty radios, I found her wedged in among hundreds of dried plants, stacks of newspaper, and plant-pressing apparatus. I couldn't help wondering where Irene and Vera K. found room to sleep; but unconcerned with the chaos, Vera K. was confidently handling the minute parts of the radio and eventually succeeded in making it work again.

In the supply tent, Liz, Alison, and Margi were giving the Sherpas their gear. The process was complicated.

"Chewang wanted a green down vest to match his green jacket," Liz told us at lunch, laughing. "I finally figured out that he could get a green vest if Pemba, the cook, could get an orange one, so he would give his yellow one to Lakpa, who would then give his green one to Chewang. I had just arranged all this when Ang came up saying he really wanted a long-sleeved down sweater instead of a down vest. But there weren't any more sweaters unless we could persuade one of the mail runners to give his back in return for something else. So off we went again."

"They're so particular about the color of the gear," Alison remarked. "Certain colors must be worth more money."

Liz and Alison's next task was almost as challenging. They had to untangle several thousand feet of red seven-millimeter nylon rope, which in transport had somehow become three solid cubic feet of knotted red spaghetti. They stretched the rope from one end of the camp to the other and, with the help of the Sherpas, followed its twistings and turnings, climbing with the end over and through other loops of rope until dusk fell on a huge unraveling tangle of rope, members, and Sherpas.

We had definitely earned our delicious dinner of salmon wrapped in dough, deep-fried cabbage (without amoebas, I hoped), French onion soup, and cheesecake. Liz read us a German article about our climb that was entitled, "What Will Their Husbands Think?" We all laughed at the title, although most of us had in fact left husbands or lovers to come on the climb. The Sherpas had already made it clear that they could not understand how we could leave our families so far away to climb a mountain. They repeatedly asked us about our children, and they always seemed surprised when most of us said we had none. They could not believe it was possible for women over twenty not to have children.

That night our families and friends were especially on our minds because Kaji, the mail runner, was leaving early in the morning. He would be taking our letters and Vera W.'s orders for supplies to Kathmandu. In about ten days he would return with the mail from home that had reached Kathmandu in the month we had been gone.

Alison wrote several long letters to her husband, Janusz, who was on an expedition to Himal Chuli, a nearby peak. In 1975 Alison and Janusz had reached the summit of Gasherbrum III (26,000 feet), which at that time was the highest unclimbed peak in the world. Thus Alison had been higher than any of the rest of us, but her slender, almost fragile appearance did not reveal her strength. She told us that she had been sickly as a child. In fact, she had suffered from such severe bronchitis, her parents had moved their family from the city to cleaner air in the southwest of England and taken up farming. "They hoped the country air would help me grow big and strong instead of being a puny weakling," Alison told us.

When she got older, Alison's parents even sent her away to boarding school because they felt she was not strong enough to make the daily bus and train trip to the local grammar school.

"At school I was totally unathletic, and I hated all games," Alison recalled with amusement. "When we had gymnastics, I would hide behind the piano so I wouldn't have to take my turn at vaulting over the horse. I did like climbing the ropes and wall bars, but that wasn't considered serious stuff at our school—just playing."

I have often been surprised by the number of climbers who are supposedly unathletic. When he was thirteen, Bob Cormack, who reached the summit of Everest in 1976, was told by a doctor that his lungs were so weak he would never be able to participate in any strenuous physical activities, and many of my male climbing friends had been rejected by the army because of various physical infirmities.

I asked Alison how she had happened to start climbing.

"It was purely by accident. Having been brought up in the country, I found college in London claustrophobic and was delighted when some climbers invited me to go to Wales for a weekend. I got myself kitted out with a borrowed anorak and army boots and piled into the coach with my sketchbooks under one arm. At some stage I was tied onto the end of a rope and dragged up a snowy hillside. I rather liked it. Besides, it was a marvelous way to get out of London cheaply.

"After that I went to Poland on a postgraduate art scholarship and met Janusz. We married in Cornwall in 1971. It was a real climbers' wedding: we wore climbing gear and left the reception through an arch of ice axes, and we belayed each other across the church lawn. Right afterward, we were invited to go on an expedition to the Hindu Kush, and there were three women climbers on the team. Wanda Rutkiewicz was one of them. To our surprise, the women performed quite as well and, in some cases, better than the men. The difference in physical strength between men and women seemed to even out at high altitudes. So we thought, if we women could climb to seven and a half thousand meters, why not to eight?

"You know the rest of the story. Wanda and I tried to go to Annapurna in 1975 with you Americans, but we didn't get a permit. So we climbed Gasherbrum III, and on that trip two men and two women got to the top." Alison then came back to the point she had stressed from the start. "For this Annapurna trip to really mean something, we've got to get to the summit alone, with no Sherpas along."

"I hope that can happen," I replied. But the aesthetics of the climb were not as important to me as its safety.

The day we spent organizing the gear had gone well, so in the morning I suggested that Liz and Alison go ahead to fix the route up to Camp I. "Hurry and get ready," I urged. "If you get up there before the fog comes up, you may be able to get a look at the north face. I want to know how much avalanche danger there is on the routes this year. Look for avalanche debris at the bottom of the icy chutes on the face."

Alison got a bowl of water from the kitchen, then carefully washed her face and brushed her teeth. Next she cleaned all of her camera lenses and slowly and neatly packed her gear. I watched impatiently, thinking what different types we were. I would have thrown my things together haphazardly and hurried off. Despite Alison's meticulousness, both she and Liz were ready to set off by 9:30, wearing large packs and big smiles. We were all happy to see the first steps up the mountain itself. I sent Lakpa Norbu along with Liz and Alison. He had been on the mountain with the Dutch the year before and knew the location of the Dutch Camp I, which we were considering as a site for our own Camp I. Lakpa was quiet and obliging by nature and, at twenty years of age and five feet nine inches, the youngest and tallest of the Sherpas. He made an elegant figure in the blue

Ang Pemba. Marie Ashton.

Norwegian warm-up suit the Dutch had given him the year before.

I enjoyed working with the six Sherpas especially as I learned more about how to communicate with them and grew to understand better how they saw the world. I especially liked Chewang, with whom I had climbed on Everest in 1976. He was the most experienced of the group, having been on ten major expeditions, including two previous trips to Annapurna and six to Everest. Chewang had helped Dyanna and Marie, our film crew, on the trek in, and they characterized him as kind, generous, and always willing to work. Chewang was the only one of our Sherpas who had a beard, which may have indicated that his ancestry differed from that of the others.

When they are climbing, Sherpas wear small packages tied with string around their necks. Chewang wore so many packages that he looked like he was wearing a stuffed shirt.

"What's in them?" I once asked him.

"Sometimes rice, sometimes medicine. Lamas pray, mountain spirits listen. No danger."

Lakpa Norbu. Arlene Blum.   *Wangel.* Arlene Blum.

Chewang Rinjing. Marie Ashton.   *Mingma Tsering.* Christy Tews.

After each expedition, Chewang stores his packages of rice and herbs until the next expedition.

Mingma Tsering, Lopsang's brother-in-law, was a less experienced climber than Chewang, but he appeared to be just as strong and just as devout. Every morning and evening I heard prayers coming from the tent they usually shared. I couldn't understand some of the things Mingma did—when he was excited he often made a series of grunts, groans, and other odd noises; and he frequently wore a small bathtowel wrapped around his head. At other times he worked on his English, reading our old issues of *Time* and *Newsweek* with intense concentration.

Ang Pemba was the expedition comedian. When he took the group picture at Base Camp, he made such a funny face that everyone laughed, and he got a very good picture. But I was uncertain about his climbing experience. His climbing record said that he had reached the highest camp on Annapurna with the Spanish in 1973. However, when I met the Spanish leader, he told me that all of the Sherpas on that trip deserted at the lower camps, and none reached the higher camps.

I also had some doubts about Wangel, a close friend of Lopsang's. He had little mountaineering experience and seemed to be an agitator. He was full of fun, though, and whenever I played rock music on the tape recorder, he would dance all over camp.

Yeshi Tenzing, our twenty-six-year-old cook "boy," was one of the most mature and likable of the Sherpas. He had been a climbing Sherpa and a good one, until he was buried in an avalanche that claimed the lives of four Sherpas and the expedition leader on the 1974 French Everest Expedition. Yeshi sur-

Yeshi Tenzing, our cook boy. Marie Ashton.

vived but wisely decided to give up the hazardous business of being a climbing Sherpa and took up the lower-paying but safer job of cook boy. Annie continued to spend a great deal of time with Yeshi.

Lopsang looked wistful as Lakpa went off with Alison and Liz to establish Camp I. He had done such a good job getting all of us and our gear to Base Camp that I thought he might like to have the day off. But he did not seem to be comfortable relaxing. I was beginning to notice that he was having leadership problems. Although Wangel and Mingma were supposed to be "his men," he was not entirely popular with the Sherpas.

Lopsang had confided to me that he hoped very much to get to the summit of Annapurna himself. Sherpas do care about summits—in part for sport and prestige—but mostly for the better job opportunities open to a famous Sherpa. And Lopsang certainly deserved to reach the top after all the hard work he had done for the expedition.

If the Sherpas did climb to the summit, they would not need oxygen, as most of them had lived at altitudes of at least 8,000 feet all their lives. They had carried heavy loads up and down steep slopes since they were children. Their bodies can use the oxygen in the air more efficiently than ours can; therefore, they function better at high altitudes where there is less oxygen. In fact, the actual physical structure of the hemoglobin in their blood is different from ours. Sherpas routinely carry loads to the south col of Everest at 26,000 feet without using oxygen, but most Europeans find oxygen useful above 25,000 feet, and the summit we were heading for was 26,504 feet high. Having a Sherpa on the summit team would be less of a logistical burden than having an additional member who would use oxygen for the last day.

That afternoon, as Christy and I were deciding which loads should be carried to Camp I first, the radio crackled and came to life.

Liz (Camp I): This is Liz and Alison at Camp I. Repeat. We are at Camp I. Can you read us? Over.

"Hurray!" I cheered and Christy let loose an incredible grunting noise that resounded across the camp—an Iowa hog call.

Alison made it official.

Alison (Camp I): The camp was established at 2:30 P.M., August 28. The altimeter reads 16,500 feet.

Arlene (Base): What's the route like?

Liz (Camp I): It's an easy four-and-a-half-hour walk up here, even with stopping to put fixed lines in three of the steep places. The campsite is rough and irregular though. The glacier must have moved a lot since the Dutch were here. No sign at all of their campsites. We've already spent several hours leveling the rock and ice—have a platform barely big enough for one tent. Damn hard work at this altitude. We'll be back down after we finish making a second tent platform. Over and out from Camp I.

Turning away from the radio, I saw that Christy had left. I went over to her tent to see if she wanted to keep working and found her close to tears.

"What's wrong, Christy?"

At first, she wouldn't answer. Finally she blurted, "I want to climb this mountain so badly that it hurts, and there's nothing I can do about it. Go away and leave me alone."

Christy had grown up on an Iowa farm and had started climbing only four years earlier when she was a thirty-four-year-old housewife in Kansas City. After a divorce she built a trailer, packed up her teenage daughter, and came out West to climb. She got a job as a masseuse at Squaw Valley and did as much skiing and climbing as she could in her free time. When she heard about our climb, she moved her trailer down to my backyard and devoted months of hard work to helping us get here. Nonetheless, she hadn't climbed any high mountains, so she could not be a climbing member of the team. It would be, I reflected, very awkward to have a base camp manager who was miserable in Base Camp. I wished I knew how to make her feel better.

"Oh Christy," I said, "you just don't have enough experience yet to climb a mountain like Annapurna. But you'll probably get to go to Camp I and Camp II. We may even need you to carry loads as high as Camp III."

Christy smiled a little, but she was still unhappy—not getting to climb wasn't the only problem. "I'm already tired of being the mother here," she said. "Everyone asks me to help

Liz and Alison, wearing delighted grins, have just returned from establishing Camp I. Arlene Blum.

when they lose things and expects me to clean up their messes."

"I know it's hard." I sympathized. I had felt like an unwilling mother myself at times. "But there are advantages to being base camp manager. You know you'll return alive from this trip, and you're not responsible for the lives of others. Sometimes I wish I could be a part of this whole thing without the life and death responsibility I feel."

I awoke on August 29, three days after we had reached Base Camp, to find Lopsang waiting outside my tent.

"One bad problem, bara memsahib. Special porters want feather bags. No feather bag, they go to Kathmandu."

Each morning seemed to begin with "one bad problem." The day before it had been the Sherpanis, who were very unhappy about having to leave Base Camp. They wanted to stay and do our laundry even though they hadn't been hired for that. A few days earlier it had been the special porters threatening to destroy the bridge they'd built because of a misunderstanding about when they would be paid.

I got up and went out, explaining to Lopsang that we had

already given the special porters all the gear Cheney had specified and that we did not have any extra "feather" bags to give them. After much serious conversation and arm waving, the porters were placated with some additional gear and the promise of down sleeping bags after the climb. Apparently the special porters were learning the bargaining process that had become traditional between the Sherpas and foreign climbers they worked for.

Our carefully timed disbursement of supplies for future use apparently looked like senseless hoarding to the Sherpas and special porters. I'm sure we looked so wealthy to them with our thousands of pounds of gear that our assertions of limited resources must have sounded crazy or dishonest or both. On the other hand, we didn't care for their tactics of stalling or striking to get more gear after we had already agreed on payment. I often felt that without our continuing resistance, many of our staff would have been happy to take what they could and go their way. But then I would remind myself that they would do this without any malice.

I got to the mess tent just as everyone was finishing breakfast. The pancakes were cold and lumpy, the syrup was turning solid, and the eggs were gone. As I mixed lukewarm milk with cocoa powder, I told the others, with some satisfaction, about how I had prevented the special porters from leaving. To my dismay, their only reaction was outrage that I had given them any extra gear at all.

"They certainly don't deserve it! They haven't carried any loads to Camp I yet."

I gingerly picked up a leaden pancake and was about to take a bite when Lopsang reappeared.

"One bad problem, bara memsahib. Sherpa loads are too heavy. Sherpas cannot carry 30 kilos to Camp I. Porters' load is 30 kilos. Sherpas only carry 25. Must make all loads 25 kilos."

I choked on my pancake. This was the sort of morning I should have stayed firmly zipped inside my sleeping bag. Did Lopsang realize the amount of work it would take to reduce each box by five kilos? We would have to unseal all the boxes, repack them, find new containers for the five kilos that had been removed, and then relist all the contents. This would mean still another day in camp, reorganizing gear we had already organized so many times.

"Sherpas very strong. Sherpas can carry 30 kilos." I looked at Lopsang hopefully.

"Just one thing, bara memsahib. Make load 25 kilos and everybody happy." Lopsang was adamant. Perhaps it was a matter of status: the Sherpas wouldn't carry the same loads as the porters.

Margi and Marie took one look at my face and volunteered to repack the loads. Lopsang left and I decided to try calming my knotted stomach with a breakfast of warm milk. Christy and

Annie watched me with concern.

"Why don't you take a day off and go up the mountain today, Arlene?" Christy suggested. "You could check out the site of Camp I to relax."

"It would be good for you," Annie chimed in.

I was pleased by their concern and agreed that they were right. It was a pleasure to imagine myself heading up to Camp I, lighthearted and relieved of all responsibility for the day. The problems at Base Camp could wait. I went back to the supply tent and hurriedly threw a load into my pack, hoping to escape before one more bad problem came up. I didn't make it. As I was tightening the straps on my pack, Lopsang came up with a worried look on his face.

"Bara memsahib, just one thing. Sherpanis leave today. They want 250 rupees extra bakshish."

"Lopsang, we have already paid the Sherpanis six weeks wages for three weeks work. That is enough."

"Better to pay, memsahib. Otherwise, Sherpanis very unhappy. I think very bad trouble if you send Sherpanis away without more bakshish."

"Please explain to them that we have already given them six week's wages and that we did not want to hire laundry women. Tell them that we wanted to teach them to climb, and we are very sorry."

Lopsang walked out shaking his head.

"I'm tempted to pay the Sherpanis," I said to Alison, who was also in the supply tent. "One of them is Lopsang's sister-in-law. I think she could make his life miserable."

She did not agree. "That's outrageous, Arlene. You shouldn't let yourself be taken advantage of like that. They'll never respect you if you pay, and they'll all ask for more and more. It's got to stop now."

I went outside and gave the Sherpanis some extra wool socks and long underwear. I never knew how much Lopsang actually told them, so I asked Mr. Gurung to tell them again how sorry we were that we could not pay them any more and to explain the misunderstanding about why they were there. The Sherpanis looked solemn as they took their gifts and listened to Mr. Gurung's explanation.

A few minutes later I picked up my pack and set off toward Camp I, following Annie and several of the Sherpas. The Sherpanis were sitting at the edge of the camp with their gear packed. As I passed them, I smiled and said, "Namaste. Have a good trip back to Kathmandu. I'm sorry we could not give you any more bakshish today."

They muttered some unfriendly sounding phrases in Nepali. After I had passed them, the muttering grew louder, and I suspected they were swearing at me. Suddenly I felt a sharp blow below my right shoulder blade. One of the Sherpanis had thrown a rock at me.

I had a split second to make a decision. The camp was silent; several porters and Sherpas had seen the Sherpani hit me with the rock. The hostility of the gesture left me weak and shaken, and my first impulse was to let the incident pass, but I was afraid that if I did nothing, I could lose the Sherpas' respect and with it my control of them.

I briefly considered picking up the rock and throwing it back, but I knew I would miss by a mile and look like a fool. Feeling clumsy with my unwieldy pack, I walked back as decisively as I could and delivered an awkward, half-hearted slap to the shoulder of the closest Sherpani. As I turned and walked away, hoping I looked more in command than I felt, I heard a volley of rocks hit the gravel behind me. I glanced back and saw the kitchen Sherpas restraining the Sherpanis from throwing more rocks.

As soon as I got out of sight, I sat down and sobbed. This seemed a very bad way to begin my first walk up Annapurna. It was the first time I had hit another human being in my adult life. And why had this happened with the Sherpanis, of all people? It was so ironic. We had wanted to help the Sherpanis, teach them to climb, give them a new opportunity. Instead, here they were, leaving feeling cheated and betrayed, and we felt the same. Our frames of reference were too different. We had probably been naive to try bringing such changes into their lives. Knowing what resistance the idea of an all-women's climb had generated in our own society, we were dreamers to think we could make changes for women in another culture.

I felt like sitting on the rock all day, but Vera Watson soon came along and encouraged me to continue toward Camp I. We traversed some grassy, flowered slopes and then dropped steeply down loose gravel for several hundred feet onto the moraine. I moved slowly, feeling the lack of oxygen and still very unhappy. Vera went on ahead, and I sat down again on a steep, rocky slope.

Soon I saw Lopsang coming along and wondered how he would greet me after this morning's scene. I felt too sad and drained for further confrontations. To my relief he came up smiling and handed me a piece of candy. "Better to forget," he said. "Now everything okay. Forget. Be happy."

Lopsang and I walked the rest of the way up to Camp I together. At one point we had to ascend a gully of loose stones over smooth rock, and for every three steps we took upward, we slid back two. Emerging panting onto a rock pass, we traversed below some ice cliffs, dodging occasional rock and ice bombardments.

The campsite that Liz and Alison had leveled out of the ice and rock the day before looked cold and desolate; the surface between the tents was rocky and irregular. Even so, the site seemed both safe from avalanches and protected from the wind. While Annie, Vera W., and I watched, the Sherpas ensured the campsite's safety by praying to the mountain gods and sprinkling the perimeter of the camp with rice the lamas had blessed.

Rain was falling when Lopsang and I sloshed back down to Base Camp. As we descended, he explained that before we could climb the mountain safely, we had to have a ceremony in which we would raise flags and make offerings of food and drink in honor of the mountain gods. Because this was an inauspicious time in the Tibetan calendar for the making of prayer flags, we would have to wait until September for the flags to be made at the Kathmandu prayer flag factory. Then it would be at least twelve days before the mail runner could return with them. Meanwhile, no one could occupy Camp II. That camp was most vulverable to avalanches, and it would be dangerous for anyone to sleep there before we had made our peace with the mountain gods.

Fortunately, the timing of the ceremony fitted in reasonably well with the timetable I had planned for the climb. The monsoon usually ends around mid-September. That would be just about when Lopsang said we could occupy the camp safely, so we had two weeks to establish Camp II and carry gear up before the flags arrived and we could officially move in. After that, we would begin to climb the most difficult part of the mountain, the steep, avalanche-prone middle section.

"Okay, Lopsang," I told him. "Very good plan—for two weeks we'll carry loads. Then we will have the ceremony to the mountain gods."

"Yes, bara memsahib. Then maybe three more weeks we reach the top of Annapurna. Everybody happy."

6 Camp II

September 3–8

As we began the two laborious weeks of load-carrying to Camps I and II, it seemed that Lopsang had been right. At Camp I everybody *was* happy. We ended each day exhausted, but we were working harmoniously and well. We were all glad to be on the mountain at last, relaxed from the pressures and tensions of Base Camp and enjoying the daily rhythm of hard physical labor. The evenings were warm and close as we crowded together into the mess tent for storytelling or singing. It was a time of gathering our strength and coming together as a climbing team.

Irene and Vera K. rest during a carry to Camp I. Arlene Blum.

The days of hard work and evenings of camaraderie were reassuring to me after the turmoil of my last days at Base Camp. And I knew that all the advance planning and technical gear in the world would count for nothing if the climbers were not united in spirit. Only about a third of the expeditions that attempt 8,000-meter peaks are successful. Some failures are undoubtedly the result of bad weather or bad luck, but many expeditions have been damaged, sometimes fatally, by expedition members who had not faced their own personal Annapurnas.

Shuttling loads from Base Camp to Camp I and then up to II provided the opportunity to fine-tune the team and learn more about how we climbed together. With Joan recovering but too weak to climb yet, we had divided into three teams of three each: Vera W., Piro, and Annie; Alison, Liz, and Margi; and Irene, Vera K., and myself. I enjoyed getting to know more about Irene and Vera K. during those long and repetitive carries.

One day at lunch Irene told us a story about a fall she had taken climbing in Peru.

"I was traversing down a steep ice mountain with a rope wrapped around my hand," she remembered, "when a fixed line gave way, and I fell 20 feet below the trail. Luckily, I got all tangled up in the rope. If I hadn't, I would have fallen thousands of feet. There I was, this little ball of misery, all wound up in the rope and hanging there trying to figure out how to get out of this fix. I just said quietly, 'Help.' But nobody could reach me. I had to get untangled and back up to the ice steps by myself. Now whenever I go down steep, icy slopes, I think of that fall and I'm afraid."

That quiet little "Help" was so like Irene, as was her emphasis on the "little ball of misery" rather than her strength or ingenuity in extricating herself. As she and Vera K. and I relayed loads up from Base to I and II each day, I watched her dealing with porters and Sherpas competently and efficiently and carrying the heaviest loads easily, while telling us she wasn't sure if she could do it.

In some ways, Vera K. was the opposite of Irene. She was competent and efficient too, but she never expressed any self-doubt or, indeed, much about herself at all. Climbing with her on the grassy flowered slopes, I waited as she stopped again and again to collect plants. High-altitude botany struck me as an excellent vocation for a climber; one day I asked whether her interest in plants came before her interest in mountains or vice versa.

"I don't know which came first," she said. "As a kid I was interested in plants, but I always wanted to climb too. I didn't do either until I was sixteen and went to the University of Prague. Then I started climbing in the Carpathian Mountains and collecting plants there at about the same time. I grew up thinking there wasn't anything I couldn't do if I wanted. I was surprised to find women in the States still struggling for equality."

Usually Vera K. was reluctant to talk about herself. Since I had her talking, I ventured another question and asked how she had ended up going to Mexico.

"Well," she said, "we were having problems getting out of Czechoslovakia to go climbing, so in 1967 some women friends and I dreamed up a great plan to get out. We walked from Czechoslovakia all the way across Europe and took a boat to New York. Then we started walking again and walked across the United States and Mexico to the Mexico City Olympics."

Vera K. said all this in a matter-of-fact tone. Though no stranger to foreign travel myself, I was flabbergasted. Vera and her companions had walked about 25 miles a day for nearly a year. I asked her for more details about this extraordinary feat.

"Come on Arlene," she said, her eyes intent on a small fuzzy plant. "I don't want to talk about it. I don't think it was that important."

I was nonplussed. "What is important then, Vera?"

"My work. I try to be serious and hardworking, and I don't want to be taken as a frivolous person."

I assured her there was no danger of that. One of the many things Vera K. had accomplished was an extremely difficult climb on Mount Dickey in Alaska the summer before.

"Oh, it was just wonderful." She smiled at the memory. "We went there in late May and spent a month climbing this 5,000-foot rock wall. It was a completely different experience from my other climbs—like being a bird living on a wall.

"We thought it would take seventeen days, but the weather was so bad it took twenty-five. At one point we spent three days just sitting in a tent hanging on tight while the snow and wind tried to blow us off. Since we spent all that extra time, we ran out of food. But it didn't matter. It was such a beautiful climb."

In some ways, my talk with Vera K. left me more baffled than ever about the woman behind the big tinted glasses. I had seen her work very hard, but had also noted that she knew how to relax. Occasionally she would spend a whole day lounging in her sleeping bag, reading mysteries and eating chocolate. I did know with certainty that she and Irene and I enjoyed working together.

The first time we three set out for Camp I as a team, Liz, Alison, and Margi stayed behind in Base Camp for the day, planning to follow us the next morning. A few more days of acclimatization had made a big difference; I found it easier to carry the 46-pound load that day than it had been to carry 20 pounds two days earlier. Piro, Annie, and Vera W. had gone ahead of us, and when we reached Camp I we found the site much improved. Working with Ang and Lakpa, Piro, Annie, and Vera W. had leveled platforms in the icy surface, pitched four tents, and built a cooking area by stacking boxes of supplies. They had also located a meltwater pond—a bonus that would save us much precious fuel otherwise used to melt snow for water. We were lucky with our water supplies on this trip. There was a running stream at Base Camp and now the pond here.

We had just put our packs down and gratefully accepted the tea Yeshi had made for us, when Vera W., Annie, and Piro came running exuberantly down the glacier. They had almost reached the site of the Dutch Camp II at 18,500 feet. On their way up, they had placed 300 feet of fixed lines across steep and crevassed sections of the new route. These lines would safeguard all of us during the hundreds of trips we would make between Camps I and II during the next months. Fifty feet before they reached the site of Camp II, they were stopped by an enormous crevasse, as they had already used all the line they had brought and had even fixed their climbing rope.

"I was so frustrated," Vera W. complained. "I could almost have touched Camp II, but we couldn't get there safely without a rope. I was tempted to go ahead anyhow, but I didn't."

"Do you want to come up again with us tomorrow?" I asked.

Vera W. looked tempted, but she prudently decided to take her scheduled rest with Piro and Annie the next day. We asked them how safe Camp II had looked.

"Well, you know nothing is absolutely safe," Piro said, "but I think it's as safe as you can get on this mountain. The camp is protected by a nice 30-foot vertical crevasse wall just beyond the place for the tents." Piro went on, "There's one place just to the right of the camp that's absolutely gorgeous. It's an incredibly graceful ridge with flutings carved out like lace. We should name it something inspirational, like Church of Christ."

I hated to tell her that a more prosaic, or perhaps hungrier, climber had already named it Cauliflower Ridge.

There was only one flaw in Piro's enthusiasm. "I sure hope those bloody Sherpas aren't going to lead us up the whole mountain," she said emphatically. "I was last coming down a little icy rib below Camp II, and by that time the steps were worn smooth, so I was going slowly, rechopping the steps. What's-his-name, Lakpa, thought I was in trouble. He came back and gave me his hand, and I said, 'Dammit! You shouldn't do that.' I was so mad." Piro laughed loudly. "I didn't need his bloody help. What was he going to do next, put his down jacket on the ice for me to walk on?"

Everybody laughed at Piro's sarcasm, but I was concerned. Good relations between Sherpas and members were vital to the success of the climb. To my relief the incident with the Sherpanis seemed to have passed without serious repercussions, and so far the Sherpas had been friendly and cooperative. Even so, some of the members were still not reconciled to their presence. Leading —making the route through untracked snow—is the prize of expedition climbing, and I wasn't surprised at the resentment that the Sherpas had done much of the leading up to Camp II. I reminded Piro that Sherpas usually do help with the leading. "The Sherpas are a lot faster than we are now," I added, "and they know the way because they've been here before. Later on, when we're better acclimatized, we'll get plenty of chances to lead." This touchy topic passed easily for the moment, as we were all delighted just to be on the mountain.

The next morning we awoke to a camp transformed by new snow that had fallen during the night. The air was clear and cold, the sky bright and pale. As I left camp at 7:00 A.M. and headed for Camp II, my boots crunched through the new snow-fall, leaving a trail that sparkled like a carpet of diamonds. The fantastic broken forms of the seracs and crevasses shifted and changed as the sun began to light them up. I was at peace in this beautiful blue and white landscape; it was so wonderful just to concentrate on the mountain and leave the bureaucratic details below.

Irene and Vera K. soon caught up; together we followed the route that the others had established the day before to Camp

The big crevasses, rock step, and upper glacier on the route between Camps I and II. Arlene Blum.

II. The only sounds, our breathing and the scrape of our boots in the snow. The first obstacle above Camp I was a maze of steep, icy crevasses.

Both crevasses and ice towers, known as seracs, are formed by the motion of glaciers as they very slowly flow down the mountain. When the glacier reaches steep, rough places, it breaks up, and much as water forms rapids, the frozen glacier forms crevasses and seracs. Crevasses are often described as bottomless, and these certainly looked it. However, I remembered a geology text which had unromantically stated that crevasses are seldom deeper than 100 feet because the weight of accumulated snow and ice pushes the sides together at greater depths.

These crevasses were wide open, so we could avoid falling in and were relatively safe wandering among them unroped. They can be treacherous if snow has crusted over the opening, leaving only a narrow slit visible at the top. Falling into a crevasse is unusual, but it's prudent to always use a rope on a glacier. In my fifteen years of glacier walking, I have been very careful but did fall into a crevasse once. I still feel cold when I think about it and am thankful that I was roped.

It happened in 1967, at 19,000 feet, just below the summit of Mount Pisco in Peru. The snow was deep and soft and the slope was gentle, so we wore overboots on top of our climbing boots, without crampons. Just below the summit, I jumped across a three-foot-wide opening in the snow. My ice axe did not hold on the soft, crumbly snow on the other side, and I scrambled desperately trying to hold on as I started sliding down the nearly vertical slope. About 15 feet down, the rope stopped me with a bruising jerk around the waist, and I found myself in an enormous, smooth-walled ice cavern. I tried to put my feet against the wall to take some weight off my waist, but my smooth-soled overboots gave me no traction. It was hard to breathe, and I was getting panicked, as I had heard that a climber hanging by the waist can continue breathing for only a very few minutes. I yelled but heard no response—only my own gasping breaths.

I fumbled in my pocket for a sling and an ascending device and attached them to my rope. Then I passed the sling through my waist loop and around my foot. At last I could stand, take some of the weight off my waist, and breathe deeply. For a brief moment I admired the magnificent icy amphitheater in which I was imprisoned. Water was glistening on the blue and green walls that dropped down vertically into the darkness below. But I suddenly realized I was very wet and cold and began to slide my ascending device up the rope. In a few minutes I was at the edge between the dark of the crevasse and the light of the outside world. Getting over the lip of the crevasse was the hardest part because the rope cut deeply into the snow there. I struggled, trying to pull myself out, but there was nothing for my flailing feet to push against. My friends pulled on the rope and feeling like a hooked fish, I managed to thrash and slither my gasping way back into the world. Numb with cold, my hands were like claws. I was bruised and shaken, unable to move, as I lay there on the open slope, gulping air and grateful to be alive.

That memory faded, as I pulled my gaze out of the blue-black depths of the Annapurna crevasse and continued on up, blinking in the bright sunlight. The glacier began to rise steeply, and we chopped steps to make the going safer. Then we cut over to a rock outcrop. On the solid rock we gained altitude rapidly and stopped for lunch at 17,500 feet. I took my pack off and put it down very carefully. Objects set down on steep slopes like this have a tendency to succumb to gravity and go zipping down beyond recovery.

Ang Pemba and Lakpa caught up and shared my marzipan bar. It was delicious. The chocolate nugget candy bars we had brought from the States seemed unpalatable up here, perhaps because they had melted and resolidified several times on the long journey. Or perhaps our appetites were getting altitude finicky.

"Let's hurry on," I urged the others, eager to reach the top of the slope for a clear view of our route before the inevitable mist came in. Above the rocks, the icy slopes were covered with a light skin of snow that made them very slippery. As I hurried, my boots slipped on the snow-covered ice, and I found myself gasping for oxygen. I didn't feel acclimatized to this altitude yet, but we made steady progress, chopping or kicking steps and improving the anchors with which the lines had been fixed in place the day before. Irene, carrying an enormous pack, laboriously broke trail through the knee-deep snow. By the time we got to the high point that Annie, Piro, and Vera W. had reached the day before, Irene was exhausted and the mist had already covered Annapurna.

We had brought along 300 feet of yellow polypropylene rope to protect the last stretch to Camp II. As we started to uncoil it, we found that once again the rolls were totally knotted. The first five minutes of uncoiling were a welcome break from the hard work of climbing the steep slopes with our loads, but soon the unsnarling with stiff, cold hands became tedious and frustrating. And Mingma's efforts to help reminded me of a mischievous kitten batting at a ball of yarn.

When the yellow rope was finally untangled, we crossed the crevassed area and found the site that the Dutch had used for their Camp II the year before. It was a level area about 30 feet in diameter. The steep ice wall above it that Piro had mentioned did look as if it might offer some protection against avalanches. I noticed something poking out of the snow.

"Look! Dutch remnants," I exclaimed.

"You mean bones?" Vera K. had a macabre sense of humor.

Digging, we found metal ladders for bridging crevasses, tent stakes, plastic bags, and—best of all—a bag of Dutch chocolate. We stomped a platform in the wet, deep snow and pitched a cheery red tent. Lopsang sprinkled holy rice around the entire campsite but cautioned us that the holy rice was not enough to ensure the safety of the camp. We would have to wait until prayer flags were raised at Base Camp before we could inhabit Camp II. After a second lunch we put our loads in the red tent and zipped them up tightly. These were the first of the hundreds of loads we would have to bring up to Camp II. This

Margi hammers in a picket to which a fixed line will be attached to safeguard the route to Camp II. Arlene Blum.

camp would eventually have seven tents and serve as an advance staging ground for our climb of the demanding upper portions of the mountain.

Rain and snow fell as we wound our way back down through the great crevasses and arrived back at Camp I wet and chilled. Irene stumbled down last. "I'm wiped," she said.

"Yeah, it's easy to push too hard now we're finally getting a chance to climb," I said. "Better carry a little less next time."

Everyone acclimatizes to high altitudes at different rates. The physiological processes are not completely understood but are known to involve an increased production of red blood cells and changes in body chemistry that allow oxygen to be used more efficiently. A really sudden increase from sea level to altitudes above 20,000 feet can cause fainting and even death. Less abrupt changes can still cause fatigue, loss of appetite, headaches, nausea, dizziness, and difficulties in sleeping and thinking rationally.

Some otherwise strong and healthy people have internal altitude barriers above which they cannot adjust. Properly acclimatized, however, most people can live and work at elevations up to about 18,000 feet for many months. People who stay above that altitude for long periods of time usually begin to lose weight and general fitness and experience some reduction of mental acuity. In Peru, miners who work at 19,000 feet stay healthy by living lower down and hiking up several thousand feet to work each day.

The rule of thumb is to go up about 1,000 feet each day to allow the body time to adapt. We tried to go up even more slowly when we could, and so far none of us had any symptoms of altitude sickness. I attributed this to several factors: our slow rate of altitude gain, our schedule of working two days and resting one day, and the lack of competition among the climbers. On other trips I had seen climbers trying to carry the heaviest possible loads as fast as they could to prove they should be chosen for the summit team. This sort of pushing would often result in symptoms of altitude sickness. In reality it didn't matter if we did a carry in four hours or six or carried a little bit less at first. The important thing was to preserve our health and to keep from getting exhausted so we would still be strong and eager to climb by the time we were ready for the summit.

The next morning, as Annie, Piro, and Vera W. carried loads up to Camp II, the peaks were clear, icy, and surprisingly free of snow. I stayed at Camp I to study the mountain looming two miles above me. This morning, finally, the issue at hand was the route by which we would climb Annapurna, not whether we could afford rum with our fruit salad or if the special porters were going to throw the bridge into the Miristi Khola. It was a welcome change.

I examined our proposed route carefully through binoculars. It was relatively safe and straightforward until Camp II, but above that, the mountain rose in a steep, avalanche-swept wall. To the left of the French route, the ice and rock rib that the Dutch had climbed last year stood out in sharp relief. That route looked safer, but it involved much harder climbing than the French route. We would have to climb the nearly vertical side of the ice rib and then walk along its very narrow crest. Still farther to the left was a route the Spanish had taken a few years ago to reach the east summit of Annapurna. We could climb the first part of the Spanish route and then traverse across to the main summit—a new variation. But it looked longer and more dangerous than the Dutch Rib.

Lopsang sat next to me and took a turn with the binoculars. I told him the Dutch route looked best to me because it seemed the most protected from avalanches.

"Dutch Route is very steep." Lopsang looked dubious. "Can memsahibs climb steep ice?"

"Yes, we can climb steep ice," I answered. "That's what we're here for."

"Sherpas are here to carry loads for memsahibs," Lopsang

told me. "We do not lead steep ice. Memsahibs must lead. Dutch route is very hard."

"Yes, we'll lead. I think we're better off making a good effort on a steep safe route than trying to climb one of the easier, more dangerous routes."

The distinction between what is dangerous and what is difficult is often subtle. Climbing an overhanging rock face in Yosemite Valley is very difficult, but the rock is sound, the weather is generally good, and for skilled climbers who use proper techniques, the risk is relatively small. On the other hand, though walking across a flat glacier may be easy, it can be very dangerous if there are unstable ice towers overhanging the glacier.

The Sherpas had already indicated they favored the French and Spanish routes, which involved little technical climbing. But there we would be more subject to avalanche danger. I favored the steeper Dutch route; once we were actually on the rib, we should be relatively safe from avalanches.

As Lopsang and I talked, the sun became hotter and hotter. It was our adversary as we labored up the steep snow slopes, making the snow wet and hard going and draining our energy. The day before on the way up to Camp II, I had worn ski goggles, a bandana over my face, a big white floppy hat, a long cotton shirt, and mittens up to my elbows. Irene had also tried to cover herself completely, but she had gotten a severe sunburn on an inch-wide gap between her shirt cuffs and the top of her mittens.

The one thing about the weather we could count on was that it would not remain the same for very long. At midday a cloud covered the sun, the temperature plummeted, and it began to rain hard. Despite the rain, the climbers who converged on Camp I from both above and below were cheerful. Liz, Margi, Alison, Christy, and Dyanna, sopping wet but with broad smiles showing from the hoods of their blue raincoats, arrived with their loads from Base Camp. Soon after, Piro, Annie, and Vera W. came skipping back down after carrying loads up to Camp II in less than six hours.

Piro laughingly told us how much easier the second trip up to Camp II had been. "That first trip we were just carrying personal gear. Every time we had a chance, we would dump a sweater or a crampon or something behind a rock when nobody was looking. It all seemed so heavy! We finally ended up with almost flat packs and still puffing. But today we each took 35-pound loads and felt great. A little time up here sure makes a difference."

All eleven of us crowded into the mess tent. We were happy to be together and excited that the real climb was underway.

"It sure feels different up here," Dyanna said. "It's lots happier than at Base Camp in the fog." Being up on the mountain was especially exciting for Dyanna. She had never been

Liz and Chewang share a snack at Camp II. Dyanna Taylor, © 1979 by
the National Geographic Society.

above 12,000 feet before this trip and was rightfully proud of
her day's climb to 16,500 feet. "Maybe I'll take climbing lessons
when I get home," she said happily.

"I could have given you a falling lesson today," Annie said,
making a comic face. Everyone laughed uproariously and asked
her what had happened.

"Well," Annie said, "I saw two wands marking something
along the track just below Camp II today. I looked at the wands
[bamboo stakes with long red flags]. I looked down below them,
and I said, 'Oh, it's a crevasse.' I saw these footprints going
across it, so I stepped right in the footprints, just like I was
walking on eggshells." Annie pantomimed walking very slowly
and carefully. "Karrumph." And she pantomimed a fall into a
crevasse, to general laughter.

"Yeah, I thought it was pretty funny at first too, and I said
to myself, 'Oh, I fell into a crevasse.' But then I tried to wiggle
out, and the more I wiggled, the deeper I went. My real mistake
was to look down. It went way, way down."

"Were you roped to Piro and Vera W.?" I asked.

"No, but it was just a hundred yards more to camp, and I

was attached to a fixed line, so I was pretty safe." Annie was unworried.

"Really?" Alison asked in a disapproving tone. "An unroped fall into a large crevasse could be fatal."

"Well, anyway, I finally bridged my legs across the top of the crevasse and pulled myself out on the rope using my feet and my arms." Annie's cheerfulness was undaunted.

"It's not sensible, wandering around without a rope like that," Liz said.

"It's okay. All of the crevasses are open and visible. This one was wanded. Everyone else walked across it with no problem. I guess I was just the straw that broke the camel's back."

Annie was still unperturbed by her adventure, and her delightful manner had most of us doubled over with laughter. I couldn't very well reprimand her because Vera K., Irene, and I had crossed the area unroped too. Although Alison and Liz were technically right that roping was safer, climbing unroped was more convenient. Each could move at her own comfortable

Alison and Margi, roped together and wearing harnesses in case of a crevasse fall, reach Camp II with loads. Arlene Blum.

pace, starting and stopping at will. With lines fixed on all the steep or crevassed sections, it had appeared safe enough to dispense with the rope between climbers, but Annie's fall emphasized again the need for extreme caution.

Christy and Dyanna went back down to Base Camp after lunch, leaving nine of us crowded into one tent. They left a little reluctantly, and Margi explained why.

"People down there are bored and depressed," she told us. "It sure is better to be up here than at Base Camp in the fog."

"This waiting for the flag raising is getting tedious," I said. "Morale will improve when we can move up the mountain and make room for the members at Base Camp to move up here." Another source of depression at Base Camp was Joan's illness. She had been sick for almost two weeks now. Piro had put her on a course of antibiotics and had told her to stop smoking, but Joan was not recovering as quickly as we had all hoped.

"If she doesn't get better," Margi said, "we may have to call a helicopter to take her out."

I heard Margi with concern. The radio reports from Base had not made it clear that Joan was still so sick.

"If it's necessary, of course, we'll call a helicopter," I agreed. My worry about Joan's health was complicated by my awareness of the spotlight of publicity focused on us. I knew from experience that the media tend to emphasize women's weaknesses rather than our strengths. Coverage of a helicopter evacuation might receive more notoriety than an announcement of our reaching the summit.

"Two years ago when I had dysentery on Mount Everest," I told everyone, "it was reported on national television on the six o'clock news. All the men on the team had dysentery at one time or another, but that wasn't mentioned. Strangers still come up to me and sympathize about my famous dysentery." The older members of the team had been denied many climbing opportunities because of their sex, and they were quite sensitive about how the world would judge us. The younger climbers had experienced little or no discrimination and were less concerned about public opinion.

"Stop worrying," Annie advised me. "Forget the world. Annapurna is enough to worry about right now."

I knew she was right; and in the warm atmosphere of our gathering there, the judgments of the outside world seemed far away. "Okay," I said, "you're right, let's forget the hassles. It's time to focus on the mountain."

Meanwhile, Annie's attention was focused on a pile of small objects that she had spread out on the tent floor. She was sorting through the Camp I repair kit: tape, rubber bands, toothpicks, spare parts, cement, safety pins, rope, toggles, metal rings, and fabric. "Speaking of hassles," she said looking up, "it's a miracle we ever got these things here."

"What do you mean?" Liz asked. This was enough encour-

agement to launch Annie into another storytelling act.

"Well," she began, "it was harder to get this stuff out of the discount store than to carry it all the way to Nepal. It took me two hours to find it all in the first place, and then the checkout girl rang up the wrong total. I had already written the amount on the only expedition check I had, and she wouldn't let me just change the amount and initial it—I had to write a new check. But they wouldn't accept my personal check and my California driver's license because the license had gone through the wash and was hard to read. They wouldn't take my out-of-state driver's license either. Finally, some fool who was running around with my check and driver's licenses *lost* them both and came back and said they wouldn't take my check because I didn't have any ID! God, give me Nepalese customs officials any time! In the end, Margi had to go back later to rescue my driver's licenses and pay for all those things."

"Listen, going back to that store to get Annie's driver's license was the second most terrifying moment of this expedition so far," Margi laughed and went on. "The worst was during the trek in. I was hiking alone down a steep, muddy part of the trail, when my tennis shoes slid out from under me and —wham!—I fell backwards and landed on my pack. I was hanging onto a little bush at the edge of a 20-foot cliff. I could see leeches crawling toward me on all sides, but I couldn't move. If I did I'd fall all the way down the cliff. Vera W. saved me —she came along and pulled me out of the bush with her umbrella before the leeches had eaten me alive."

Margi's story set us off on a favorite climbers' pastime: fishermen tell fish stories, pilots tell flying stories, and climbers tell stories of their near escapes. Most seem to have a dramatic fall if they keep climbing long enough, and most survive by stopping just in the nick of time.

"It's amazing how long a fall you can take on ice and still not get hurt," I said.

Margi agreed. "I think I've come closer to killing myself bicycling than I have climbing, though I've had a few long falls." Margi had done most of her climbing in California where fatal accidents are relatively rare.

Liz's experience was chiefly in the European Alps, which offer more hazards. The rock is frequently rotten, and the weather changes abruptly and often. Access to the high Alpine peaks is so easy that many of the fatalities there occur to inexperienced, ill-equipped hikers who go for a walk on a glacier in the sunshine and find themselves in real trouble when a storm comes up suddenly. Others are climbers who make mistakes or have bad luck. Liz told us two stories that explained why she had reacted so strongly to Annie walking among the crevasses unroped.

From Camp I, at 16,500 feet, we had a clear view of the route to the summit, 10,000 feet above. Arlene Blum.

"Just last summer," Liz recalled, "I was climbing behind a Spanish team who were roped but not belaying. All of a sudden, I heard a piercing scream. One had slipped and had pulled the others off. They all went tumbling down, one over the other. There was no way they could have survived that fall. I felt sick, but we continued on to the summit.

"Then, a week later when we'd just finished a long, vertical rock climb and were coming down a couloir, a friend yelled, 'Rock!' I ran out of the couloir as fast as I could. A rucksack went flying about two yards over my head, its owner with it."

We were silent for a moment. We all knew that climbing in the Alps can be risky, yet climbers have more control over the dangers there than we did over the avalanches on Annapurna. If the Alps are to be taken more seriously than mountains in the States, the Himalaya command even more respect. Though we never discussed it, we had all heard that one out of ten climbers who attempted mountains like Annapurna did not return. There were ten of us. The idea that one of us would remain here was unthinkable. We assumed that nothing would happen in our case. We would plan carefully and try not to make any mistakes.

Freezing rain fell on the tent, but inside we were warm and close. Cuddled in my sleeping bag and talking with my friends, I felt at last that being leader was not so isolating. Too often I had felt as though I had a scarlet "L" emblazoned on my parka that set me off from the rest. I was very happy now to be part of this group of friends. Although Annapurna loomed large and cold outside, the sharing of experiences and growing understanding within would help unite us into a team that could face the challenge.

7 The Mountain Gods

September 10–12

Once on Mount Everest I was traversing a treacherous flake of rotten ice with Norbu, a Sherpa. He yelled to me, "Wait, memsahib." Watching him rummage through his pack, I assumed he was looking for ice screws to anchor us to the slope. He finally found what he was looking for—holy rice. He prayed, tossed the rice over his shoulder, and then informed me that now we could cross the rotten ice safely.

"What about some ice screws?"

"No problem, memsahib. Mountain gods happy."

The flag-raising ceremony. Arlene Blum.

Though many Sherpas are expert at using modern techni-
cal-climbing techniques and equipment, they still believe that
their survival in the mountains depends primarily on fate and
the goodwill of the mountain gods. They ready themselves for
the most severe climbing not only by perfecting their skill, but
also by praying and making offerings to these gods. The time
had finally come to make offerings to the mountain spirits who
lived on the slopes of Annapurna.

On the morning of flag-raising day the Sherpas got up at
dawn and built a four-foot high, rectangular stone altar between
our camp and the stream. The day before they had carried birch
branches up from the banks of the Miristi Khola. Right after
breakfast they piled the branches on the altar and set them on
fire. As we watched, Chewang meticulously tied brilliant
streamers, each composed of dozens of red, blue, green, and
white prayer flags, from the center altar to three large stakes
spaced out on the ground about 50 feet from the altar. Pasang
stood near the flames, praying intently, while the other Sherpas

sprinkled holy rice on everyone with great enthusiasm. After Pasang had prayed for fifteen minutes, the others raised the stakes upright so that the strings of flags radiated out above us from the central altar like the spokes of a wheel. Just at that moment the sun came out, revealing the summit of Annapurna far above us. A good omen! Apparently the mountain gods were pleased with the ceremony.

The Sherpas moistened the corners of the flags with rum and butter and sprinkled them with holy tsampa. Then they ceremoniously poured rum and butter into our cupped palms. Next the Sherpas sprinkled us with rice, sugar, and holy tsampa, laughing gleefully as it coated our hair and trickled down our backs. I wasn't sure if this was done to impress the mountain gods or just in fun. We ate the rum and butter and scratched the tsampa from our hair. Our morale was high as members and Sherpas laughed together in the warm sun with Annapurna smiling down on us.

Lopsang made a speech urging the Sherpas to do their duty, work hard, and climb the mountain. Then it was my turn to speak.

"All this time members and Sherpas have climbed very well. We have reached the mountain with all our gear. We have established and stocked Camp I and Camp II. Perhaps one month from now we will reach the summit of Annapurna together. I hope that anyone who wants to get to the summit will have a chance and that members and Sherpas can climb as friends to the top of Annapurna and return safely."

I looked up at the tip of the mountain poking through the clouds and wondered if the fine-sounding hopes I had just expressed would be realized, if everyone who wanted to reach the summit would indeed have that opportunity.

On most mountains any climber who wants to lead or to attempt the summit usually gets the chance. This cannot be the case on large Himalayan expeditions, because resources at the high camps are sufficient to support only a few climbers. Sections of the route are led once; then dozens of trips must be made to build up the supply pyramid. Often only two climbers can reach the summit, even though their success is based on the hard work of the whole team. Most of the climbers are capable of reaching the top, however, and the selection of the summit teams is often dictated by circumstances at the last minute.

These questions of who will lead and who will make up the summit teams invariably cause problems on large expeditions. Frequently the climbers divide into competing factions, and sometimes the losing faction has actually given up and gone home. More than one expedition has been seriously weakened by the bitterness resulting from these difficult choices. It was time to start thinking about how to handle these inevitable problems, for we would soon be tackling the hardest climbing on Annapurna.

All the members were tired of packing, repacking, and carrying loads day after day; and all wanted to share in leading this section. Up to now our three teams of three members each had alternated between leading and load-carrying—everyone had been equal, and if we kept to this arrangement everyone would get a chance to lead. But the steep, difficult ice rib above Camp II had to be climbed as quickly and safely as possible. I believed that our four best ice climbers supported by two Sherpas could climb this dangerous section most efficiently and safely. That way only a few climbers would be up in the hazardous area at one time. Logistics would be simplified, too, and including the Sherpas in the leading should increase their sense of being part of the team.

I did not expect this plan to be popular with the members. Designating the four best ice climbers as "lead climbers" would divide the team into two classes of members, which was bound to be painful for those not selected and uncomfortable for those who were. It also presaged the later and even more difficult division into summit and support climbers.

I believed that including the Sherpas in the leading and promising them a place on a summit team was both fair and necessary to maintain their loyalty. But many of the other members did not agree with me, and in the past few days various annoyances and frustrations had begun to strain relations among the members and between members and Sherpas.

The problem had first come to my attention four days earlier, when Liz and Alison stomped into the mess tent at Base Camp where Irene and I were quietly working on logistics.

"Something's got to be done about the Sherpas," Liz asserted. "The situation is outrageous. We've been delegated to come down to Base Camp to talk to you about it."

"What's the matter?" I asked as calmly as I could. The word *delegated* bothered me, as it implied that the problem —whatever it was—was widespread.

"Those bloody Sherpas!" Alison said vehemently. "It's not worth having them. They're carrying exactly the same loads we are and making the round trip in half the time. They're not exerting themselves at all. Lopsang said they would carry 18-kilo loads, but they're carrying closer to 12."

"What's their argument?" I asked.

"Well, they said that the day before they had carried more than they should, which they didn't," Liz answered. "Yesterday they took their loads out of the boxes, so Piro and I had to carry the boxes for them."

"Three pathetic pounds of box," Alison added. "And these guys are acclimatized. They don't have the problems we do getting used to the altitude. And besides, they're being paid to do it—paid very handsomely. We ought to trot out all the gear we've given them just to show them exactly what they're getting out of this trip."

Margi and Liz commiserate about Sherpa stubbornness at Camp I.
Alison Chadwick.

"That doesn't sound very good," I agreed. "I know it's easier for me to be calm about it because I wasn't up there, but you could deal with the situation better if you could get over your anger. Try to treat it as a rational problem, not an emo—"

"But it *is* a rational problem," Alison insisted. "If they're not carrying what they're contracted to carry, we can't afford to keep them hanging around as parasites. We should give them the push."

"Come on, Alison, you know it's not unusual for members to carry the same as the Sherpas or even more. On the Dutch expedition the Sherpas carried 15 kilos, and the members sometimes carried 25 kilos low on the mountain. Higher up, the Sherpas carried the same or even more weight than the members."

"We'd be better off with six more women climbers than with these six Sherpas," Alison insisted. "I've always said we shouldn't have Sherpas on the climb, and this proves it."

"Besides, they're getting awfully obnoxious," Liz added. "They keep pointing at us and giggling all the time. I know they're making obscene comments."

Because of my status as "bara memsahib leader," I had been spared the Sherpas' rude remarks, so I was surprised to learn of this.

"How do you know?" I asked.

Well, for one thing, they keep drawing phallic symbols in the snow," Liz said. "And when Vera W. asked them to stop, they just said, '*Yeti* make pictures in snow—not Sherpas.' "

We all laughed, easing the tension a little.

"Anyhow," I said, "phallic symbols are holy to Hindus, and this is a Hindu country after all."

"The Sherpas are Buddhists, though, aren't they?" Alison pointed out, provoking another laugh.

"I don't think they're ever going to develop any loyalty to us," Liz stated.

"Sherpas have developed loyalty on most other expeditions," I said.

"Yeah," Liz agreed, "but that's different. On male expeditions it can work on a man-to-man basis, but I don't think the same thing will happen with women. The jokes and snickering are getting worse every day, and real hostility is beginning to develop at Camp I."

"When we all go back up to work on the Dutch Rib, we'll have members and Sherpas climbing together—two of us and two of them working on a common problem. As we cooperate more, loyalty should develop," I suggested.

But Alison objected strongly. "We definitely do not need any Sherpas helping with the lead climbing above Camp II. They haven't earned the right."

"I don't think things will get any better if all the members are climbing above Camp II and all the Sherpas are carrying loads lower down. They've got to feel that they're part of the team," I urged.

"That's the problem. They're not part of the team. They're employees." Alison was adamant.

"Everybody gets bored carrying loads day after day. The Sherpas have got to share in the interesting climbing if we want their cooperation," I countered.

"If the Sherpas help with the leading, this climb will be meaningless as a woman's climb." This was Alison's familiar argument.

"I don't agree with you," I said. "Most successful Himalayan expeditions have included Sherpas. We put this whole thing together, made all the decisions, and did most of the work. Including the Sherpas in the climbing won't detract from all that."

Though we disagreed on this issue, I sympathized with Alison. She had wanted and expected this climb to be more of an all-woman effort than her climb of Gasherbrum III, on which she had reached the summit with men. Still, I was getting tired of having this same discussion over and over and was relieved when Marie and Dyanna yelled from outside, "It's Kaji with the mail!"

Everyone ran out and rifled through the large pile of letters. Kaji, the mail runner, had made the round trip between Base Camp and Kathmandu in just ten days—the same time it had taken us to go one way.

I walked back to my tent with a handful of mail, including a letter from my boyfriend, John Percival. I saved it for last and read the letters from my other friends and family first. I picked up his letter last and looked through the envelope, trying to see what it said. Finally I opened it. John cared for me and supported me, urged me to be strong, to believe in myself, and to follow my instincts. It was just the advice I needed.

I went for a walk around Base Camp in the cold rain. A few hundred yards beyond the camp, I was out of sight of the tents in the fog and total quiet. Taking strength from John's letter, I decided to use whatever tactics necessary in convincing the rest of the team to accept my plan for leading the Dutch Rib. I considered but then rejected the idea of first proposing the plan at an expedition meeting, fearing the members' personal ambitions and current hostility toward the Sherpas might defeat it. I decided to do some lobbying in advance—to talk to each climber individually and try to win her support. Then we would have a meeting.

I hoped that Margi and Annie, the two youngest members, would agree to my plan. When I stopped by their tent to lay it out to them, they were ready for me.

"Rumors are floating around about different climbing plans. Is it true that the Sherpas are going to do most of the leading?" Annie asked as I crawled into the tent.

"Of course not," I reassured them. "But only the strongest ice climbers should lead now. The two of you haven't had that much ice-climbing experience, so I want you to keep carrying loads for a while."

Both women looked unhappy. "I sure never realized how little you get to climb on Himalayan expeditions, that you mostly just hassle and carry loads," Margi said. "I guess if I really wanted to do a lot of climbing, I should have stayed home and climbed in the Sierra."

I told them I hoped they would get a chance to do some lead climbing later on and to be on a summit team. "If worse comes to worst, at least you'll have the experience to get invited

Arlene, Marie, and Irene read mail from home.
Unknown expedition photographer.

on other expeditions, later on."

"Yeah, I know," Annie tried to look more cheerful. "I'm having a good time, and I'm glad I came."

"I am disappointed," Margi said, "but I can understand. We have to consider what's best for the whole climb, not just for us."

I crawled out of the tent, impressed by the unselfish, mature attitude of our youngest climbers.

Vera W. did not accept the plan so readily. "I want to climb this mountain myself," she said angrily. "I've worked two years for this opportunity, and all the Sherpas have done is grumble and complain. They don't deserve a chance to climb. I do." Vera was even more adamant than I had expected.

"The Sherpas are impossible!" she went on. "Yesterday was my first rest day in four days, and Lopsang came along, saw me sitting down resting, and said, 'Members must carry loads or we must hire more Sherpas.' Outrageous! We're carrying as much as the Sherpas even though they're stronger. Later on we were sitting having a sip of Scotch to warm our bones, and Lopsang told us, 'Members drink Scotch, then no climb mountain.' It's none of his damn business what we drink."

Vera W. *had* worked hard for this trip, and I reminded myself that this would probably be her last chance to climb in the Himalaya. By contrast, it was easier for me to give up the chance to lead or even to attempt the summit. Being the leader was satisfaction enough, and I would doubtless come to the Himalaya again. I told her I would make sure she got a chance to lead later on when the route did not require so much expertise in technical ice climbing.

From Vera K. I heard the Sherpas' point of view. Her voice was low and her tone conspiratorial. "I've been talking with the Sherpas, trying to find out why they're unhappy. First, they think Lopsang treats them badly. They get tired of his continual lectures about duty, and they don't respect him. Second, they want a chance to climb and reach the summit themselves. I think they will be pleased to help with the leading."

I visited each tent and discussed the Sherpa problem and my lead plan. Reactions ranged between Margi and Annie's philosophic acceptance and Vera W.'s resentment, but no one questioned my right to make the decision.

On the night of the flag raising we threw a party for Margi, Annie, Marie, and Joan, as all had birthdays that week. Margi was twenty-one and Joan, fifty. A whole sheep had been bought for the flag-raising ceremony, and we had fried sheep liver at the party. Even people who detested liver at home liked it here, appreciating any fresh food. Best of all, though, was the salad —the most desired and least available of all foods on mountaineering expeditions. Joan had solved that problem; she'd brought four varieties of seeds to sprout, and she grew them in plastic water bottles, keeping them warm inside her sleeping bag on cold nights. The times she shared them with us were definitely the culinary high points of the trip. She had nearly recovered from her pneumonia, raising our spirits even more.

With dinner we had concentrated wine made by Margaret Young, a remarkable climber who had been on the all-woman McKinley expedition and was Vera W.'s and Annie's frequent climbing partner. She had recently become paralyzed in a horseback-riding accident, leaving her unable to climb. But she had participated in our expedition by designing and making our pickets and flukes (used to anchor a rope to a snow or ice slope), and making this superb concentrated wine. For dessert Pasang had managed a birthday cake with candles. My contributions were noisemakers and a bottle of champagne; however, I'd neglected to consider the problem of opening a champagne bottle at 14,000 feet, and most of it ended up on the roof of the tent, where it froze solid. We sang happy birthday, shook the noisemakers, and told stories as the champagne thawed and dripped off the roof.

Finally it was time to present the climbing plan to the whole group. I took a deep breath and began.

"Only the four most experienced ice climbers should lead the next section. Liz and Alison will lead one day and Vera K. and Piro the next. The other five of us will carry loads between Camp I and Camp II. Ang and Lakpa will support the two women who lead each day. I believe this will be the fastest and safest way for us to climb the rib."

I went on, explaining that since the Sherpas could work more days consecutively, less food would have to be carried up, and logistics would be simplified. I expected some resistance, but when I finished talking, there was dead silence. I knew that some of the members who were not included as lead climbers were unhappy, but no one voiced any disagreement. But then, no one expressed any support either. Would my pushing the decision through undemocratically lead to further resentment? Apparently it did, for as I blew out the candle in my tent that night I heard someone say, "All Arlene cares about is public relations with the Sherpas, not about giving women a chance to climb." I went to sleep wondering if my plan was the right one and whether my way of getting it accepted had been too costly.

The day after the flag raising, Liz, Alison, Vera K., and Piro prepared to leave for Camp I on their way to begin the demanding lead climbing on the Dutch Rib. The mood at breakfast was tense. Neither the climbers who were to take the lead nor those left out seemed comfortable with their positions. My tactics obviously had caused a lot of unhappiness.

The usually taciturn Piro brought the matter into the open. "I think we should have a discussion about how decisions are made in this group."

Immediately all chatter about passing the jam stopped. The

Outdoor breakfast at Base Camp the day after the flag-raising.
Arlene Blum.

thirteen women around the breakfast table listened intently, and I felt my mouth go dry.

"I think the climbing plan was made undemocratically and should be changed so that everyone gets an equal chance to lead," Vera W. immediately asserted.

Margi disagreed. "No, if the plan is best for the expedition as a whole, then we should try it."

Vera W. looked doubtful. "If I get to the summit on someone else's fixed rope all the way, I'm not going to feel like I climbed the mountain. I want to lead myself."

"I'm disappointed, too, not to get a chance to lead now," Margi said. "But remember, it's just as important to get the stuff to Camp II. We can't all be a bunch of prima donna climbers and lead the whole mountain. We're all going home afterwards, and we can climb something really hard there if we want to. Why can't we just enjoy doing the work that's needed for the expedition?"

Joan answered, "Because a lot of us are unhappy about the way that decision was made."

As she so often did, Vera K. made a reasonable comment tactlessly. "For most of us this may be the only opportunity in our life to climb a mountain like this, so why not try and make it a nice experience instead of fighting all the time over these stupid issues." Everyone cringed when Vera used the word *stupid*.

I was hurt by the criticism even though I knew it was deserved. My lobbying had been found out, and the group was angry at the methods I had used to get my plan accepted. My intentions had been good, but the result was devastating. Some people strongly supported me; others were equally strongly opposed. I struggled with my own emotions—concern that I had divided the group and damaged the joy of the climb and hurt that my intentions had been misunderstood—but managed to say calmly, "Well, some mistakes have been made in the last few days. We can learn from this experience and try to make decisions more openly in the future. From now on when we have to make decisions, I'll try to get a consensus from the climbers at each camp, which will be transmitted over the radio to the other camps."

"We'll never reach a consensus," Annie interrupted. "You're supposed to be the leader and decide what's going to happen."

Here was the essential paradox again. I was supposed to be the leader and decide what was going to happen, yet everyone wanted decisions to be made democratically. It was possible, just barely possible, but still a very difficult task. In this instance, my climbing plan had been accepted by the group—at too high a price. Their anger and the loss of support hurt me a lot. But the strain and unhappiness I saw now among the group was even worse.

Irene had been silent throughout the discussion, but I noticed that tears were forming in her eyes. Margi noticed too. "I'm sick to death of this wrangling about who's going to lead," she said firmly. "I think Arlene's plan is good. We should try it—if it doesn't work well, we can always change it. Irene, do you want to say something?"

Everyone turned toward Irene, who unsuccessfully tried to steady her voice.

"I think that most of us have forgotten how hard Arlene's job is, and I don't think we're giving her adequate support. She's getting pressure not just from us, but from many other directions too, every day, every hour. She gets continual demands from the Sherpas and the liaison officer and the cooks, and on top of all that these continual complaints from the members." Irene's tears spilled over. "I'm bummed out on groups, and I can't cope with it. I offer to resign."

This brought gasps of shock from everyone, and then a

chorus of protests. We all liked Irene and no one wanted her to go home.

"You can't leave, Irene, the group would suffer if the only nice person quit." Everybody laughed at Vera K.'s outrageous way of voicing her support.

"Irene, what you need is to go to Camp I. People are much happier up there," Vera W. suggested.

"I'd be very sad if you left, Irene," Christy moved around the table next to Irene and hugged her. "I want you here. What do you need so you can stay?"

Irene said, "More support and less criticism. I feel like everything I do is wrong."

"No one has ever said that!"

"Irene, that's ridiculous."

"I got all the equipment wrong. I brought too many pairs of crampons, too much hardware." Tears were running down Irene's cheeks.

Margi said, "You've done the best job on equipment that's ever been done on any expedition."

Alison said, "No one in this group harbors ill for anyone else."

"Especially for you," Vera W. added. "You did a fantastic job and you're still working like hell."

Irene's and Vera K.'s decision to bring extra crampons and technical gear had been criticized by some of the more frugal members. This criticism, though not particularly harsh, had apparently hurt Irene badly.

As everyone chimed in to reassure Irene, I was so full of emotion I couldn't say anything for fear my voice would break. Irene's support made me want to cry, and ordinarily I cry easily. But the group had said they wanted a strong leader, and I believed that such a leader wouldn't cry. Summoning all my control to keep my voice even, I said, "This is a good example of a common problem at high altitudes. The higher we go, the more sensitive we become to our own feelings and the less sensitive to other people's. We should all be very careful about other people's feelings."

The conversation shifted to other cases of hurt feelings: Christy's resentment at being treated like a mother; Margi's and Annie's feeling that Christy bossed them around; Vera W.'s disappointment at not being selected to be a lead climber. Considering the trying five weeks we had already worked together in Nepal, the complaints were few. The leader of the Dutch expedition once told me that if they had not managed to reach the summit when they did, the accumulated psychological strain would have forced them to abandon their attempt. Perhaps this meeting would release enough tension so that, psychologically at least, we could stay as long as we needed to reach the summit.

We sat around the breakfast table for several hours as the oatmeal congealed, bringing out all the small tensions we had felt. As lunchtime approached, Vera K. looked increasingly impatient. "Let's quit this blabbing and get up to Camp I and start climbing the mountain. This psychological crap is a waste of time."

I looked around noting the reactions to this latest of Vera K.'s blunt pronouncements, and I saw that Piro was gone. After initiating the whole discussion, she had left a little while after Irene started to cry. Piro was uncomfortable with emotional scenes.

Christy, sitting next to Irene with an arm around her shoulders, asked "Well, how do you feel about staying now?"

"Better," Irene said, "though sometimes I still don't feel like I'm a good enough climber to be here. And I'm terrified of the avalanches."

"We're all afraid of them." There was general agreement on this, and the discussion shifted to our common and individual fears. As one of us would share her fears about avalanches and her own private mountain demons, the rest of us felt the courage to express our doubts too. We all experienced great relief in sharing what we had been keeping inside ourselves.

Three hours after we had started having breakfast, Pasang came in to clear the table. As he took away the dishes, he announced, "Sherpas not going to Camp I today. Did laundry yesterday. Clothes still wet. Must wait another day till clothes are dry, then go to Camp I."

Incredible! All that fuss because the Sherpas were to share in the lead climbing, and here were the Sherpas, totally unconcerned, with their clothes still wet from laundering. They wouldn't be able to go up today anyway. A smile that turned

Nuru Wanchu, one of the special porters, reads some of the high-quality literature in the expedition library. Dyanna Taylor.

into a laugh spread quickly around the breakfast table. Even Irene looked amused.

"Well, that takes care of the Sherpas for the moment," I said.

Liz said, "Let's try not to get bummed out about the problems of the last few days. Up to now it's been going marvelously well. I mean, consider that we've gotten up to Camp II with extraordinary group cooperation and haven't had any major conflicts. In my mind this expedition has been a success even if we don't get any higher."

Everyone seemed to agree with Liz, and as I looked at the smiling women still sitting around the table, relaxed and talking warmly, I suspected that we'd just weathered the worst conflict of the entire trip. And I had learned another lesson about leadership: if there had been an open meeting, my plan would probably have prevailed, and at a much lower cost. I'd had the confidence in my plan to get it accepted, but had lacked the confidence in myself necessary to do it openly.

Fortunately we had not simply buried our hurt feelings and gone marching stoically up the mountain. It had been worth it to take the time to face each other and expose our vulnerability, hurt, and anger, and then our fears. We realized again how much we cared about each other, and our shared laughter had been the final healing touch.

The Sherpas had prepared for the hard climbing ahead by prayer and ceremony at the altar to their gods yesterday morning. This long morning's talk around the breakfast table had been our preparation. A reunited team was now ready to face the Dutch Rib.

The Dutch Rib 8

September 13–17

D amn, that looks tough," I said. "I almost wish we hadn't come to scout out the route. Now I'll worry all year."

It was December of 1977, and I was surveying the Dutch Rib from the site of Camp I during my reconnaissance of Annapurna. What I saw was discouraging.

"I'm glad *I* don't have to climb it," my companion, Richard Isherwood, commiserated. "Annapurna looks harder than Mount Everest."

Annapurna East
26280

Center Pk
26415

V ▲
24200
Probable
accident site ☩

IV ▲
23000

III ▲
21000

Northeast

Buttress

Dutch Rib

IIIa ▲
20500

Annapurna

North

ANNAPURNA I
26504

kle

Northwest

Ridge

Sickle

Glacier

H
18500

cier

© 1980 D MOLENAAR

Coming from a veteran climber who lived in Nepal and had many years of Himalayan experience, this was a sobering statement.

"Too bad you didn't pick an easier mountain," Richard said.

"There are no easy 8,000-meter peaks."

I couldn't help having second thoughts—maybe we should try to change our permit to another mountain. Makalu was safer and easier to climb, but it was higher, requiring more oxygen and more complex logistics. We had originally selected Annapurna because it was a "low" 8,000-meter peak and because we could get a permit. Most of the other relatively low 8,000-meter peaks are either located in Moslem Pakistan, likely to be an uncomfortable place for an all-female team, or they are politically inaccessible, like Gosainthan located in Tibet or Cho Oyu on the sensitive Tibet-Nepal border.

The two prior expeditions that had climbed the north side of the mountain reported that the climbing was relatively straightforward. But a photograph from Herzog's first ascent in 1950 showed a very different mountain than I was looking at now. Twenty-eight years of glacial movement and high-mountain storms had considerably changed the appearance of the north side, and the route climbed by the French in 1950 now looked highly unstable. We would probably have to follow the safer but more technically difficult route pioneered by the Dutch in the fall of 1977.

Using binoculars, I carefully examined this route between the previous sites of Camp II and Camp III. Three major problems stood out. First, we would have to cross below the massive, overhanging Sickle Glacier to get to the base of the Dutch Rib. Technically an easy walk, this area was exceedingly dangerous because the Sickle dumped tons of ice across the route at random times. The second problem was the steep, difficult thousand-foot slope of snow and ice we would have to negotiate to get from the base to the crest of the rib. Finally, there was the crest of the rib itself—an undulating knife-edge of snow which we would have to balance along for nearly a mile.

"If we can just get up the rib, we can probably make it to the top," I speculated. "But Annapurna does look harder than Everest."

"Be sure you invite some expert ice climbers," Richard advised. "That shiny ice up there is going to be damned hard to climb at these elevations."

"Things always look steeper from a distance."

Richard handed me the binoculars. "You see those blue green striations on that great crevasse? Those marks mean vertical ice."

"I know." I sighed. "Well, maybe we can find a different route, or maybe it'll be easier next year."

Scenic view of a climber above Camp II. Arlene Blum.

Well, here it was next year, and the Dutch Rib shone fierce-ly in the sun, as menacing as it had been the year before. The lead climbers—Liz, Alison, Piro, and Vera K.—had all gotten up at 2:00 A.M. and, along with Chewang and Lakpa, had broken trail below the Sickle to the bottom of the rib. Now they were back at Camp II, resting in the sun and studying the details of the rib. Margi and I, who had just arrived with loads from Camp I, joined them and asked about their morning's work.

"Well, we finally got a close view," Vera K. said, "and it looked awful. Steep, hard climbing."

"It's the avalanche danger crossing to the bottom of the rib that bothers me the most," Alison added. "It took us an hour to cross beneath the Sickle this morning, and I was bloody uncom-fortable the whole time."

"What about the other routes?" I asked. "Do any of them look possible?"

Piro said that the route to the crest of the rib from the other side looked easier. But to get there we would have to cross an exposed avalanche gully the Dutch had nicknamed the "Bob-sled," even more dangerous than crossing below the Sickle. The Sherpas favored the Spanish route farther east because it would be easier to climb; but there, too, the avalanche danger was very great.

I concluded once again that the Dutch Rib was the safest alternative. "But no doubt about it, it's going to be tough, and you all know that getting to the bottom of the rib is going to be dangerous. Do you still want to try it?"

The response was unanimous. Of course we would try.

I was confident that our top ice climbers could eventually climb the rib but worried about how long it might take. The year before, the Dutch had spent two weeks climbing from their Camp II to Camp III. Today was September 16, and the days were already getting shorter and colder. Some time in October the jet-stream winds would drop down over the summit, making climbing virtually impossible. If we didn't climb the rib soon, it might be too late by the time we did get up there.

When Margi and I got back to Camp I after leaving our loads at Camp II, we learned that a very large snowslide had come down the chute just to the right of the Dutch Rib about three o'clock that afternoon. The footprints made by the six climbers earlier that day had been obliterated by tons of snow and ice. Our first reaction was horror. We hoped, however, that this timing indicated a pattern: if avalanches always occurred in the late afternoon, we would be safe if we climbed in the early morning and laid low on the days after heavy storms.

This tactic had worked when I was on Mount Everest in 1976. Almost all the avalanche fatalities on Everest had oc-curred in the Khumbu Icefall—the great jumble of glacial ice blocks at the base of the mountain—in the afternoons. (For ex-ample, the six Sherpas who died on the 1970 Japanese ski expeddition were resting below a serac at 2:00 P.M. when a large section of the icefall collapsed.) We had minimized the danger by climbing in the icefall only in the morning, when the ice was frozen solid, making sure we were safely down by the time the sun hit the cliffs in the late morning. I had been encouraged by this to attempt Annapurna despite the mountain's bad reputation for avalanches. But so far the theory did not seem to apply on Annapurna for we heard the rumblings of avalanches at all times of the night and day. In fact, no one even looked up at the sound anymore, unless it was very close and very loud.

Despite our worry about avalanches, everyone was excited at the thought that tomorrow morning we would finally come to grips with the Dutch Rib. The general high that was building through Camp I reached a climax with the six o'clock radio contact, when Base Camp told us that our mail had just arrived from Kathmandu. The call also brought word that a group of Japanese who were climbing Nilgiri, across the valley, were coming to our Base Camp for lunch the next day. Impetuously, Margi and Annie decided to march down to Base Camp that night to get their mail and meet the Japanese.

"Why don't you wait and go down in the morning when it's light and you can see where you're going?" I suggested as they threw things into Margi's pack.

"The adventure is in going down now."

Lopsang was upset at the peculiar behavior of these young memsahibs. "You have light?" he asked anxiously.

"There's a full moon."

Annie and Margi started down to Camp I just before sunset, gleeful and giggling. I smiled and waved adieu as they set off at a jog.

Annie later described the episode in her diary:

Peaks rising above the valley mist were colored orange and rose by the beautiful sunset. The sky was a deep shade of blue, Venus rising in the west. We quickly dropped a few hundred feet down the rocky glacier out of sight of Camp I and put on our headlamps and warm clothes. Darkness came immediately and the only light was from our headlamps. Winding down and across the cliffs at a half-run was exhilarating, but the mist was lying very low, making the beams of our lights almost useless, bouncing back at us from the water particles in the air. We knew it was going to be hard to navigate a course on the glacier. Even in daylight the trail is obscure, so we decided just to use the sound of the flowing river to keep us oriented. Our field of vision was only 2 feet. All these small glacial pools and things we'd never seen before kept appearing out of the murk. Once we reached a very weird old deserted camp. Fumbling for what seemed forever we finally sighted the familiar "Buddhist" trail marker in the distance. We both knew we were "there." After that it was relatively easy to find the base of the cliffs, ascend the river gully, and wind down the grassy slope to Base Camp. Walking back up the next day, I discovered to my amazement that our route of the

Climbers moving from Camp II to the base of the Dutch Rib.
Christy Tews.

night before was almost a straight line from start to finish. No back-tracking or meandering. I am always confident about Margi's and my ability to do things well together, but this was amazing considering all the things that could have messed us up.

That night I awoke at 3:00 A.M. and stepped outside my tent. Above the mist countless stars and the full moon illuminated the immense peaks around us; it was almost as light as day. The splendor of the scene filled me with awe and a measure of peace.

The climbers at Camp II were awake at the same time, getting ready to tackle the Dutch Rib. By climbing early and returning to camp before the heat of the day, they hoped to minimize the avalanche risk. At 6:00 A.M. I went outside and saw two tiny dots standing below the 60-degree hard ice slope, menaced by enormous overhanging icicles and multi-ton blocks of ice. The first climber moved right below the steepest part of the rib and paused for a very long time. I watched impatiently, mentally cheering them on. At last the small figures began to move up—slowly, steadily.

"They're doing it! They're climbing the rib!" I yelled, waking the camp. While we watched through binoculars, the dots crawled a third of the way up the face. Then a cloud obscured our view.

The day was hot, and by noon the distant rumblings of avalanches began to sound around us. We waited eagerly for the two o'clock radio call to assure us that all was well with the climbers on the rib. Meanwhile, I decided to take advantage of the heat to clean myself. I got a pail of hot water and a sponge from the kitchen and, limb by limb, began to expose and scrub off all the soot, suntan lotion, grit and grime that had accumulated during the past days. As I looked at my body for the first time in weeks, I was delighted to see that I was becoming rather bony. All of us were losing weight; in particular, our bosoms were vanishing. I would probably lose even more weight as we moved to the higher altitudes where appetite disappears and eating becomes difficult. A favorite expedition joke was the "fat farm in the sky"—a scheme whereby wealthy patrons could shed extra pounds at 20,000 feet in the Himalaya while helping us pay off expedition debts. Spectacular scenery, basic accommodations . . .

The radio interrupted my mental ramblings.

Vera K. (Camp II): What a great day! Piro and I won the coin toss this morning, so we got to lead first. Piro did the bottom pitch—nearly vertical front-pointing [using only the front points of the crampons to climb steep ice]. I led the second, which was 55-degree snow—good challenging climbing. Then Chewang led a rock and snow pitch. Looks like we're nearly halfway up to the crest of the ridge.

Arlene (Camp I): How dangerous was crossing the plateau below the rib?

Vera K.: Well, we were exposed for forty-five minutes. Just after we'd passed, an avalanche came down right over our tracks. It looked awful, but we just put it out of our minds while we climbed. We wanted to stay up on the face and keep climbing but decided to come down before the heat of the afternoon increased the avalanche risk. Over and out.

I was elated as I switched off my radio. We were finally climbing the steepest slopes and would perhaps finish leading them all in the next couple of days.

Liz front-pointing on "Piro's pitch," the bottom of the Dutch Rib.
Arlene Blum.

Piro later translated the following description of the climb from her diary:

> Vera K. and I reach the snowrib. Snow is bloody deep—have to lean into the slope to pack it down for each step—even have to lift my leg with one hand under my thigh. I'm breathing like a terminal cardiac case, but don't feel tired. Wow, this is really it—I can't believe where I'm climbing. I turn my head a few degrees, and I can see the summit pyramid more than 6,000 feet above me. I'm all alone on the rib; it's so great I let out a yell of sheer pleasure. I put in two pickets and bring Vera K. up. She leads up the next 150 feet and then it's my turn again. Get stumped halfway up. It's steep rock covered by ice and snow, and I'm out of anchors. Lakpa has all the pins—he is sunbathing 500 feet below on the glacier, God bless him. A bit of yelling and gesticulating—up come the two Sherpas. Lakpa belays Chewang, who continues to lead until just below the green icicles. Never used a pin or screw. Around noon now—we decide to go down and leave the rest of the fun for Liz and Alison tomorrow.

At dinner that night there was great rejoicing. The Sherpas were delighted. "Memsahibs are very good climbers. Climb steep ice on Dutch Rib. Also Sherpa Chewang is a very good climber. Together memsahibs and Sherpas will climb Annapurna. Very good."

As I walked to my tent after dinner a few snowflakes tickled my face. The air felt oppressive and heavy, and the altimeter was rising. My elation at our success on the rib was becoming mixed with unease, and I hoped it wasn't going to storm.

I began to read *The Thorn Birds*—a six-hundred-page escape into the Australian grasslands. The incongruous sounds of Indian movie music drifting over from Lopsang's tent on my left, and Russian folksongs from Radio Moscow from Wangel's on my right, would occasionally remind me that I was still here on frigid Annapurna. As I continued to read through the night, the snow began to fall more heavily and accumulate on the tent. I couldn't hear it falling, but every half hour the heavy wet tent fabric would sag close to my face and I would reach up and knock the snow off. At 3:00 A.M., just as I closed my book, I heard a great crash. A pole supporting the mess tent had broken under the weight of the new snow. With shouts and turmoil the Sherpas went out to right the tent. I stayed warm and snug in my sleeping bag, trying to retain the feeling of being in Australia.

Just as I was finally about to doze off, my thoughts turned to kerosene. We had ordered forty quarts two weeks earlier, but none had arrived yet. Without kerosene we could not melt snow for water at Camp II, and without water we would not be able to continue the climb. I suddenly realized that we had not sent along any containers when we had sent for the kerosene. The storekeeper in the village probably didn't have containers, and that must be why we weren't getting our kerosene. Right now we were burning wood at Camp I and the remaining kerosene at Camp II. If we were to run out, we would have to retreat down the mountain. So I resolved to have some containers sent down first thing in the morning. The solutions to yesterday's problems often stand out sharply at 3:00 A.M.

In the morning when Pemba brought us tea, the snow had stopped falling, but the skies were gray and cloudy. After the seven o'clock radio contact with Base Camp, Annie and I began to trudge toward Camp II with heavy loads. The going was hard in the foot of newly fallen snow, and at one place we had to walk on an ice blade that was about four inches wide with enormous gaping holes on either side. If we were to slip, we would spiral down into a funnel of ice a hundred feet deep. Stepping cautiously across the ice blade, we finally gained the rock; it too was slippery with new snow. When we stopped for a snack at the top of the rock, angry black clouds pressed around us, and the light was dull and ominous.

"Looks like a big storm coming in," I said unhappily.

Annie agreed. "What a different world from Base Camp. It's hard to imagine there are grass and flowers and running water just a few hours below. I'm glad I went down for that day."

"How was lunch with the Japanese?" I asked. I hadn't talked with Annie since she and Margi had returned from their sudden trip to Base Camp.

"Fantastic. It was great to have somebody new to talk to."

"I'm sure glad we've got neighbors. Maybe they'll help keep the Base Camp people from going crazy with boredom," I said.

"It sure is better to be up here where things are happening," Annie affirmed. "Poor Christy's sick and tired of being stuck down there. And I felt so sorry for her when the Japanese came for lunch."

"What happened?" I asked.

"Well, she was so excited before they arrived that she changed her shirt three times. She even put on a bra." Annie laughed. "Then after lunch we sang songs and played games with the Japanese. The Sumo wrestling did it. The object is to get the opponent out of the ring. Christy was paired up with Mitsua, the leader of the Japanese expedition, who is quite a small man. They faced each other in the ring, and then Christy just went over, picked Mitsua up, carried him to the edge of the circle, and deposited him on the ground. Everyone, including Christy, was amazed at how fast and how well she did it, but Christy told me later that she realized immediately what a mistake she had made. She said it was just like when she was a little girl and did things better than the boys. It just wasn't allowed.

"Later, when she happened to walk past Mitsua, he jumped as if she was going to kill him. Then the next day, when the Japanese liaison officer came back to our camp, he said that the Japanese had decided Christy was really a man who had been given a woman's body. Christy was terribly hurt. Of course she's a woman, and the fact that she happens to be stronger than some men doesn't give them the right to say she's not."

I knew how Christy felt. Women who are stronger or smarter or taller or better at things than men often must pay a price. On our expedition we were spared the price of being better than men, as well as the price of not being as strong—the doubts about whether we were carrying our share or going fast enough. We could be ourselves and do things at our own pace.

Finishing our snack, Annie and I continued to Camp II. Large, heavy snowflakes were falling rapidly, covering our tracks in minutes. Irene and Vera W. had brought loads up the day before and had stayed in hopes of getting a turn at the lead, so almost the entire team was at Camp II—a good chance for a meeting. We all crowded into a tent for a powwow and lunch. Liz, Alison, Irene, and Vera W. were exhausted. They had planned to get up at 2:30 that morning, but it was snowing so heavily then that they decided to go back to sleep. At 3:45 Vera K. woke them again. "It's nice out there. You ought to get

Fog rises daily from the valley of the Miristi Khola to cover Base and Camp I; Camp II is in foreground. Vera Watson.

up." They had dragged themselves out of bed again with guilty consciences for having slept in on a possibly good day, and hurried to make up for the lost time.

"It was against my better judgment," Liz told us, proffering a kipper. "The altimeter had risen over 100 feet, and the air was ominously warm—almost like a spring night."

By the time they reached the rib, the clouds had closed in again, and it had begun to snow lightly. As they got ready to go up the fixed line, the snow flurries turned into a storm. They turned around and hurried back down over the avalanche area in a whiteout, unable to tell up from down and hoping that what they couldn't see wouldn't come piling down on their heads.

"Two hours after we got back," Liz said shakily, "an avalanche came down right over where we'd crossed in the storm."

"I don't think we should climb tomorrow with all this new snow." Alison looked tired and tense with worry.

Vera K. disagreed. "I think the avalanches are random. They come down whether or not it's snowed recently." Vera K. was a fatalist. "We should just go ahead and climb tomorrow if the weather's good." She was still energetic after having gotten up at 2:00 A.M. for three nights in a row. Irene had been right when she said Vera K. was a powerhouse.

"Nearly all the people who have died on Annapurna have been buried by avalanches during or just after snowstorms," I pointed out. "The plateau above Camp II is a dangerous place, and we shouldn't be there the day after a storm. We have food for six weeks and enough supplies right here to wait several days before beginning to climb."

"But there was a morning avalanche a few days ago. Avalanches can come down any time," Vera K. insisted.

"That's true, but there are more during snowstorms. We have to do everything we can to climb safely," I said. "What about the Sherpas? Are they helping much?"

"The Sherpas have been working out well after all," Piro said. "At first I was worried. You know I like to be self-reliant, and the Sherpas just about blow your nose for you. I didn't like that on the trek. And I was afraid that they'd want to take over and do all the leading, but yesterday Vera K., Chewang, and I shared the lead. Good cooperation."

"At night we all play cards together," Liz went on. "Actually, the game is Macao, but the Sherpas renamed it Annapurna. Every time you're left with one card, you have to say 'Annapurna,' and if you don't, you get penalized and have to pick up five more cards. The Sherpas learn fast, and now they usually win."

I didn't say anything out loud, but I was delighted that the members and Sherpas were enjoying their climbing together. Apparently loyalty and group spirit were developing just as I had hoped.

Liz went on to describe the fine cuisine at Camp II. The previous night, Vera W. had cooked mushroom soup and chicken with peas in an herb—sour cream sauce. "And what a dessert —a chocolate cake with white cream topping. We called it Annapurna Cake."

"But when Yeshi was shaking the snow off the kitchen tarp," Vera W. continued, "it poured down all over the Annapurna Cake. Yeshi said, 'Ah, Annapurna avalanching.' I wonder if that's prophetic."

After lunch Vera K. translated some off-color stories from her native Czech. In some cases the translations worked well and the stories were uproarious; in others we couldn't understand what Vera K. was laughing at. While we talked, a lot of new snow was accumulating. I asked the residents of Camp II whether they planned to go down the next day if the storm kept up. The consensus was that they would prefer to stay. "We like it up here and don't want to come down unless it's definitely too dangerous," Liz summarized.

It was time for Annie and me to head back to Camp I, but Annie had disappeared to chat with Yeshi. I stuck my head out of the tent and called her.

"Why don't you start without me, Arlene? I'll be along in a few minutes," she yelled back.

It was a good idea. Our earlier tracks were rapidly filling with snow; by starting now I could make fresh tracks that Annie could easily follow. As I plowed through the knee-deep snow along the fixed line down to the rock, blowing snow obscured my vision. The rock itself was iced over and nasty to walk on. I was inching my way down, as Annie caught up with me.

"Am I glad to see you," I called. "My glasses are so fogged up I can hardly see anything."

Annie took the lead as the snow fell thicker and faster. The wind picked up, and suddenly we were fighting our way down in a blizzard. Earlier we had placed wands every few hundred feet along the route so the way would be visible in just such a storm. But now the blizzard was so intense that Annie and I could barely make out the wands in the upper icefall.

Down the glacier the light was flat and weird, so that up and down were indistinguishable. We could see neither the wands, nor the trail, nor the crevasses we knew were all around us. Very cautiously, we moved a few feet in what we hoped was the right direction, straining to see the next wand through the featureless white surrounding us. We were soaking wet from the snow and had few warm clothes along with us, but I tried not to dwell on this. If we couldn't find our way down to Camp I or back up to Camp II, we would have to walk all night to avoid freezing. And walking all night would be impossible because of the crevasses all around us. I had just started contemplating the possibility of having to jog in place all night—in a blizzard, wearing our damp cold clothes—when the next wand appeared, a vague red blur in the distance.

"Thank God!" We headed toward it, then strained ahead to see the next wand. A few steps out into the unmarked murk, the next red blur was barely visible. Each time we reached a wand, we would just manage to see the next.

Suddenly I saw the vertical wall of a crevasse dropping down hundreds of feet just inches to the left of my foot. I quickly took a couple of steps to the right and noticed another large crevasse on that side too. In this blizzard, crevasses were invisible even when they were only a foot or two away, and the glacier, a safe and easy place to walk in the sunlight, was a terrifying maze.

Just at dark we reached Camp I where a smiling Pemba greeted us with steaming mugs of hot tea. As we gratefully drank it, Annie and I admitted to ourselves that we might very easily still have been lost on the glacier instead of warm and safe in the mess tent. The snow continued to fall heavily, and our concern about the climbers at Camp II increased. We waited anxiously for the next radio call.

At 6:00 P.M. they radioed that heavy snow was weighing down their tents, and they were worried about avalanche danger at Camp II. Annie took the radio from me and said, "There's a Wyoming song that's appropriate for this occasion. It goes like this." And she began to sing, " 'Take this job and shove it / I don't wanna work no more / Take this job and shove it / Push it out the door.' Over and out."

9 Storm

September 18–21

Irene *(Camp II):* There's 20 inches of new snow here and—

The 7:00 A.M. transmission was drowned out by heavy static. I couldn't understand Irene's words, but I was alarmed by the tension in her voice.

Arlene (Camp I): Repeat, please, Irene. Are there avalanches coming down near Camp II?

Irene: Yes. We've been getting wind and spray from avalanches since 4:00 A.M. One of the tents has collapsed, and we have to dig the others out every few minutes.

Arlene: The storm is probably going to get worse—the barometer's still falling. How soon can you come down?

Irene: We think it's too dangerous to come down now because we'd have to cross too many avalanche slopes.

I was about to say that I wanted them to come down right away when the transmission was again interrupted by a crackling, rumbling noise. I listened impatiently. When Irene finally came back on the air, her voice was urgent.

Irene: There was a huge avalanche right beside the camp. I've got to dig out the tent again. Call us back at eight o'clock. Over and out.

Irene's abrupt sign-off left me worried and frustrated. Of

the nine climbers killed on Annapurna, seven had died in avalanches in the vicinity of Camp II. I wanted the climbers at Camp II to come down immediately, but they had to make this decision for themselves. I could not order them to risk descending possible avalanche slopes.

I called Base Camp to get a weather forecast: it was for continued wind and snow. Christy also warned me that they had spotted several avalanches between Camp I and Base Camp. We had tried to place our campsites so they would be protected from avalanches, and so far the snowslides had come down between or beside the camps, not on them. For the moment, the climbers were better off staying at Camp II than risking the descent. But as the storm worsened and more snow accumulated, and the avalanches grew larger, there was no guarantee that any camp on the mountain would remain safe. The safest place for all of us was Base Camp, although getting there could prove as dangerous as staying put.

The snow continued to fall in thick, wet flakes as Annie and I dug out the tents. By the time the last one was free of snow, the first one was partially buried again. I knew that even more snow was falling up at Camp II. At 8:00 A.M. I called Irene again.

Arlene: This is Camp I calling Camp II. What's happening up there?

Irene: We're having bacon, hash browns, freeze-dried

Digging out the tents at Camp II during the storm. Irene Miller, © 1979 by the National Geographic Society.

strawberries, and more avalanches up here.

Arlene: Breakfast! What about coming down?

Irene: We still think it's safer to stay here than to risk the descent.

Arlene: I disagree. Coming down you will be exposed to avalanches for an hour. If the storm continues, it will become even more dangerous to come down and also impossible to stay where you are. Is there any damage from avalanche debris hitting the camp?

Irene: Not much. But the avalanches are getting closer and closer. Spindrift and enormous gusts of wind are hitting the camp every few minutes.

Arlene: The storm's supposed to last at least another day. I want you to come down as soon as you can.

Irene: Okay. We'll start packing now, and if it keeps snowing we'll come down. We'll call again at nine o'clock with our final decision. Over and out.

As Annie and I went to shovel snow off the tents again, I worried about the loss of momentum this storm was causing and the tremendous amounts of energy it would take us to get back to where we had been. Even if the climbers were able to stay at Camp II, the trails would have to be rebroken through deep new snow, and all the fixed lines would have to be dug out. If they came down, the camp would have to be leveled to prevent damage to the tents by the heavy new snow. Afterwards we would have to dig out the tents and start all over again with a new climbing plan. We could still climb the mountain if everyone got down safely, and if there were not too many storms, but the storm was definitely a setback.

In a letter to her husband Alison described that wild night at Camp II:

> I didn't get much sleep. Avalanches were rumbling all around us. At about 2:00 A.M. a giant hand shook our tent—I thought Yeshi was shaking the snow off for us, but when I tried to look out, the tent was buried so deeply I could hardly open the zip. Since there was no one around, I concluded it was an avalanche. Later I went out to dig out the tent. Piro was doing the same thing when suddenly a hurricane hit us. I bent over my shovel to avoid being blown off my feet. The air was full of snow, and I could hardly breathe—it was very frightening. As I didn't hear any rumble, I didn't realize until afterwards that it must have been the wind from another avalanche. Piro thought I'd been blown off the plateau as my headlamp suddenly disappeared.

At 9:00 A.M. the radio crackled out its signal.

Irene: This is Camp II. It's still snowing; we've leveled the tents, and we're coming down.

Arlene: Good. I'm relieved.

Irene: I'll be more relieved when we get there.

Arlene: The route down isn't too bad. You should be able to see wands most of the way. The main problem Annie and I

The tents at Camp II had to be collapsed when the climbers abandoned the camp during the storm, to prevent the weight of new snow tearing the fabric. Irene Miller.

had yesterday was when we first reached the glacier. We couldn't see any wands, so we listened for the little glacial creek and headed toward the sound. After about five minutes we finally saw a wand in the distance. I'll ask the Sherpas here to start breaking trail toward you. We'll have lots of tea and soup ready. And be careful. Over and out.

I had tried to sound matter-of-fact over the radio, but I knew as well as they did that their descent could be a desperate business. Annie and I had barely managed to get down yesterday, and today the storm was much worse. Plowing down through the several feet of unstable new snow would drain the climbers' strength. The steep rock section would be slippery and treacherous. And the new snowfall would conceal the crevasses, making the descent risky even in decent weather; in this furious gale the climbers, roped 30 feet apart, would barely be able to see each other—partially filled-in crevasses would be virtually invisible until someone's foot broke through. Even more menacing was the snow accumulating unseen on the steep walls of the mountain above, perhaps to slough off in a giant avalanche that would sweep the entire face and bury the climbers.

When the Camp II climbers made it down—I was careful to think *when*, not *if*—the rest of us here would have to go down to Base Camp so there would be room for them. Normally that would be a two-hour stroll. But Christy's earlier report of avalanches along this stretch meant that no part of the mountain was safe today. I called down to Base Camp for the latest word.

Arlene (Camp I): What does the descent route from Camp I to Base Camp look like?

Christy (Base): Oh, Christ! Looks like an awful, awful trip.

A one-quarter chance of rock falling down on you and a one-half chance of snow falling on you.

Arlene: What's Joan's opinion about our coming down now?

Christy's words had confirmed my own fears about the descent, but maybe she was being alarmist. After all, this was her first big mountain.

Joan: I don't think it's wise to come down now. There was just an enormous powder avalanche across the route between Camp I and Base Camp, and more are likely. The footing is insecure on the glazed rocks. I recommend that you stay up at Camp I if that's possible.

Arlene: Okay, we can stay, but it's going to be real crowded here tonight. Over and out.

One of the large tents had collapsed and torn badly the night before, so there were only two large and two small tents left at Camp I—uncomfortably close quarters for sixteen people. And we were having to work like hell to keep these four tents intact. But with avalanches above and avalanches below, it looked like we were trapped at Camp I. Somehow we would have to manage to stay here.

The winds picked up, and the snow was falling more heavily than ever. Just knocking the snow off from the inside of the tents didn't work, so we had to go outside every few minutes to shovel it off and resecure the guy lines against the wind. Each trip out I would peer anxiously in the direction of Camp II, but all I could see was whiteness. The storm muffled all sounds except the roar of avalanches. Each time I heard one, I strained to figure out the direction of the sound. Some were below or from peaks across the valley, but a good number sounded from the direction of Camp II. The descending climbers had a radio but could not stop in the storm to use it, so we would just have to wait until they arrived to know that they were safe. The time crawled by, as we listened anxiously to the howling wind and the roaring avalanches.

I asked Chewang and Mingma to start breaking trail up from Camp I to meet the descending climbers. With surprisingly little reluctance they agreed, roped up, headed off into the storm and were invisible in minutes.

Finally, just before noon, we heard shouts from above, and shadowy figures began to appear out of the storm. I counted ten. They were all safe. Thank God! The climbers unroped slowly, dropped their packs, and straggled into the mess tent for hot tea and soup. Only Alison stayed out in the storm to coil the climbing rope. In spite of the heavy snow falling on her, she arranged the strands slowly and meticulously. Only when the rope was perfectly coiled did she join the others in the mess tent.

After numerous cups of sweet milky tea, the climbers had some energy to discuss our situation. I said we would have to

Alison neatly coils the climbing rope at Camp I after the terrifying descent from Camp II in the storm. Arlene Blum.

spend a crowded night here because the avalanche danger was so great down below.

"Not me," Piro stated emphatically. "After coming this far, I want to go all the way down to where it's comfortable. It's Base Camp for me today."

Alison and Liz agreed that going down to Base Camp was nothing compared to the ordeal they had just survived. So the three of them, along with Lopsang, Chewang, and Lakpa, roped up and set off again into the storm. After they left I began to worry again, but once more, all I could do was wait. Two hours later they called from Base Camp to say that they were safe, but that it was not as luxurious as they had anticipated. The snow, even wetter and heavier down there, had knocked down several of the tents, and everything was soaking wet.

Liz, Vera W., and Irene in the mess tent at Camp I, recovering from the descent. Arlene Blum.

In storms as severe as this one, water in the tent can be as great a problem as wind and cold outside. We had chosen to use down gear because it is lighter and less bulky than synthetics, but once down is wet, it loses its insulating properties and is worthless for keeping warm. And during a storm there's no way to dry it out either. Keeping the inside of a tent dry is, therefore, of vital importance but very difficult when it's necessary to go out every few minutes and shovel the tents off. As a result of my half dozen trips in and out this morning, everything in my tent was getting disastrously soggy. Before going back into the tent each time I would try to brush all the snow from my clothes. Then as I squeezed back through the tunnel entrance, I would get a neck and back full, and invariably carry half of it into the tent. Squatting at the door with a whiskbroom I would carefully brush my clothes and put the snow back out; still, a little more snow stayed inside each time. By now the moisture had condensed on the walls and was dripping onto the floor.

Things were a bit drier in the mess tent where we all met for dinner. Yeshi had not been able to fix much of a meal in the storm so, as is the habit of hungry climbers, we all began talking about what we would eat for our first meal back in Kathmandu.

"I'm going to eat a whole rhubarb pie at KC's pie shop as soon as I get back," Annie said.

"The apple pie's better," Margi countered. "I'm going to eat three apple pies."

I laughed. The thought of eating pies till I had a stomachache sounded delightful to me. It seemed amazing that only a few hours ago our main concern had been survival; now it was the relative virtues of KC's apple and rhubarb pies. We discussed food endlessly that evening, perhaps to avoid talking about the storm and what we were going to do when it ended. I felt some pessimism in the group about all the ground we had lost. But I was sure that when the sun came out, people would be eager to go up again. At least I hoped so.

The next day was a rest day at all camps. Even though the storm had abated, I awoke feeling anxious. Our old logistics plan would no longer be workable because of the delays due to the storm. I would have to present a new logistics plan to the group today. The four women selected as lead climbers had not had much opportunity to lead and were not eager to give up their places. And, of course, the rest of the climbers all wanted their chance. After the unhappiness the last plan had caused, I was not looking forward to another round.

On the four successful ascents of Annapurna, only two men had reached the top each time. When I had invited each woman to go on this expedition, I had emphasized the possibility that only two climbers might make it, and that would be a triumph for the whole team. Back home, everyone had readily accepted that. Here on the mountain, though, it was another story, and while I told myself it was not surprising, I was still disappointed. I wanted our group spirit to outweigh our individual-achievement ethic—a lot to ask. To get here had required extraordinary perseverance, even aggressiveness. Now that the final pay-off was close, how could we be expected to let go of the very qualities that had got us here in the first place?

At 7:00 A.M. I started trying to contact Base Camp to get the other climbers' input for the new plan.

Arlene: This is Camp I calling Base Camp. Over.

No response.

Arlene: Camp I calling Base Camp. Camp I calling Base Camp. Please come in, Base Camp. We really need to talk with you.

No answer.

Arlene: This is Camp I calling Base Camp. We have found twelve cases of Dutch chocolate up here at Camp I. We are going to eat them all. If any of you would like some Dutch chocolate, come in at once.

Still no answer. Maybe they just weren't listening.

After calling several more times over the next few hours, I began to worry that something might have happened to Base Camp. There had been a small avalanche near the camp the day we had left to come up here. Perhaps a larger avalanche had come down there after all the new snowfall. Vera K. hiked partway over the hillside, looked down, and reported back that Base Camp was still there. Apparently their radios weren't working, or else they weren't interested in talking to us.

Here at Camp I the members stayed in the mess tent after breakfast to discuss logistics. We decided to make a preliminary plan without the input of the Base Camp climbers. I began by saying I wanted this new plan to be decided upon democratically to avoid all the unhappiness caused by the last one, and everyone agreed. There was a great deal of work left to be done carrying loads from Base Camp to Camp II; since the storm had used up so much of our time and resources, we would have to be even more efficient than we had been up to now. The climbers here could go up tomorrow to dig out Camp II if the weather stayed stable. The day after that the two Veras would work on the route to Camp III, followed by Liz and Alison, who would come up and take their turn leading. With little discussion the plan was accepted; my early morning worries had been unfounded. We would start undoing the storm damage tomorrow.

After lunch Vera W., Mingma, and Ang volunteered to dig out the tent that had collapsed and been buried two days ago. Digging the heavy snow off the buried tent was strenuous. At first the Sherpas were unenthusiastic about working so hard on a rest day, but then Mingma dug up a bottle of Nepalese rum someone had left in the tent. He jumped up and down with glee at this treasure and went through a hilarious pantomime of how he had shoveled and dug, doubled over with his hand pressed to his aching back, until he found the rum, which instantly cured his backache. As he pantomimed, he grunted and groaned and made his peculiar noises of pleasure.

After the tent had been resurrected, we gathered in the kitchen, and Mingma shared his bottle of rum. Soon we were all laughing and joking. Vera K. took out her mirror and studied her face intently. As usual it was covered with the thick pancake makeup she used as sunscreen.

"Let me look," I said, taking the mirror. I saw an unfamiliar, relatively slender sunburned face with prominent cheekbones. I wondered if John would recognize me when I got home.

"I don't want to see my new wrinkles," Vera W. said. But she couldn't resist the mirror for long. "Well, maybe I'll take just a peek." I handed her the mirror, and Vera looked at her face for the first time in several weeks.

"Oh," she complained, "I look so old."

"No, no, Vera. Your suntan is very becoming. You look beautiful." And she did indeed look classically lovely. In fact, the higher we climbed, the better we all looked—slim, tanned, and healthy. Many men, in contrast, take on a haggard look after a few weeks at high altitude.

But not all of us saw it that way. Annie made a face at herself in the mirror. "I look like a red-nosed booby," she laughed.

Margi took the mirror next and ruefully surveyed her short blond hair. "Blah! It looks like straw," she grimaced.

"It's great," Annie laughed. "You could be an English rock star."

"But I can't sing worth shit."

"Doesn't matter. Most of them can't either."

The Sherpas took the mirror and began to make faces at themselves. They were all clowning and wrestling on one side of the tent. Just then a mighty roar from an avalanche across the valley shook the tent, and the mood suddenly changed. Yeshi, who had been a climbing Sherpa on the 1974 French expedition to Everest in which an avalanche had killed six people, was reminded of that tragic event and told us the story.

He had been at Camp II, making tea in front of a tent occupied by the expedition leader and several other Sherpas when "whoosh! Big avalanche comes. Everything under snow. Tent buried. Barasahib lies under snow. I say, 'barasahib, do not die, not finish yet.' But barasahib says, 'I am finished, Yeshi, finished,' gurgles and dies. Then Yeshi is alone. Friends under snow. Other Sherpas, members come and dig. Dig out best friend, five Sherpas, barasahib, all dead." After hearing this, it was easy to understand why Yeshi had changed his job to that of cook boy. "Never climb again," he declared.

Meanwhile, I was still concerned about Base Camp and tried to call them again.

Arlene (Camp I): This is Camp I calling Base Camp. Camp I calling Base Camp. A dozen salamis for anyone who comes to the radio. Do you read me?

Suddenly there was an answer: "This is Lopsang calling. This is Lopsang calling. Over my signal."

But it wasn't Base Camp; it was the other Sherpas in our own camp playing with another radio outside. As the day went on, I wondered and worried about what was happening at Base Camp. At the six o'clock radio call it occurred to me to try another channel.

Arlene: This is Camp I calling Base Camp on channel two. Can you read me?

It worked!

Christy (Base): Yes, we can read you. Where have you been all day?

Arlene: Where have *you* been? We've been calling all day —you've had your radio on the wrong channel. That's why we couldn't talk. There's a lot to discuss.

Christy: Can you wait a few minutes? I want to finish my dinner first. I'll call back in half an hour. Over and out from Base.

My surprise at this somewhat cavalier attitude made me slow to react, and Christy signed off before I had a chance to object. When she called back, I explained the climbing plan for the next days. The climbers at Base said they needed a second rest day down there but agreed that we should go up and start digging out Camp II, assuming that it didn't storm. Then Christy said that the porters had finally arrived with supplies from Choya—360 pounds of potatoes, onions, squash, and cucumbers. I asked her about the forty quarts of kerosene we so desperately needed. She said a second group of porters had brought kerosene—but only five quarts. They had also brought two hundred lemons and 50 pounds of sugar. At least we could have lots of cold fresh lemonade.

On the way up to Camp II the next day, the glacier was a different place from when Annie and I had stumbled down a few days earlier, barely able to see our hands in front of our faces. High-mountain environments are always totally determined by the weather: one minute the sun is out and everything is heat and light; then a cloud covers the sun, the temperature drops 50 degrees, and snow begins to fall within minutes. Now it was scorching hot, with a sun that was fierce and unrelenting. Its reflection on the new snow was so intense that my eyes hurt in spite of the dark goggles I wore over my extradark sunglasses. Carrying heavy packs, Vera W. and I followed the trail that Vera K. and Annie had broken to Camp II. Enervated by the light and heat, we stopped to rest and eat snow to cool off. Vera W. confided some of her worries to me.

"You know, I feel that my carrying loads like this isn't helping the climb that much. The Sherpas can carry more than I can, and faster."

I tried to reassure Vera that her early work in fund raising and organization had been crucial. And now it wasn't important that she couldn't carry as much as the Sherpas. "If you just carry moderate loads and are strong enough to try for the summit, that'll be fine," I said.

I feel like I'd be helping the climb more if I were still in Palo Alto raising money." Vera W. still seemed very downcast. "I doubt that I'll be on a summit team."

"You've been doing at least your share all along and you still are. Don't worry so much, Vera."

"It's hard not to." She paused. "You know, I had a really weird dream one night during the storm. I dreamt that someone did reach the summit, but there was some danger. You didn't want to mount a second attempt. I was trying to persuade you in my dream. And then, 'bang'—the tent was on my face. The pole had broken. It was just awful."

"Oh, Vera," I sighed. "The summit's a long way off yet. Who knows what will happen by then?"

I felt drained too. Carrying our heavy loads through deep snow and the intense heat was taking extraordinary effort. This was my fifth trip to Camp II; it should have been easy because I was acclimatized by now, but it was the hardest so far— discouraging to feel so lethargic after nearly a month on the mountain.

We finally reached Camp II where we spent several hours digging out the tents, scooping away the snow with shovels, pots, snowshoes, and our hands. The tents had survived their burial remarkably well. They were mostly intact, though sopping wet. One of the poles had broken, but Irene and Vera W.

splinted it with strips of metal and hose clamps from the repair kit. I wondered if any further remnants of the Dutch expedition would be found in the camp. I thought of Dutch chocolate and dug industriously. Mingma likewise dug with great enthusiasm, perhaps hoping to unbury more rum. But all we found were our oxygen cylinders, ice axes, and pickets—nothing good to eat.

By the time the camp was dug out, it was cooler, and my energy had returned. Irene and I decided to start breaking trail above Camp II, as that would make the going easier for the others the next day. Plowing through two and a half feet of fresh powdery snow at 19,000 feet was like running a marathon with lead weights on each ankle. Irene went first, chugging along like a very slow but steady locomotive. As I followed her, it became clear we would have the energy to dig out the camp and remake the route only so many times. If Annapurna kept dumping storms like this one on us, we would never reach the summit. I had read of years when more than two feet of fresh snow fell every night on expeditions in the Nepal Himalaya. Each day the climbers would dig out and break trail through thigh-deep snow, but the overall upward progress was negligible. Very few summits were reached in those years, and if this were such a year, the mountain would not be climbed.

Crossing a narrow snowcrest, I heard an ominous crack and stopped instantly. A block of snow four inches to the side of my left boot slid down the steep slope, gathering mass and speed until it was swallowed by a large crevasse. When we had arrived three weeks earlier, the mountain was bare and icy. Since then many feet of new powder had fallen, with little respite for consolidation. The likely conclusion: high avalanche danger during the next weeks. I continued on, placing my feet deliberately so as not to start any more snowslides. The afternoon mist came in and with it a sense of unease. We couldn't see how close we were getting to the avalanche slopes below the Sickle Glacier.

"Let's turn back, Irene," I yelled to the red rope disappearing into the mist. "I don't like the feel of this place."

Irene agreed. As we walked back down together she told me, "I don't think that being high on this mountain after a snowstorm is any place for me. Teresa is only thirteen, and she still needs a mother. I'd rather carry loads between Camp I and Camp II for the next week and think about whether it's right to expose myself to avalanches from the Sickle. Someone else can have my turn in the lead."

I okayed her going down. There were still lots of loads to be carried between Camps I and II, and no one should be up there leading unless it felt right to her. In fact, I wished we could all wait a week before crossing below the Sickle. But it was September 21, and in less than a month winter gales would begin to scour these peaks. We would have to resume climbing very soon.

10 Avalanche

"Avalanche!" A boiling cloud was rolling down the Bobsled, over-flowing the edges, growing larger and larger as it headed straight toward us. We couldn't hear the roar or feel the wind yet, but after one look at the huge cloud, everyone ran to their tents and zipped the doors tight. We crouched inside, our minds racing with the dreadful possibilities. In the past five days there had been numerous avalanches from the heavy snow-fall of the big storm. Until now our camps had appeared safe, but this avalanche was bigger and moving faster than any of the rest.

Finally we heard the roar and felt the wind driven by the gigantic mass of flying ice. Pellets of spindrift rained down, but the tents protected us. Alison crouched at the back of the tent with her pocketknife open, ready to cut our way out of the tent should it begin to get buried. For an eternity of less than a minute we waited for the buffeting to end.

Silence. The avalanche mass had stopped above us. We crawled cautiously out of the tents to see that here the only sign of the avalanche was a layer of spindrift pellets two inches thick on the ground.

"It looks like it came from the plateau above the rib," Margi said, noticing a fresh scar above the Bobsled. "If that one didn't hit us, I'd say this camp is pretty safe."

Alison looked more dubious about our safety as she folded the blade back into her pocketknife.

"What a lovely little campsite," Vera W. said cheerily, as she crawled out of the tent.

"What are you talking about?" I asked incredulously.

"Camp IIIa, of course," Vera W. said.

Then I remembered that she and Vera K. had just come down from establishing Camp IIIa on the crest of the Dutch Rib a few minutes before the avalanche. Camp IIIa was to be a temporary camp. From it we would climb along the crest to the permanent Camp III, nearly a mile farther. When Camp III was established, Camp IIIa would be phased out, and loads could be carried directly from II to III without an intermediate stop. For the time being, the lead climbers could stay at Camp IIIa and work on the route to Camp III without going all the way down to Camp II each night.

"I can't wait to move up to IIIa," Vera K., coming out next, agreed.

The avalanche might not have happened, so delighted were

Vera W. reaches the crest of the Dutch Rib on her way to establish Camp IIIa. Vera Komarkova.

the two Veras with their day of leading on the mountain.

"Thank God you two didn't come down twenty minutes later," Annie said soberly. "The avalanche debris covered your tracks. You could have been buried."

When the rest of us had calmed down, the two Veras told us about their day on the rib.

"On the crest I put my ice axe in and there was nothing, nothing," Vera W. said, pantomiming a swimming motion. "I couldn't bring myself up on the axe, so I just had to kick, kick, kick with my feet and flounder up. I led all the way to below the serac, and then there was this lovely little platform. We decided to put Camp IIIa there."

"The first lead beyond IIIa looks like good, hard climbing," Vera K. said.

The conversation shifted to the subject of who was going to get this lead. Everyone was eager for the chance, and since it seemed that most of the hardest pitches had already been climbed, I decided the next turn could fall to anyone. We drew lots among the climbers who had not yet led on the rib, and Margi and Liz won. Annie and I would carry loads in support.

The next morning was crystal clear and the peaks resplendent. I enjoyed the walk up until I reached the piles of debris from last night's avalanche down the Bobsled. However, as I concentrated on picking my way through the unstable blocks of

View of the Dutch Rib showing four climbers leading the traverse pitch and avalanche couloir on the right side. Arlene Blum.

rubble, I relaxed. After all, the chute had avalanched last night; it should be safe this morning. Then the track passed below the chute on the right side of the Dutch Rib, which had not had an avalanche recently. I crossed the stretch as quickly as possible and joined Liz, Margi, and Annie at a flat spot next to the face where we had left our crampons, ropes, and harnesses. We did not need this technical gear below the rib, so it was left in a cache at the foot of the face. Leaving things in caches can be risky, especially on an unstable mountain like Annapurna. But this cache was right next to the face and thus presumably protected from avalanches coming off the Sickle.

I spent several minutes there putting on my seat harness

Telephoto picture of four climbers on the traverse pitch.
Irene Miller.

and jumars (devices that clamp onto a rope and aid in ascending), and tightening my crampons for an exact fit. Then I put my backpack on, adjusting the straps with care so it wouldn't shift and make me lose my balance, and walked slowly behind Liz for the last steps to the Dutch Rib. After months of anticipation, I stood in the shadow of the great wall of ice. Carefully attaching my jumar to the yellow polypropylene rope Piro had left in place when she had led the pitch, I started up the 65-degree, hard-ice slope. On her lead Piro had chopped small steps for the front points of our crampons; they helped, but I still had to use both arms to pull myself up on the jumar attached to the rope. Then I would step up on my crampon points, slide the jumar higher, and pull myself up again. My right bicep ached from the repeated strain, and I was glad for the weight training I had done before the trip to strengthen my arms.

As the angle of the face decreased slightly, I began to relax and enjoy the climbing. The higher I went, the more magnificent the view of immense peaks surrounding me. Finally I reached a little platform where ten-foot-long, fanglike icicles blocked my direct upward progress. The route then traversed through a two-foot-wide gap between the icicles and the ice face. I moved through it deliberately, carefully not touching the icicles for fear they would crack off and shear through our fixed lines.

Next I moved delicately across the difficult ice traverse, putting my crampons in slowly so as not to crack the brittle ice. I was full of admiration for Annie's lead the day before, which she described in her diary:

> After following the last pitch, a vertical piece of ice, I saw what I was to lead: a traverse of about 60- to 70-degree ice leading to the ramp. Jesus Christ! I had never climbed ice like that before, much less led it. I tried to act noncommittal, while I arranged the ice screws, and adjusted my ropes and other equipment.
>
> With the "Do's and Don'ts" from Chouinard's *Climbing Ice* flashing through my memory, I began. I found about three inches of granular snow on top of hard ice, I could not get a secure enough stance to put in an ice screw, so I kept going without an anchor. Next I was faced with a bulge of even steeper hard ice. I tried repeatedly and finally succeeded in putting in an ice screw from my precarious position. With that adored security, I continued traversing and finally reached a gully with about one foot of powder snow covering ice. The fixed rope and "people rope" (as the Sherpas say) were pulling me back too, so I would take one step up and slide down two. I buried a "deadman" in the snow to anchor us and belayed Vera K. over. She continued up to just below the crest of the ridge. She thought there might be a large cornice, so she placed a deadman and belayed us up. Mingma then continued to the ridge and up it until the length of the fixed rope ran out. Many times in the past I'd thought about climbing at 20,000 feet and wondered how it would be. To think that's what I was actually doing blows my mind.

Beyond Annie's pitch I followed the ramp Vera K. had led. Soon I left the shadow of the rib face for the bright sunlight of the crest, where there was an incredible 360-degree panorama —peak after peak as far as I could see, ice mushrooms and seracs, the Cauliflower Ridge to the west, large tumbling glaciers, improbable features and forms like an ocean of enormous frozen waves. As always, the beauty of the mountains quieted my doubts and anxieties and filled me with contentment. This was where I belonged.

I slogged the last few hundred feet along the ridge in the hot sun and dropped my pack at Camp IIIa. While Margi melted water for tea, Liz gave us a tour of the camp—a simple task, as

Margi jumaring up the rib. Arlene Blum.

it was only 15 feet square. On one side of the tent was the area where we could collect snow to melt for water; on the other, the toilet area. On both sides, the slopes dropped off a thousand feet to the glaciers below. Behind the tent was the hundred-foot, vertical ice wall with the shiny striations that had looked close to unclimbable during last year's reconnaissance. From up here, however, it looked as though Liz could get around it by traversing far to the left and then up a shorter, less steep stretch of ice.

Leaving Liz and Margi to make themselves comfortable for the night, Annie and I went back down. Rappelling, which is the usual way to descend a steep slope, always makes me uneasy. Though it requires less exertion and technical skill than climbing, the danger is greater. The climber's weight is mostly borne by a rope tied to an anchor, and the climber is attached to this rope with one of a variety of mechanical devices. Anchors can pull out and mechanical devices can fail; I much prefer to have my weight in contact with the mountain and my safety more directly under my own control.

Today as I came down the rib, I was trying out a new type of descender. At first I put it on the rope backwards, but Annie patiently showed me the right way. I soon got the knack and began to enjoy weaving effortlessly down the steep ice slopes that had required so much energy to climb. Instead of descending the ice traverse that Annie had led, we rappelled down an ice gully on a single red climbing rope. I'm heavier than the others, and the descender didn't slow me enough, so I wrapped the rope around my body for additional friction as I rappelled down the overhang amidst the brittle icicles—again careful not to brush against them. I landed on a two-inch-wide ice ledge behind the icicles and moved cautiously to a larger ledge to wait for Annie.

The rest of the descent was relatively straightforward. At the base of the ice wall Annie and I put our crampons, descenders, and jumars back in the cache. Exhilarated, we ran back through the avalanche area in about fifteen minutes. I had climbed the Dutch Rib at last!

The next morning I sat with my binoculars fixed on the striated ice wall beyond Camp IIIa, watching Liz and Margi climb. The face looked almost overhanging, with great ice bulges around the two climbers.

Liz, who has climbed some of the most severe ice faces in the Alps, described it as the hardest day of ice climbing she had ever done:

> I started out traversing in loose snow to the Bergschrund. The powdery stuff fell off steeply, and the route was slippery and insecure. The first pitch was the most awe-inspiring technical ice on the climb so far. Sixty to 70-degree ice and very crappy.

> Kicking both feet in hard, my ice hammer in my right hand placed firmly in the slope and my dagger in my left, hoping the ice would hold. . . . I didn't feel secure enough to stop on my front points to put in protection. My heart was pounding and my lungs were burning. Finally I got my first good ice screw in. Then two-thirds of the way up I got into some hard snow, which allowed me to put in a snow stake and relax a little. The worst part was over. After the ice wall was conquered, Margi, Mingma, and Ang Pemba took turns breaking trail through the deep snow over ice until we got to the crest.

That evening a tired, bedraggled Margi stumbled into Camp II, having come all the way back down from their high point. She reported that she'd been coughing blood all day, decided to rest, and gave up her lead to Alison. So Liz and Alison, good friends who climbed well together, would continue with some of the most challenging climbing on the mountain.

Vera W., Alison, and Annie also had an eventful day taking loads to IIIa as Annie described in her diary:

> I was just beginning to cross the mounds of avalanche debris when I saw, but didn't hear, a great cloud of snow and ice coming down from the right side of the Sickle. It looked as though the three members ahead of me were directly in its path. I turned around and ran, occasionally looking back at its progress. I got so winded running full speed with my pack that I had to slow to a fast walk. When I felt I was out of the way, I looked around for

Climber ascending "Liz's pitch" above Camp IIIa. Alison Chadwick,
© 1979 by the National Geographic Society.

the others. All I saw was a great cloud of snow engulfing the area
where they'd been. I knelt down, breathing fast and hard. I didn't
know what to do. Should I go probe for them? What if another
avalanche came down? Should I run back to Camp II for help?
What if I forgot the place where I'd last seen them? Oh, shit.
What should I do?

Then I saw someone 200 feet up the face on a fixed rope. I didn't
know who it was, but that person remained motionless—neither
up nor down to give me a clue about what she knew. I rose from
my knees, breathing returned to normal, and started back to the
avalanche area to look for them. I saw two figures slowly ascending from a depression. My relief was indescribable. It was Vera

W. and Alison. They'd run down a hill toward the rib to get away from the avalanche, which explained why I couldn't see them. The third member, Vera K., was the one on the fixed rope and out of danger.

Vera K. says she is a fatalist. This leaves her free of worry about avalanches. Well, I don't worry about them when they're not there, but when they are, they scare the bejesus out of me.

The avalanches were coming down night and day, dominating our existence here. The Everest tactic of climbing in the morning would not work on Annapurna, and there was no certainty that even our campsites were safe. That night I was awakened at 2:00 A.M. by what sounded like the largest avalanche yet. Our tents shook for several minutes from the wind and flying debris, much longer than ever before. After that, I spent most of the night wide awake with fear. Occasionally I would doze, dream of an avalanche, then yank back to consciousness only to find myself in a waking nightmare.

Ever since my friend John Henry Hall and his three companions had been killed on Mount St. Elias, I have been extremely afraid of avalanches. It now seemed particularly ironic to be attempting a venture whose success was so important to me in one of the world's most avalanche-prone places.

By morning I was exhausted and more reluctant than ever to cross the avalanche chute, but loads had to be carried to Camp IIIa, and today it was my turn again. Piro and Irene were moving up to Camp IIIa to take over the lead from Liz and Alison, while Vera K. and I carried loads in support. As I made my slow, rhythmic way up the hill, my fears began to recede. I was a hundred yards from the bottom of the face when Irene shouted down to me. "The cache has been avalanched. Everything is gone." My heart sank. We had left our twelve pairs of crampons, jumars, descenders, and other vital gear there, and without that technical gear we couldn't climb any higher. As I hurried toward the cache site, Irene yelled again, "Avalanche! Run!"

I heard the familiar roar close by, spun around, and ran down the track, propelled by a surge of adrenalin, until I was completely winded and had to stop short. I crouched down, my axe dug in to keep myself from being swept away, and waited, mentally reviewing the instructions for what to do if hit by an avalanche:

> If caught in an avalanche, the victim should attempt to stay above the snow by swimming. If the snow starts to pile up on the victim after he reaches the bottom, he should attempt to thrust a hand up as high as possible before the snow sets up. The other arm and hand should be in front of the chest and face to form a breathing space. In order to conserve oxygen, the victim should relax and not fight the sensation of blackout. (*Avalanche Handbook*, R. I. Perla and M. Martinelli, Jr., Agricultural Handbook 489, U.S. Department of Agriculture)

Piro reaches the rib crest on her way to Camp IIIa. Irene Miller.

Fortunately the avalanche stopped just above us, and I didn't have to try following any of these directions.

Laboriously, we slogged back up through the avalanche debris to where our cache had been, and where now there was nothing but an enormous hole, as though a great explosion had destroyed the entire ice slope. All the gear we had left there was lost. The previous night a huge block of ice had apparently split off the overhanging ice bulges on the face above, dropped straight down 500 feet, and smashed through to a crevasse 50 feet wide and 50 feet deep. The snow surface had disintegrated into the whirlwind of flying ice particles that had pelted our camp a mile away and a thousand feet below and had also splashed back up onto Camp IIIa, 800 feet straight above.

The loss of our gear meant that we could not continue up the mountain today, and for a time I thought it might even mean the end of the whole climb. Before going back down, Vera K. and I spent several minutes poking through the debris to see if we could recover anything. Only a few light items that had apparently floated to the top of the moving ice—one hard hat, some foam pads, and a few wands—were left from our entire cache. As we began walking down, still stunned by our near escape from today's avalanche, I wondered if we would indeed have to give up our attempt. Then Vera K. reminded me of the

Irene and Vera W. watch with horror from Camp II as an enormous avalanche threatens to bury the film crew at Camp I. Arlene Blum, © 1979 by the National Geographic Society.

twenty extra pairs of crampons she and Irene had insisted on bringing in spite of our objections about the extra weight. Even while praising Vera K. for her foresight, I was inwardly less than delighted. Without those damn crampons we could honorably go home and escape the avalanches of Annapurna. At that moment I wanted nothing better. But virtue won out, and I started making plans to get the extra crampons up here and resume climbing as quickly as possible.

At Camp II there was no discussion of giving up the climb. Ang Pemba was sent right down for the crampons. I was in my tent reworking our logistics plans to allow for the time we had lost when I heard Piro yell. "My God! Look at that avalanche!"

I jumped out of the tent to behold the largest avalanche I had ever seen sweeping down from a 23,000-foot peak across the valley. The cloud must have been two miles across and was growing larger by the moment. My first thought was, how beautiful—then suddenly I realized that it was big enough to cross the entire glacier and possibly hit Camp I. We all ran to the far end of the plateau and saw to our horror that Dyanna and Marie, accompanied by Joan, Christy, and two porters, were filming out on the glacier—six tiny spots directly in the path of the gigantic, foaming mass of snow. Within seconds, the avalanche swept across the glacier, burying the spots and blanketing Camp I.

For several terrible minutes we could see nothing but the boiling white cloud. When the snow finally settled, we could see the little spots begin to pick themselves up and move about erratically, like ants whose home has been stomped. We counted six—and allowed ourselves to breathe again, reprieved from an almost intolerable horror.

Christy wrote of the experience in her diary:

> With a great crack a giant chunk breaks off on top of the chute across the valley. At first we're delighted. Dyanna starts filming the avalanche as it rushes down, growing menacingly. Suddenly I realize *we're going to get it.* We're miles away, but that thing is moving like fury. My God! I look for a depression. Can't find one—dive for the glacier and thrust my axe in. Marie screams, "Christy, what do we do?" "Get down!" It's the last thing I can say before the rush of wind begins. The first blast picks me up from flat on the glacier and carries me twenty feet through the air. Next come tons of snow and ice driven by eighty-mile-an-hour winds. Miraculously my hat is still on my head, and I snatch it to cover my face and breathe through. Every bit of exposed skin is abraded by the driven ice and hurts like hell, but I just keep breathing. As the wind dies to about twenty miles an hour, I look out to pure white. My glasses are plastered inside and out. I take them off, but it's still wind-driven whiteout.
>
> When it finally dies down, I check people. Joan is okay. Pemba and Kaji buried by twelve inches of snow but fine. Marie is screaming now, pouring out her terror, so I know she is alive and well. Dyanna is quieter and harder to find. She was blown into a crevasse. One or two feet in either direction would have been straight down—we couldn't see the bottom. Luckily she landed on a snow bridge only six feet down. The power of this mountain overwhelms me.

After they had made it back to Camp I, Christy radioed up that the camp was a shambles, the mess tent badly torn and the other tents intact but leveled. Base Camp reported that the cloud and the wind had gone all the way down there, but had not caused any damage.

During those few moments when the enormous avalanche had covered the glacier, all my personal desire to reach the summit of Annapurna was swept away. I felt as never before the tenuousness of our habitation here, the fragility of our existence in the face of these incredible forces. Should we stay or leave? The weather was perfect, and after years of planning and struggle we were only a few weeks from the summit. But the size of the crevasse that had opened where our cache used to be was so staggering, the avalanches so relentless. Big mountain. Small people. I just didn't know if we should be there.

We had placed our camps in locations that had previously been regarded as safe from avalanches. But this year was different. The day after the flag raising, the first avalanche in the recorded history of Annapurna ever to threaten the area of Base Camp swept down the gully where we got our water. Pasang ran out in front of the avalanche and threw holy rice in its path, and it stopped, but not before the moving snow had dammed the stream that supplied our water. We left Base Camp delighted by Pasang's ability to stop avalanches but shaken by this historic event. Then there had been the huge ice avalanche that obliterated our cache, this latest monster at Camp I (another historic first), and the avalanches across the route to Camp III at all hours.

Every few minutes that afternoon we heard another avalanche. Until now I had been able to ignore the sound, but after the day's near catastrophe, I jumped up each time I heard that all-too-familiar roar to make sure it was not coming toward any of our camps. At 6:00 P.M. Base Camp radioed up the tragic news that three Japanese climbers had been killed in an avalanche on Dhaulagiri, across the valley, raising to six the toll of climbers who had died this month in avalanches in Nepal. Ordinarily fewer people than that would die in avalanches during a whole season here.

The avalanche danger had become so grave, it seemed to me that we seriously had to consider giving up and going home. I decided to poll the climbers on the subject and crawled into the large blue tent where Vera K. was reading a murder mystery, Annie was writing in her diary, and Piro was sorting medical supplies.

"These avalanches are getting to be too much. Do you think it's safe for us to stay here?" I asked.

Each one concentrated on what she was doing, and no one answered me.

"Things that aren't ever supposed to happen are happening twice a day right now. I feel as if something is telling us we should give up before one of us dies."

Still only silence. Finally Annie said, "I don't feel like talking about it. I just want to climb this mountain." No one else said anything.

At the time, I couldn't understand why no one would talk about the possibility of giving up, but Alison later offered what seemed like a reasonable explanation.

"The problem with talking about it at all is that if we admit we are really worried and try to have a rational discussion, we would inevitably come to the conclusion that we should give up. After years of work to get here, nobody wants to go home now. So they just won't talk about it."

I went to another tent, where Irene and Margi were more willing to voice their fears. "I've been climbing for twenty years," Irene said, "and I've never been on a mountain that's so

The sinuous crest of the Dutch Rib, showing the sites of Camps IIIa, III, and the plateau beyond. Irene Miller.

unstable. The avalanches are completely random. Sometimes it seems almost immoral to keep going."

I agreed. "Everest had lots of them, too, but it was safe enough in the morning. That's not true here. No time is safe. There have been avalanches at eight in the morning, five in the afternoon, noon, three in the morning—any time. That avalanche today swept from 23,000 feet to 16,000 feet in a few seconds."

"If an avalanche as big as that one came down from the Sickle, we could be hit here at Camp II," Margi pointed out.

"I'm not sure I want to stay at this camp—it's dangerous."

"It makes me heartsick," I told them. "I feel like we did everything right except selecting our peak. I know we've got the ability to climb the mountain. We've already done the hardest part, but I don't know if we can stay here for three more weeks and keep walking under these avalanche slopes day after day without someone getting killed. It's not worth it if anyone dies."

Irene felt the same, but voiced a stubborn conviction that seemed to prevail in the group. "I've never felt good about Annapurna because of the avalanche danger. I wish we'd picked another peak, too, but we're here now. I guess we'll have to make the best of it."

And so we did. The momentum of the ascent overwhelmed our individual or collective doubts, and even while we talked, the climbing went on. Two thousand feet above us, Liz and Alison were perched, tired and sun scorched, on the rib. They were overlooking the catastrophes below and encountering problems of their own. Liz wrote in her diary,

> Ali was leading a delicate traverse when the whole valley below us filled with flying snow—it was the largest avalanche I had ever seen. I watched with horror, sure that Camp I would be destroyed. When we saw that everyone was okay, we breathed a great sigh and continued up.
>
> When I reached the crest I was in for a bad surprise—every two yards there was a new cornice with an enormous cavern beneath —put me back two steps every time I took one up. I kept hacking away at the soft snow and cornices hoping to come to more solid snow below. It was grueling and scary work. I attempted to detour from the narrow crest but found myself out over sheer edges. The caverns kept increasing in size, numbers, and instability, just when I thought they were ended.
>
> I started to panic—the whole slope was soft, totally insecure, and there was a thousand-foot dropoff on either side. I looked for a place to put in a rappel anchor, but the snow between the caverns wouldn't hold more than one shaky step up. There was no turning back until the crest. Finally, with only one deadman and three snow stakes left, I reached the crest and drove them all in, then rappelled back down to Alison.

The news later came over the radio that Liz, Alison, Mingma, and Ang had just made it up to the top of the rib and established Camp III there at 21,000 feet. The most technically difficult part of Annapurna had been climbed!

Considering the extraordinary avalanche danger, I was surprised that no one was leaving or inventing excuses not to climb. We weren't trying to act heroic—everyone was bitching and saying they were afraid, that they hated it, or else refusing to discuss the avalanches at all. But we were still climbing. I'm not sure it was particularly intelligent or laudable of us to stay. But it definitely was heroic.

11 Sherpa Strike

"This is the worst expedition I've ever been on." Wangel was nearly shouting at me and gesticulating wildly.

"What's the matter?" I asked.

"Equipment is very bad. Food is very bad. Members are very bad. You tell us, leave our sleeping bags at Camp IIIa. Sleeping bags belong to Sherpas. Members cannot tell Sherpas what to do."

The intensity of Wangel's outburst surprised me. In recent weeks the tension between members and Sherpas had eased considerably. Earlier I had been greeted each morning with the refrain, "Just one bad problem, memsahib," but lately things had seemed fine, and we had been able to focus our attention on the mountain rather than on problems with the Sherpas.

A suggestion of this renewed discontent among the Sherpas had come only a few hours earlier at Camp IIIa. I had carried a load up and joined Liz, Alison, Chewang, and Mingma there. They had finished several days of working on the rib and were heading back to Camp II for a rest. When I reached Camp IIIa, the Sherpas were stuffing their sleeping bags into their packs to take them down to Camp II, as Alison and Liz looked on in concern. We had planned to leave most of the high-altitude gear, including the down sleeping bags, up at the high camps, to avoid the extra work of carrying the bags up and down between camps. We would use fiberfill bags at Camps I and II.

Alison now reminded the Sherpas of this and was trying, so far in vain, to get them to leave their down bags at IIIa.

"No, memsahib, we want our feather bags at Camp II. We will carry them down and then back up. No problem."

"But if you carry your sleeping bags up and down each trip, then you can't carry as much of a load, and it will take longer to climb the mountain." Liz's reasoning likewise failed, and the Sherpas stubbornly continued to stuff their bags.

"We told you when we gave you the bags that they were to be used only at the highest camps and you agreed." Alison's voice grew sharper, and the exchange became quite heated. I didn't contribute much because I had already had a similar discussion with the Sherpas the preceding day.

Wangel, who had come up just for the day and whose own bag was still down at Camp II, was taking Mingma's and Chewang's part vociferously. "We will leave our bags here at Camp III if you can give us feather bags at every camp. Sherpas do not want to sleep in nylon bags at Camp II."

Alison and Chewang lunching at IIIa before heading back down to II.
Irene Miller.

"Members sleep in fiberfill bags at Camp II," Liz told him.
"They are very warm."

"I do not care!" By now Wangel was furious. "Feather bag
is Sherpa bag, and we take them down." The Sherpas stomped
off angrily toward Camp II, and when Liz, Alison, and I arrived
back there, we found Chewang sitting in front of his tent with a
sullen expression on his face.

Vera W. rushed up to us. "The Sherpas came down from
IIIa really angry about something. They threw their ice axes
down and started stomping around. What's going on?"

I went over to the corner of the camp where Wangel was
haranguing the other Sherpas, his eyes flashing and his arms
waving in the air. This was the point at which he informed me
that the expedition was the worst he had ever been on.

"I've been on twelve expeditions," he ranted, "none like
this."

I remembered that, in fact, Wangel had been on only three
previous expeditions, and smiled. It occurred to me that the
Sherpas' reluctance to leave their bags at Camp III was in all
probability based on fear that we might leave the mountain
suddenly, forcing them to abandon the valuable bags. I apolo-
gized about the scene at Camp IIIa.

"You can bring the bags up and down if you insist. As for

Chewang protests against leaving his sleeping bag at Camp IIIa.
Christy Tews.

your complaints about food and equipment, members and Sherpas have the same food and the same equipment. Both are very good."

I was tired from the day's carry and went to my tent to take off my boots, thinking the Sherpas would soon simmer down. Complaints about food and equipment are not unusual on expeditions and frequently mean that the Sherpas want more money. At the moment I was more concerned about the thickly falling snow that was beginning to blanket the camp. Piro and Irene were camped in a tiny tent at IIIa with only a few supplies. They were scheduled to move to Camp III tomorrow, and most of their food was already up there. If it continued to snow heavily, they would not be able either to descend across the avalanche slope or to go up. They would be marooned at Camp IIIa until several days after the storm ended.

Annie interrupted my reflections. "You'd better get out there right away. The Sherpas are packing up to leave." This sounded serious, so I wearily went back out into the storm.

Vera W. was saying to Ang, "You say we are bad people. Why do you say we are bad?"

Wangel overheard her and retorted, "You always call us Sherpas bad. Why do you call us bad?"

Vera W. was surprised. "No, I never call you bad."

But Wangel insisted, "I heard you. You just called us bad again."

This present exchange was obviously caused by a language problem; Wangel heard only a few of Vera's words and misinterpreted her meaning. Even international expeditions composed of climbers from various European countries who speak different languages but share basically the same cultural background have a history of misunderstandings. Between Sherpas and expedition members the potential for misunderstanding is compounded by totally different backgrounds and expectations.

I said to the Sherpas, "Very bad for everyone if you leave. Bad for the expedition—it will take us a long time to climb the mountain. Bad for the Sherpas—you will not get a good recommendation if you desert us in this snowstorm."

But the Sherpas still looked angry and hostile. Standing in the heavy, wet snow, I tried to seem calm, but my mind was racing, trying to determine whether we would be able to climb the mountain without them. It certainly would be harder. Our logistics plan had counted on their help with the load carrying. They just couldn't leave.

But leave they did. The five Sherpas stomped off down the mountain shouting furiously over their shoulders, "See you in Kathmandu." Only the cookboy, Yeshi, remained, and I suspected this was more out of loyalty to Annie than to the rest of the expedition.

I radioed down to Camp I to warn them what to expect.

Arlene (Camp II): This is Camp II calling Camp I. Five angry Sherpas are coming down the mountain. Please put Lopsang on.

Lopsang (Camp I): This is Lopsang. Let me talk to those Sherpas on the radio. I will explain they must stay and do their duty at Camp II.

Arlene: It's too late, Lopsang. The Sherpas have already left. You'll have to talk to them when they get there. They say they're going to Kathmandu. Don't feel bad. It's not your fault. You're a good sirdar.

Lopsang: If these Sherpas come down to Camp I, they are bad Sherpas. I will send them back to Camp II right away. Over my signal.

I was skeptical of Lopsang's confidence that he could turn the Sherpas around. An hour later Christy called back to tell us that the Sherpas had just stormed cursing through the camp.

"Ang and Wangel are the two chief troublemakers," she said. "They were swearing at me in perfect English. Lopsang talked to them, but he could only persuade them to wait at Base Camp until tomorrow. They drank some tea and then went down to Base Camp in the dark."

Lopsang had failed. This meant my having to go all the way down to Base Camp the next day to try to persuade the Sherpas to stay. That night at dinner I was complaining about my trip down to the others.

"Have you considered just letting them go?" Alison suggested. "I'm sure we could climb the mountain without them."

"They're not all that useful," Liz agreed. "The day Wangel and Lopsang were supposed to help us on the rib, Lopsang led one good pitch, but Wangel seemed afraid to do anything. Finally Lopsang said valiantly, 'I'm an old man. I can climb no more. We must go down.' But I'm sure he was just covering up for

Wangel. I asked Wangel if he would at least bring the second rope up to the end of Lopsang's lead, and he wouldn't even do that. Lopsang did do a fine lead, but waiting for them both to get straightened out took longer than climbing it by ourselves."

"Yes, the Sherpas did slow us down that day," Alison qualified Liz's criticism. "But the next day Ang and Mingma did about half the leading. That climbing wasn't as hard as the first day, though."

"We probably could climb the mountain without the Sherpas," I speculated. "Let's go over the logistics and see if it works."

So Alison and I made a new plan and calculated that we could climb the mountain by ourselves in an extra week. Alison was delighted. "Think how much better it will be not having to deal with these stubborn Sherpas."

"Even that extra week may lose us the summit," I cautioned her. "If it storms again or the winter winds begin to blow, we might not make it." I again reminded Alison that the Sherpas would provide an extra measure of both speed and safety on the highest part of the climb, and she finally agreed that I should go down the next day and try to talk the Sherpas into staying. "But don't worry if you can't persuade them. We can still do it on our own."

Meanwhile, we called up Piro and Irene to find out how they were weathering the storm at Camp IIIa and to get their opinion on continuing without the Sherpas.

Piro (Camp IIIa): We wouldn't mind giving the climb a go without them. But with this blizzard, it doesn't look like we'll be going anywhere for a while. The snow is accumulating in the gullies on both sides of the camp, and avalanches are bombing down a couple hundred feet away every few minutes. I feel like I'm living on a freeway divider. I doubt if we'll be able to climb for several days. Over and out from Camp IIIa.

The snow fell heavily all night; I had to go outside and dig out the tents several times. The demons of the night were out in force as I worried about Piro and Irene, isolated in that tiny camp up on the ridge. They were safe there for now, but it would be very risky for them to come down with all this new snow. If the rest of us were forced to abandon Camp II again, Piro and Irene would be far away and very much alone. Then it was finally time for the early morning radio contact.

Piro (Camp IIIa): There's a foot of new snow, avalanches coming down on either side, but we're in good spirits.

Arlene (Camp II): Is there anything you need up there?

Piro: Yes—crampons and tampons. Irene's crampons aren't fitting too well, so could you send us up a new pair? Also, both of us need tampons all of a sudden, and we don't have enough. Oh, and the only book we've got is a Spanish grammar Irene brought—not too inspiring. We've been keeping ourselves entertained by playing "name the composer" and telling jokes, but we've run out of jokes. Could you dredge up a few?

Christy (Camp I): I've got a joke that'll help you forget the storm. I promise.

Piro (Camp IIIa): Go ahead, Christy, we're ready.

Christy: The prince was getting married, and he asked his father, the king, for advice about the wedding night. The king told him, "You should escort your wife to the bridal chamber and then stand in front of her and bow, saying, 'I offer you honor.' Then she'll curtsy and say, 'I honor your offer.' You should drink a glass of wine and repeat, 'I offer you honor.' She'll hold your hand and repeat, 'I honor your offer.' And it'll go on like that all night. Honor . . . offer . . . honor . . . offer." A good morning to all—over and out from Camp I.

Groans came from the lower camps and hysterical laughter from the upper—an indication of the effects of high altitude on good taste.

Vera K. came over to my tent and offered to go down with me to help negotiate with the Sherpas. Since she seemed to have a good rapport with them, I accepted. We threw a few things in our packs to take down with us and organized the rest in waterproof bags in case the storm got worse and the camp had to be abandoned. I feared the Sherpas might leave for Kathmandu early in the day so we left before breakfast.

Vera K. roped up first because she was lighter; I could hold her more easily if she were to fall into a crevasse than she could hold me. In the heavy snowstorm this was a real possibility —visibility was about two feet, and our earlier track was completely buried.

"Can you hook the radio onto your sweater so you can call for help in case I fall into a crevasse?" Vera K. asked.

"Sure." I put the radio in the pocket of my wool shirt. It was not very comfortable because the antenna tended to poke up my nose as I walked.

Vera K. set off at a run. I lurched along behind her clutching a bundle of wands in each hand. I wanted to mark the trail more clearly in case the others had to follow us later in the storm. My glasses were so fogged over I could barely see. The deep snow-over-ice was slippery and difficult to negotiate, and the radio antenna bobbing in and out of my nose added to my misery. I felt like a reluctant dog being hauled on a leash.

As we crossed the glacier an avalanche thundered off the rock face ahead of us, threatening to bury the route between Base Camp and Camp I. Then all of a sudden the snow stopped and the sun came out. We were instantly too hot, so we stopped to take off some clothes and put on our dark glasses.

"Let's have a bite of breakfast and collect ourselves so we'll be composed when we first see the Sherpas," I suggested.

We drank iced tea out of our water bottles, nibbled mint cake, and discussed whether the Sherpas might already be gone when we reached Base.

"I wouldn't be surprised if they've left," Vera K. said. "But Annie doesn't think they actually mean to leave. She bet me a steak that this is just a move to get more money."

"A steak? Where are you going to get a steak?"

"A buffalo steak at K.C.'s, after the trip."

When we had finished eating, Vera K. suggested that I walk first and look as "leaderlike" as possible entering Base Camp. As we approached to within sight of Base Camp, I looked eagerly for some sign of the Sherpas and realized that I very much did want them to stay. I decided to do whatever I could to convince them to do so, for the sake of making the climb safer.

The Sherpas were still at Base Camp when we reached there about noon, and although all was quiet, I could feel the tension in the air. Joan came to greet us and told us that at a meeting with the Sherpas that morning, they had demanded more equipment and more voice in the climbing plans. But since we did not have the equipment, they said they would accept money instead. So it was as simple as that—if we paid them more money, they would continue to climb the mountain.

I was relieved that the Sherpas had not left and was willing to pay them the extra money. Though high by local standards, their daily wage of about $2.50 did not seem so to us, considering the perilous work they do. We had already planned to give them a lot of extra pay in the form of bakshish at the end of the trip. What I objected to were the tactics they were using to get their extra pay early.

Next, I visited our liaison officer, Mr. Gurung, to get his version of the morning bargaining session.

"Namaste, Mr. Gurung. What's happening with the Sherpas?"

"They came down in the dark last night very furious. They said they were going to Kathmundu at once. I suggested they eat first and told the cook to fix them a special dinner. After that they were less angry. Then I told them they should wait until today for you and Lopsang to come down, and they agreed."

I praised Mr. Gurung for his tact in calming the Sherpas, and together we proceeded to the smoky kitchen tent where Lopsang and the other Sherpas were eating. From everyone's serious demeanor it seemed this was going to be a business luncheon.

Lopsang listed their demands as he peeled, buttered, and ate small potatoes. "The Sherpas say they need another sweater, wool shirt, down mittens, down booties, a pair of jumars, towel, a bar of soap, and ten cigarettes a day. Otherwise they cannot climb."

"But, Lopsang, we gave the Sherpas wool shirts and sweaters in Kathmandu. You have ensolite booties instead of down ones. And we already gave out the whole cigarette ration on the trek, like you told us to. I don't know what to say about towels and soap."

"The Sherpas did not bring the wool shirts and wool sweaters from Kathmandu. A good expedition gives sweaters and shirts two times, once in Kathmandu, once at Base Camp. But if you pay extra money instead, then everybody happy. Sherpas will forget and climb the mountain without rest."

High-altitude climbing is a regulated industry in Nepal. The mountaineering rules of His Majesty's government specify that members and Sherpas must have equipment and food of equal quality. Problems nonetheless arise because the Sherpas can always cite some expedition that had given out more and better gear. Ours now told us of a Japanese expedition that had given them instant cameras, transistor radios, and alarm wrist watches, implying that they hoped for that much loot from every expedition to follow.

In fact, the Sherpas had more new personal gear than we did; the members used mostly clothing brought from home. Our sweaters, for example, were not so warm as the heavy new ones we had given the Sherpas. But only Mr. Gurung had brought his sweater to Base Camp; the others had either sold their sweaters or left them behind, apparently expecting a second issue.

I shrugged in acquiescence and began assigning values to the list of items the Sherpas demanded: ten dollars for a wool sweater, ten dollars for a wool shirt, one dollar for soap and towel. No one questioned these values. The total came to about one hundred dollars, nearly forty days' pay, for each of the Sherpas.

"Okay. The expedition will pay each Sherpa 1293 rupees. Now you must go up to Camp II at once and continue to carry loads."

But another issue was bothering the Sherpas. "Men are men and women are women. You should have men along with the first summit team. We don't want you women to disappear on the mountain," Lopsang told us paternalistically.

"No. The first summit team must be all women," I said firmly. "After all, this is a women's expedition. The second team can have both women and Sherpa climbers."

"Maybe snow waist deep. Can women climb through waist-deep snow?" Chewang asked.

"If the snow is waist deep, then the first team may not reach the summit. The second team with Sherpas will be able to use whatever trail the first team has broken and will have a better chance." The matter was left unresolved as, just then, the cook brought in another big tub of boiled potatoes. Fresh potatoes with chilis and salt are a delicacy after a month of high-altitude food.

The next afternoon we paid the Sherpas, and the strike was over. They were happy, but I was not pleased that they were in effect being rewarded after having deserted us in a snowstorm. Although this sort of behavior was becoming more usual on expeditions, I was not reconciled to it.

That evening Pasang had just served a delicious tuna casserole when the Sherpas filed into the mess tent where Mr. Gurung, Vera K., and I were eating. One by one the Sherpas made lengthy, platitudinous speeches about working without rest until the summit was reached.

I simply said I was sorry there had been so many misunderstandings between us and hoped they were over. As the speeches continued, our dinner got colder and colder, and I got hungrier and hungrier. The Sherpas kept telling me that I should go ahead and eat my dinner while they talked, but I felt uncomfortable eating with all those eyes watching. What a crazy world! One day climbing a 60-degree ice slope at 20,000 feet with avalanches crashing down on all sides, the next day at Base Camp—two members of an all-woman expedition surrounded by men, eating fresh vegetables, and trying to solve a labor dispute.

High on the mountain the storm was still raging. Annie, Margi, Liz, Alison, and Vera W. had to abandon Camp II because of avalanche hazard and retreat to Camp I in the blizzard. And Irene and Piro were still up at Camp IIIa, now even more isolated from the rest of us. But their spirits remained high—as long as we kept telling them jokes over the radio. The quality of the jokes was getting even worse, but they didn't seem to mind.

Christy (Camp I): Here's a joke for Piro. Why do Polish dogs have flat noses?

Piro (Camp IIIa): I don't know. Why?

Christy: From chasing parked cars.

Arlene (Base): That's even worse than yesterday. Be careful, Alison might start thinking you're bigoted about Poles.

Christy: Bigoted? I just wish I could climb as well! Over.

I smiled, thinking how right Christy was. I wished I could climb as well too. Some of the best women climbers in the world came from Poland. Wanda Rutkiewiez and her compatriots, in addition to climbing Gasherbrum II and III, had climbed the infamous Trollryggen Wall in Norway, the north face of the Eiger, the north face of the Matterhorn in winter, and many more of the world's most challenging routes.

Arlene (Base): How's the food holding out up there?

Piro (Camp IIIa): We have lots of candy bars and Instant Breakfasts, but not much else. There's one hot tuna dinner, but we're saving it. Today we each had a Mounds bar for breakfast, an Almond Joy for lunch, and a Milky Way for dinner, but we're doing fine. Just keep those jokes coming. Over and out.

After their rest day, the Sherpas were ready to go back up the mountain. Just before leaving, they went over to pray at the shrine where we'd had the flag-raising ceremony. Though somewhat faded, the flags still fluttered in the wind—a reminder to the mountain gods to be merciful. After saying the prayers, burning some juniper wood, and sprinkling the area with blessed rice, the Sherpas marched solemnly back up the mountain. By afternoon they would be back at Camp II, ready to resume the climb. As I watched them go up, a lone figure emerged from the mist and headed slowly down toward Base Camp.

It was Liz Klobusicky. She had told me earlier she had to be back in Germany to start teaching on October 15, and now it was time for her to leave. I hated to see her go. Liz was one of the strongest, steadiest members of the team. After her outstanding work on the rib, she deserved a chance at the summit.

"If you stay you have a good chance of making it to the top," I told her.

"If I knew I'd make the summit, I could probably get away with being a week late for work, but there's no guarantee. If I'm not back on time, I might lose my job," she told me sadly.

"Doesn't all your hard work on the rib count for anything?"

"No. Only the summit makes any difference to the German school system. In all honesty, I'm not that sorry I'm leaving. I keep getting letters from Nicko urging me not to take any risks, to come back to him. And you know that staying here means taking even greater risks. Imagine, in two weeks I'll be home with Nicko."

I assured Liz that I understood, and indeed I did. The thought of being back home with John seemed preferable in many ways to shivering up at Camp IV.

"I have a lump in my throat about the next two weeks," Liz said. "I'm terrified for all of you."

"Me too. I've never seen conditions like this on any other mountain. Do you think the avalanches have anything to do with the Sherpas going on strike?"

"I doubt it. They didn't mention avalanches at all, did they?"

"No. In fact, the day before the strike Lopsang said, 'Tomorrow weather bad. Sherpa rest day.' I wonder if the Sherpas knew there would be a storm and decided they might as well rest at Base Camp during the bad weather and make some money at the same time.

"That's an interesting thought," Liz laughed. "The Sherpas do have a good sense of weather. This strike didn't slow the climb that much, and it got them what they wanted. But I'll bet that they did it partly because we're women. They don't seem to resent taking orders from men like they do from us."

"I guess they're not used to working for women," I said. "I suppose we'll never know whether the strike happened because we are women, or was manufactured to get more money, or was based on genuine anger."

That night, when Piro called down on the radio from Camp III it became clear that our Sherpa problems were not entirely over.

Piro (Camp IIIa): Today Irene and I broke trail through

Liz bids goodbye to Mr. Gurung before her departure. Arlene Blum.

two feet of new snow from Camp IIIa to Camp III, and we were planning to move up tomorrow and begin leading the ice step. That's why we've been sitting here waiting for five days. Then Ang and Mingma marched up our broken trail, camped at III, and told us they were going to lead the route themselves the next day. We're furious. Over.

There wasn't anything I could do from Base Camp. Apparently the Sherpas' promise to climb the mountain without rest implied that they were going to climb the mountain on their own, ignoring our logistics plan. Liz and I went to ask Lopsang for advice about how to handle the Sherpas' disobedience.

"Those bloody Sherpas," he fumed. "I will tell them they must do their duty."

I knew that wouldn't work. The Sherpas weren't listening to Lopsang anymore. Perhaps it was because he was too different from them: he was formally educated in India and had been an army officer. The authoritarian way he dealt with subordinates might have worked well in the army, but it antagonized the Sherpas, who seemed to no longer like or respect him. Lopsang in turn had reacted to his loss of control over the Sherpas with high blood pressure, incipient ulcers, and insomnia. He told Liz and me that he was through with climbing; in the future he would only lead trekking trips or accompany expeditions as far as Base Camp.

Liz and I both liked Lopsang and tried to cheer him up. "Don't worry, Lopsang, you did a wonderful job getting all the loads to Base Camp. Rest now, and you'll be strong again soon."

Lopsang smiled weakly and told me he wanted to stay at Base Camp for the rest of the expedition. I agreed that he could, though I did not relish trying to manage the five unruly Sherpas myself.

The next day as Liz left, I walked with her a few hundred yards below camp and thanked her again for all her hard work on the expedition. "Don't take any risks you don't have to" were her last words as she turned and walked off down the hill.

Liz was going back to the world today. She would be seeing trees, animals, perhaps even some of our friends who were trekking into Base Camp. For me it was time to return to the ice, snow, and avalanches. Even though I no longer wanted to go to the summit myself, I would go up again at least to Camp III to coordinate the establishment of Camps IV and V, and the final summit push.

Slowly I walked back to Base Camp, picked up my pack, and set off across the green meadows above the camp, all too soon leaving the flowers and grass for the rock and ice of the Annapurna moraine and glacier. How would we feel when we saw those meadows again, if we all saw them again? Would we be elated or in despair? In either case, it would be over.

Plans and Changes 12

October 3–8

Arriving back up at Camp II, I was greeted with the welcome news that Irene and Piro, rather than the Sherpas, had taken over the lead above Camp III. They were making good progress on the 400-foot ice step which was the first major obstacle on the route to Camp IV.

Piro's diary records the details:

Irene and I sat in our little tent at IIIa for four days waiting for the storm to end. When it finally cleared, we spent the next day breaking trail through thigh-deep powder up to Camp III, planning to move up and start leading the next day. Then Ang and Mingma came up the trail we had broken and announced that they were going to stay at Camp III. "Sherpa lead. Climb mountain. In three days summit."

We tried to explain to them that the steep ice above Camp III was ours, that we had been waiting for five days to lead it. No luck. They just smiled at us and settled in for the night up there. We stomped back down to Camp IIIa, showering blessings on all Sherpas, their mothers, nannies, grandmothers, and unborn children.

So we weren't too sad when Ang Pemba got altitude sick the next day, and he and Mingma had to come down. The lead of the ice step was to be ours after all.

October 4: Morning windy and incredibly cold. Irene led out on a nasty, steep traverse on rotten snow, and came to a very awkward corner of steep ice deeply covered with powder. She spent a long time getting protection in, finally managed to place a small deadman high up on the left, then oozed around the corner onto more stable snow. Every once in a while her ice axe would disappear into a hole—better you than me, I thought. She brought me up, and I had a chance to lead a short, steep pitch on ice, then an easy slog to the mouth of a steep rock and ice chimney. At first I was nice and warm, even though I was out of the sun by a few yards. When Irene climbed up to me and took the gear for the next lead, she looked up into the chimney and grunted. I was grinning the grin of the righteous because I had done my bit for a while.

The chimney had vertical walls of hard blue ice and a sloping back. Irene put her crampons into the back and used her hands on the sides to jam and slither up to the top. She tried to put in an ice screw, but the ice was too brittle. Finally she got a sling around an icicle for protection.

The grin froze on my face as I stood there belaying Irene. After fifteen minutes I was barely comfortable, then cold and finally shivering and shaking. I didn't dare make a move to put on more clothes. I was thinking about death by hypothermia when Irene

Piro emerging from the top of "Irene's chimney" during the leading of the ice step. Irene Miller.

Annie, Vera K., and Lakpa at Camp III, getting ready to lead the route to Camp IV. Note the "deadmen" anchors Annie is taking out to secure the fixed lines. Irene Miller.

gave her "belay on" call. I tried to move fast to get warm and scrambled up the chimney admiring Irene's lead. As I poked my head out at the other end, the sun hit my face and my belayer took a casual picture of my arrival. We both felt good until we looked at the next ice pitch—not too steep but apparently very rotten.

I started out and found that the ice was easier then I had feared— I actually had more trouble with deep snow on the steep upper part just under the rim of the plateau. The usually uncomplaining Irene yelled plaintively up to me, "What's taking you so long?" After considerable floundering in the deep snow, even using the dog-paddle technique to get ahead, I got a picket in and brought Irene up. She led off to the plateau. No sooner had she disappeared than I found that I was getting hypoglycemic. Boy, P.K., I thought, what a winner. First you get cold, then hungry— next thing you know, you'll be calling for your mommy. I felt disgusted with myself and almost oblivious to some of the most spectacular scenery I'd ever seen. Then I saw Irene poke her nose over the edge of the plateau. The ice step had been climbed.

The next day Piro went down to Camp II, and Annie and Vera K. joined Irene in the lead on the plateau. The three of them put in a long, strenuous day plowing through very deep snow and finally reached the foot of another, shorter ice step where fixed lines were needed again. The next day Irene descended, and Mingma and Chewang came up to help lead the terrain beyond the plateau—short, steep ice pitches alternating with deep snow.

Annie, Vera K., Chewang, and Mingma put in two long hard days of climbing to establish Camp IV. Vera K. described the first day in her diary:

> We start early, have a long way to go with heavy packs. Annie and I carry the wands—a particularly awkward load. We pass the site of the Dutch Camp IV which is too low—we want to put our Camp IV much higher. At about 3:30 in the afternoon we have used up all our fixed rope, and Chewang in particular is disappointed because he wants so badly to get there today. I explain it is too late, but he is inconsolable. Finally, we give up and go down, knowing we'll reach the camp tomorrow for sure. Back at Camp III the four of us cook dinner together and talk until very late. We make ice cream and set it outside to cool, and we joke forever about how a baby yeti is going to come and eat it.

The next day Mingma easily and elegantly led a nearly vertical 40-foot ice wall, and the four climbers reached Camp IV at 23,000 feet early in the afternoon. The campsite was a small platform in the shadow of an enormous serac. It was a cold, cramped place but with a spectacular view. Once there, they found they had used up all of their anchors, so Annie contributed her ice axe for the last fixed anchor, and she had to descend the plateau without an axe.

With Camp IV established, the question of the day at Camp II was: "Who's going to be on the summit teams?" I invariably answered that the final decision would best be made at the last minute, because circumstances often change summit plans right up to the end. I told the story of our Everest climb, on which the two climbers who reached the summit on the first team had originally been slated for later teams. In fact, one of them had been so discouraged by his exclusion from the first team that he had almost given up and gone home.

I had assumed all along that by the time we were ready for the summit push, natural selection would make the choice of the summit teams obvious. On many expeditions, after months of hard work at high altitude, some climbers are too tired physically or psychologically to try for the top. But there had been little attrition on this climb. Indeed, most of the members were growing stronger and more determined by the day.

Physiology may have been a factor in this. The average woman's body is 25 percent fat, while an average man's is only 15 percent fat. This extra fat is an energy reserve that can help women to remain strong and healthy under the most severe conditions; it is said to give women a higher tolerance for cold, exposure, and starvation. Joan Ullyot, in her book *Women's Running,* notes, "Among the survivors of shipwrecks, mountaineering, and similar disasters, women generally outnumber men . . . endurance rather than power seems to be their natural strength." Women excel in athletic activities such as long-distance swimming in cold water, where their fat provides in-

Two climbers carry loads up "Liz's pitch" above Camp IIIa.
Irene Miller.

sulation and can also be mobilized for energy. It has been suggested that women may have superior ability to utilize fat for energy and consequently do relatively better at events that demand stamina more than sheer power.

Whatever the explanation, after forty days on Annapurna, seven of the ten members—everyone but Joan, Liz, and me —were still eager to try for the top. Though I was delighted that we had such depth on the team, it did mean that the summit decision would not be made by attrition, and I spent hours considering how two or three summit teams could best be made up of the seven eager climbers.

The women could be grouped in pairs: Margi and Annie, Vera W. and Alison, Vera K. and Irene were natural combinations since they had climbed together, were close friends, and had told me they hoped to be on a summit team with the other. This left only Piro, who got along with everyone and could climb with any of the three pairs. No one could be eliminated from consideration on the basis of not being fit. What Vera W. might lack in speed, for example, she certainly compensated for in determination.

The vital psychological factors were harder to assess. No one was clearly unfit for the top, although Margi had been severely shaken by the avalanches. She had quickly recovered from the illness that stopped her from continuing to lead the rib with Liz and joined Vera W. and Alison to carry a load to Camp III. But a few days later, when it was her turn to carry a second load to the camp, Margi was very uncertain about crossing the avalanche slope another time. She left with a load but was back after a few minutes, saying she had forgotten her toothbrush and had returned for it. It took me a while to realize that she was joking to cover her nervousness. She had walked up, taken a look at the avalanche chute, and turned around. Margi and I discussed her misgivings about continuing to climb.

"Remember how before the trip you told us that expedition climbing was boring?" she asked. "You said the hardest thing is going over the same dull slopes day after day carrying heavy loads? But this trip is a thrill a minute. It's certainly not monotonous with that ice hanging over us all the time. I think I've had enough. I want to go down and take a break, think about whether I really want to climb this thing. I'd rather carry loads between Camps I and II for a few days than face the avalanches."

"Fine, Margi," I agreed. "Go down and make up your mind about whether you want to keep climbing."

"But I don't feel comfortable doing that either," she went on. "Alison thinks it's not fair for me to get out of carrying my share of the loads to Camp III. She says she's doing carries to Camp III every other day, even though she's afraid, and that if I want to climb the mountain, I should too. She says that I should do things in the proper way."

"There's no 'proper way,'" I reassured her. "You should do what you feel comfortable doing. It doesn't matter that much if you don't carry one of your loads to Camp III. Now go on down and relax and try not to worry."

Three days later Margi was back up from Camp I looking calm and confident. She had made her decision.

"I want to go on up," she told me, "even though I'm terrified of the avalanches, I can't resist. I want to climb this mountain, see the view, and find out how I feel up there."

I had to give Margi credit for a lot of courage. On other trips I had seen climbers pass their fears on to others in the party and so undermine group morale. Margi admitted she was frightened but went on anyway.

Margi's friend, Annie, was climbing strongly and accepting the avalanches without complaint. I wondered if part of her calm was based on Yeshi's support. Annie had taken to helping him cook our meals, and we could hear them talking together in the cook tent until all hours of the night. They made an attractive couple, but I was concerned that their romance might strain relations between members and Sherpas. The Sherpas were very conscious of the relationship between Annie and Yeshi and apparently couldn't understand why the rest of us were not similarly inclined. Marie complained that the Sherpas kept looking at her in a way that made her feel very uncomfortable.

I had asked Annie several times to wait until we got back to Kathmandu to be with Yeshi, but she was noncommittal. Otherwise, she was proving to be an ideal expedition member: unselfish, uncomplaining, strong, and hard-working.

Vera K. was another member whose strengths were becoming more evident the higher we climbed. Annie told me that when they were together at Camp III, Vera K. made sure that she and Annie put in four consecutive days of hard work. After a grueling day Annie would sometimes just want to go to sleep, but Vera would insist that they melt snow and eat dinner. The peculiar mannerisms we had all noticed in Vera K. at lower altitudes faded away higher up, where she was solid and amiable.

Irene, too, had shed her self-doubt and was certain she wanted to try for the top. After all her agonizing about the risk and about her own abilities, she and Piro had spent five days sitting out a storm at Camp IIIa and then several more leading the steep terrain above the rib. Both had come back full of enthusiasm for the summit.

Piro returned to Camp II a day before Irene, who stayed up at Camp III to film. Generally Piro worked hard and talked little, but coming down from the rib, she was positively voluble.

"It's fantastic up there," she beamed. "Leading that steep ice step was one of the best things I've ever done. I'm so glad Irene and I got the lead from the Sherpas. It was everything climbing should be—just two climbers working out a route, good weather, solid ice, spectacular surroundings. The pleasure was so intense that it more than made up for all those days of waiting out the storm."

I asked Piro how she and Irene had managed during their long confinement.

"No problem. We decided early on that we were only going to have what we were wearing and the two sleeping bags inside the tent, and we didn't cook much. We just melted snow whenever there was a break in the storm. For entertainment we had ice avalanches, powder avalanches, and rockfalls. And Christy's fine jokes.

"Things would have been better with more to eat, though. On the third day we had to go out and repitch the tent. By that time our body heat had melted the snow beneath us, and the tent floor was like two bathtubs. We began shoveling snow to level the surface underneath the tent, but a couple of strokes sent us sprawling into the snow gasping. That pushed the panic button. Those three days of lying around not eating must have weakened us. We dove back into the tent and started scarfing those terrible candy bars; then we cooked up the last tuna din-

ner. After we ate all that stuff, we went back out to repitch the tent. Damn hard work in thigh-deep powder."

Piro coughed deeply. "And we both had these high-altitude coughs most of the time and had to take codeine to sleep. Then, of course, we had to deal with the side effects of codeine, like constipation. Trying to contend with that at 21,000 feet with a fresh wind whipping the new snow around wasn't fun. But it was all worth it."

Physiological studies have shown that climbers deteriorate physically and mentally when they spend prolonged periods above 19,000 feet, but Piro and Irene didn't seem to have suffered unduly. They were obviously strong contenders for the first summit team.

Vera W. and Alison were less happy about the way the climb was progressing. Vera W. had not led as much as she had hoped to and was very conscious of being somewhat slower than most of the others. Alison had done some of the best leading but was still dissatisfied with the style of the climb and extremely concerned about the avalanche danger. In a letter to Janusz, her husband, she wrote:

> Life here is a constant game of Russian roulette. It's the most dangerous mountain I've been on. Between Camp II (a relatively safe site, although we sometimes get shaken by avalanche winds) and the foot of the Dutch Rib, you have to "run the gauntlet" for over an hour on the way up. Each side of the rib is a great gully topped by ice cliffs, and the floor of each gully is polished green ice with some bare rocks, testifying to the frequency with which they are swept from above. Threatening our route is the great Sickle couloir above.
>
> Vera W. and I are carrying to III again tomorrow, a prospect I don't enjoy. It's a hard day. Yesterday we left at 7:00 A.M. and got back at 6:00 P.M., and the worst thing is the continual avalanche fear. Hopefully, if we survive tomorrow, it's the last time we'll have to go up and back. Next time we'll go to stay at III and carry to IV and on to V and the summit. If the weather holds.

With dogged persistence, if little pleasure, Vera and Alison made the dangerous carry to Camp III every other day. Besides aiding the progress of the climb, their hard work was a means to a personal end: they were counting on being chosen for summit teams.

Eventually I worked out what I considered a fair and flexible strategy for the summit attempts, though I had not yet decided who should be on the teams. During the 6:00 P.M. radio call on October 8, the day Camp IV was established, I presented the general plan to the members and Sherpas at all the camps.

Irene taking telephoto pictures of the four climbers on the traverse pitch on the Dutch Rib. Note the shiny avalanche gullies to the right and left of the rib and the piles of debris below the gullies. Arlene Blum.

Alison and Annie approach the crest of the Dutch Rib.
Vera Komarkova, © 1979 by the National Geographic Society.

"The first summit team will consist of three members using oxygen," I began. "The second will be two members and two Sherpas, but there may not be oxygen available for them. A third team is a possibility if anyone else still wants to try for the top. The first team will make their attempt between October 14 and 16; the second, two days later; and the third, two days after that. Of course, this plan may have to be changed in case of further storms or other problems."

At Camp II the reactions were varied. Alison, for one, was not pleased. "I think all the members of the team—all nine of us now that Liz has left—should have a reasonable chance for the summit. Your plan gives only five members positions in the first and second teams. And I doubt there will be a third. What about the rest of us? Everyone should have some guarantee of being on a summit team after they've risked their lives doing carries to Camp III."

"I can't guarantee anyone that they will be on a summit team," I responded. "If you feel you need that promise to do carries to Camp III, then you shouldn't do them."

Margi said, "If anyone gets to the summit, even if it's not me, I'll be really happy."

"Of course, so will I," Alison agreed. "I just want everyone to feel they have a chance for the top. I think we ought to have three members and one Sherpa on the second attempt. Members deserve places much more than Sherpas. We've invested so much more in this expedition than they have. And there should definitely be a third team so everyone gets a chance."

"I'm sorry," I said, "but there's no way all nine of us are going to try for the top. Joan isn't acclimatized enough after her illness, and ever since the avalanche at Camp I, I haven't cared to try. That leaves seven at the very most."

The other members seemed willing to go along with my plan. But Lopsang, who was feeling better and had come up to Camp II to discuss the matter with me, objected strongly.

"No, bara memsahib, bad plan. Too many people going to summit. Annapurna is very dangerous. When one member and one Sherpa reach summit, then we all are very happy and go home. Everything okay."

"No, Lopsang. All the members want to climb to the top, and many Sherpas do also. They've all worked very hard. Before we go home, we must give them a chance."

"No, bara memsahib, one member, one Sherpa enough. You are leader. You are responsible for what your members do. You must tell members that everyone cannot climb mountain. They will do what you say."

I smiled, thinking of the problems Lopsang had in controlling the Sherpas. "Lopsang, you cannot make Sherpas do what you want. I cannot make members do what I want." We both laughed.

I could see Lopsang's point of view, though, just as I could see Alison's. Lopsang was sick and tired of this climb and wanted to go home before anyone was hurt. I was inclined to agree with him but respected the team's request that everyone who wanted to would get a chance for the summit. The weather was stable, and snow conditions were getting better daily; it was beginning to seem possible that everybody might get that chance.

The climbers contending for summit teams were not the only ones who were adapting well to the altitude. Joan, Christy, and the film crew were also getting stronger all the time. Since that morning at Base Camp when, with tears in their eyes, they had filmed the emotional scene around the breakfast table, it was clear that Dyanna and Marie were truly part of the team. Subsequently they had also managed to shoot some excellent climbing footage. The first time they had ventured onto the ice by Base Camp, they had been very nervous—it was their first glacier after all. But now they were walking confidently among the enormous crevasses of the Annapurna North Glacier. After the avalanche above Camp I that had nearly buried them, they had naturally been afraid. But they were professionals and needed climbing footage high on the mountain; they particularly wanted to film us climbing the steep slopes of the Dutch Rib. So they suppressed their fear of avalanches and climbed up to

Annie, Christy, and Dyanna filming above Camp II. Vera Komarkova.

and above Camp II to film. For these two young women who had never climbed before, this achievement was as great as reaching the summit would be for the rest of us.

Marie and Dyanna had already tried unsuccessfully to get up to Camp II a few days earlier. When they finally made it, after dragging their unwilling bodies through the deep snow and the heat, they were ecstatic. "We did the hardest things we've ever done today—to think we were dragged through it all by women!" Dyanna marveled. "And I just love being roped," she continued.

It had never occurred to me that being on a rope represented anything more than security, so I asked her why.

"Well, even though it's awkward for everyone to have to move at the same pace, your energies are linked. You're 75 feet apart, but you're connected. You have to be sensitive to the movement of the others on your rope and notice when someone is slowing down because of a hill or difficult part. The movement of the line in the snow tells you about your partners and their movements, and that makes me feel good."

"I can't decide whether I love climbing or hate it," Marie commented. "I'm in ecstacy over the beauty but exhausted by the hard work, and I'm terrified of the avalanches."

"Those five hours slogging up here were like the five-hour drive to our summer vacation when I was a little kid—endless." Dyanna sighed. "But we're here now, and we'll stay and do what we have to. But, God, am I afraid of the avalanches."

Dyanna's diary reflects how she and Marie reacted to being high up on Annapurna.

I was exhausted and weak and afraid. But when you must you must. Learn not to resist the inevitable, not to bitch and moan, just to start the works rolling. We got all our gear ready, and by 3:30 in the afternoon the brave but humble film crew made it to its goal—19,000 feet. I was glad I wasn't expected to go any higher or farther. We felt great pride in having made it, despite exhaution.

Got one mag of Irene and Piro on the steepest part of the ice wall, and then we hustled down before frostbite set in. Being up there made me want to yell. It was so stunning. Coming down I noticed how colorful Camp II is: orange and blue dome tents, bird-shaped yellow and blue tents, the green mess tent, brightly colored sleeping bags draped everywhere.

We slept in mounds of fiberfill and down that night. Nothing was familiar like at Camp I, our cozy home. New tent, new tent-door zippers, no flashlight, where on earth is the pee bottle, how to avoid stepping on someone's head, endless coughing, claustrophobia, tossing Marie, and the dreaded snow falling thicker and thicker all night. But morning finally came and the snow stopped and an avalanche hadn't swept us away.

The film crew heads towards 19,000 feet. Arlene Blum.

Even after their miserable night, Marie and Dyanna decided to go up to 19,000 feet a second time to get more footage of the climbers on the rib. Dyanna wrote:

> Vera K. and Annie were anxious to get across the chute before it got too late. By sheer will I tore up the ridge the last 500 feet and managed to delay them until I got the rig set up.

> Damned if we didn't shoot synch at 19,000 feet in this incredible place. We really did it—our very best.

They certainly did. Many people were incredulous that these two nonclimbers were able to become part of the expedition, climb to 19,000 feet, and shoot synchronized film and sound the whole time. Their success reinforced my belief that mountain climbing is not just the province of a few superb athletes, but can be enjoyed by anyone for whom the mountains hold an attraction.

Joan had recovered from her pneumonia and pleurisy and had been slowly but persistently conditioning. Although she would not be strong enough for the summit, she was diligently carrying loads to Camps I and II, helping to manage the lower camps, and generally doing whatever she could to make the climb run smoothly.

And Christy was another success story. It was hard to imagine that she was the same woman who had been so grumpy on the steaming trek. Up here in the snow she was in her element, eyes shining and cheeks rosy. I don't know how, living on the plains of Kansas and Iowa for most of her life, she had discovered her love for high places. Four years ago Christy had never set foot on a mountain. Now here she was at 19,000 feet on Annapurna in Nepal, and couldn't have been happier.

Joan, who had just turned fifty, and Christy, now thirty-eight, were striking demonstrations that age was no barrier to achievement. Many women have told me they felt they were too old to take up a strenuous activity like climbing. These women are probably unduly influenced by the competitive versions of sports like swimming and gymnastics, in which the participants are in their early teens. But women of all ages can enjoy these sports, if they can avoid becoming intimidated by the media's emphasis on youth. Mountaineering and hiking, too, can be enjoyed at any age. The Mazamas, a Portland-based climbing club, have sponsored well-attended climbs of Mount Hood in Oregon for people sixty years and older. Climbers tend to keep active all their lives and to be more alive because of it.

Both physically and psychologically, then, all the members had adapted well to life high on Annapurna. This was, in itself, an achievement, and I wondered again why more women did not have the opportunity to climb the highest mountains. Clearly, the reasons for the paucity of women on expeditions are more psychological than physical. What are considered admirable traits in men—assertiveness, independence, ambition, competitiveness—are still often seen as undesirable in women. Yet most successful climbers, male or female, possess these characteristics.

Our leadership qualities need to be developed as well. For example, it was difficult for me to go against my upbringing, which taught me to be accommodating, soothing, and likable, when I had to be a strong leader. Until there are confident women leaders, women will have to depend on men to invite them on expeditions—and this is unfortunately rare. So a major requirement is to believe in ourselves and in other women.

What we had already accomplished on Annapurna, both individually and as a team, was an example we could point to with pride. I remembered Liz's words at breakfast on the morning after the flag raising: "In my mind this expedition has been a success even if we don't get any higher."

The Highest Camps 13

October 9–13

Margi and I started out for Camp III early and in reasonably good spirits. Once there, we would at last be above the avalanches. We both were getting spooked—always wondering when the next avalanche would hit—and had doubts about making this last trip to Camp III today. I would not go unless she went and she wouldn't go unless I did. For the two of us, at least, the drive to climb higher was slipping away, but after all this time and effort, we just had to get on with it. In another six days someone could be on the top.

We decided to put on our crampons and harness before crossing the avalanche slope and so decrease the time we would spend at the old cache site below the rib. As I fumbled with my crampon straps I wondered: Will stopping here for a few minutes save my life by keeping me from being hit by an avalanche, or will it delay me so I am hit, or won't it make any difference? It was strange to realize there was a chance I might die on this simple half-mile walk. Perhaps one in ten, one in a hundred, who could know? Avalanches crossed that path every day.

My stomach fluttered queasily, and as she started across the slope before me, Margi confessed that she was so nervous she felt like throwing up. Still she walked on toward the rib. Just as I finished strapping on my crampons, I saw a large avalanche coming down the Bobsled, overshooting the curves and spilling over the sides. "Avalanche! Run, Margi! Avalanche!"

There was no time to run. Margi could only crouch off to the side of the trail with the pick of her ice axe dug deeply into the snow. The avalanche stopped above us, and the air cleared. We were both trembling, unsure whether to go up or down.

"Will you go on if I do?" Margi yelled to me.

With no outward hesitation I called back, "I'm going on today, no matter what!"

As I spoke, I felt a strong pull from the world of living things below. But I had to continue up to select summit teams and oversee logistics. I had to force myself to cross the avalanche slope one more time.

"If you're going on, I'm going too." But Margi looked unhappy.

As we picked our way through the debris of the recent avalanche, my stomach ached and my legs trembled. I kept thinking, this is the last time I'll have to go up across this slope —down will be faster; if I can just make it across safely this time, I will probably survive. No more avalanches came down as we crossed, but five minutes later, just as we reached safety a few hundred feet up the face, another large one boomed down just below us. We had barely made it across in a window between two avalanches.

Now that we were safe, we climbed slowly, taking movies and still pictures, reaching Camp IIIa in time to join Vera W. and Alison for a sunny lunch. The north side of a Himalayan mountain in October is a cold place. Most of our camps were in the sun only between 10:00 A.M. and 2:00 P.M. Camp IIIa, located on a projecting ridge and so out of the shadow of the mountain, was the most pleasant campsite on the north side of Annapurna.

Above IIIa the route went up steep ice to the left of a large crevasse for 60 feet, then traversed 400 feet of deep snow to gain the knife-edged ridge crest. The crest snaked upward like the sinuous tail of a dragon for nearly a mile, widening slightly at the site of Camp III. Just above this camp, a 400-foot ice step marked the end of the Dutch Rib and the beginning of the upper section of the mountain.

Beyond the ice step we would ascend a low-angled slope —almost a plateau—and then find an intricate way among the crevasses and seracs that interrupted the face on the way to Camps IV and V. Our path would roughly parallel the curve of the Sickle—the great wall of rock and ice topped by a hanging glacier that sweeps from 23,000 to 25,000 feet, dominating the upper part of the mountain—keeping a few hundred yards to the left of it. The route was similar to that climbed by the Dutch the preceding year and just below Camp V we would intersect the route pioneered by Herzog's French team in 1950.

Technically, the climbing would be easier up high than on the Dutch Rib, but the thigh-deep snow that Irene, Annie, and

Vera K. had encountered on the plateau worried me. If we were forced to plow through deep snow all the way from 21,000 to 26,500 feet, we might not make it. But the snow was consolidating daily, and above Camp V it looked like the classic "easy walk" to the base of the final rocky summit pyramid.

I asked Alison how difficult the climbing on the ridge crest had been.

"It's not bad now," she responded, "but when I first led it, the snow was bottomless, just awful. Then overnight it firmed up, so the route is like a sidewalk now."

"A sidewalk?" I was incredulous.

"Well—a very narrow sidewalk with a thousand-foot drop on either side."

As I climbed the next pitch, a hundred feet of nearly vertical crumbly ice, I noticed no resemblance whatsoever to a sidewalk. I at least was able to pull myself up on a fixed line; when Liz had led this pitch, she'd had no such advantage. I was impressed

The route approaching Camp III on the crest of the rib. Arlene Blum.

once more with her skill at climbing steep ice and wished she hadn't had to leave us.

I placed my feet carefully in the foot-wide track on the windswept ridge crest, especially when I came to what looked like the place where Annie had fallen off the day before. She had been caught by the fixed line, of course, but it had been hard to climb up again. Occasionally the ridge widened, and I would dare lift my eyes from the narrow path to admire our magnificent surroundings. All around us rose the peaks of the Grand Barrier. A bit higher, perhaps, and I might be able to see the brown hills of Tibet off to the north, which had been a dream of mine for years. On the 1976 Everest expedition I had reached 24,500 feet—only a few hours from the South Col, where I would have been rewarded with that view. I still hoped to climb high enough on Annapurna to see Tibet. This, rather than the summit, had become my personal goal.

It was bitter cold and blowing hard when we reached Camp III. The crest broadened just enough to accommodate three platforms, each six by eight feet, which had been terraced for our tents. They were pitched with their sides only a few inches from the thousand-foot drop. From outside, the tents looked warm and inviting, but inside was another matter. When I crawled into one of them to get away from the cold and the wind, I found two of the Sherpas relaxing amidst chaos. Gear was strewn about, and noodles and beef stew were solidly frozen to the tent floor.

"Namaste, Mingma and Chewang. Where is tent space for Margi and me?"

"No empty tent. You move in tent with Sherpas." Mingma smiled knowingly. After some discussion, the four Sherpas agreed to move into the largest tent, so that the six members could use the two smaller ones.

All six of us crowded into the larger of these for dinner. Repeated freezing and thawing had left the surface underneath the tent floor so irregular that there was no level place to put the stoves, so I sat by the door balancing a simmering pot on my knees and leaning out from time to time to get more snow to melt. My feet, trapped in double boots, were freezing cold, but the tent was too cramped to take off my boots. I was trying to get down a clotting bowl of macaroni and cheese before it froze, when Vera K. and Annie cheerily asked me for the latest details of the logistics plan. I nearly choked on the disgusting mess. At that moment I couldn't have cared less about logistics, but I promised to discuss it in the morning.

Finally extricating myself from the wretched tent, I was about to squeeze into the one I was sharing with Vera W., when I was waylaid by an invitation from Ang Pemba.

"Noodles, bara memsahib?"

"Sleep."

"Please come."

Cramped quarters at Camp III. Arlene Blum.

Reluctantly, I crawled into the Sherpa tent. They too, wanted to know the details of the summit plan, but all I could do was repeat the general scheme I had already announced.

"The first team will be three memsahibs, the second team two Sherpas and maybe four memsahibs." I had reworked the logistics to give all the members a chance.

"Oh, no, bara memsahib. Very important to have Sherpas on the first team. Best team is two Sherpas, two members."

Once again I explained that because this was a women's expedition we wanted the first team to be all women. The Sherpas still looked dubious as I crawled out into the night.

The next morning, while the Sherpas, Vera K., Annie, Alison, and Vera W. took loads to Camp IV, Margi and I stayed at Camp III and tried to relieve the squalor. After we had dug out some loads that had been left out in the snow, and smoothed out the hummocky surface under the tent floors, it was time to melt water for cooking and drinking. I sat on the edge of the snow ridge with my feet dangling over the thousand-foot dropoff, melting pot after pot of snow and ice and enjoying a fine view of Dhaulagiri across the way.

This undemanding chore left my mind free to mull over the details of the summit plan. By the time Margi came over to make some lemonade, I felt ready to discuss my ideas with her.

"I think we'll be ready for a summit attempt in three days. First, somebody has to establish Camp V, and whoever does it may be too tired to try for the top."

Camp V, our highest camp, would be located at nearly 25,000 feet. There is less than half as much oxygen there than at sea level, and exertion can lead to deterioration rather than to enhanced acclimatization. The longer a climber stays at 25,000 feet, the weaker she becomes; therefore, whoever established this camp was less likely to be strong enough to reach the summit.

"How do you think people will react to being asked to do the job?"

"I'd like to try it," Margi promptly offered. "Establishing a camp above 24,000 feet would really be an accomplishment for me. And if I feel strong enough after that, I can still go back up again with the second summit team."

I was pleased that Margi had volunteered to establish Camp V, and I felt comfortable about her doing it. She was twenty-one, and if she climbed to 24,000 feet now, she would undoubtedly be asked to take part in other expeditions to high peaks.

As we talked, Mingma arrived back in camp, frowning. "Sherpas don't like food. Bad food."

Margi asked, "What's wrong with the food, Mingma?"

"We don't like memsahib food. We want more chilis and more noodles." He stomped off angrily toward the Sherpa tent.

"Well, Margi, do you think we're going to have a Sherpa strike over noodles?"

She giggled. "I don't know. We could climb the rest of the way without them. But I want to get this over with as fast as possible and get the hell away from these avalanches."

I couldn't have agreed more.

At 3:30 Joan and Christy arrived with loads from Camp II. Camp III was an altitude record for both of them, and they were delighted to be there. Christy had been tense throughout the day's climbing, later noting in her diary:

> Worry drained my strength during our snail-like progress across the avalanche track. I was prepared to be dead but not prepared to go through the process of dying in an avalanche. I already knew what it meant to be caught—panic, cold, pain. I struggled against my fear, tried to think of something else—love, hugs, kisses. It worked.

Now that they were safe in camp, Christy was exuberant.

"What a route, what a camp! This is the hardest day's climbing I've ever done. My first time with crampons on all day, and my first climb to 21,000 feet. It's a long way from Kansas City."

Joan and I greeted each other with real warmth, both eager to put our earlier conflicts behind us. She had accepted me as leader, and I truly admired her extraordinary perseverance. Joan had been training conscientiously since her illness, and she was now strong enough to accomplish the very demanding carry between Camps II and III.

Joan and Christy headed back down the mountain after a brief rest. At the 6:00 P.M. radio broadcast I made the long-awaited announcement—the names of the summit climbers.

Arlene (Camp III): The first team will be Irene, Vera K., and Piro. The second team will consist of Margi, Annie, Alison, and Vera W., with Chewang and Mingma, if all of them still feel strong enough to try for it.

"Margi has volunteered to establish Camp V. Tomorrow she, Mingma, and Lakpa will go as far as Camp IV, and Irene and Piro will come up from Camp II to join Vera K. here at Camp III. The following day Margi and the two Sherpas will put Camp V as high as possible, and the three summit climbers will move to Camp IV. The first summit team will carry on to Camp V and the top, while Margi and the Sherpas come back down to III to rest and wait for the second summit attempt."

The plan met with general approval, as everyone who wanted it would have a chance for the top. Vera K. reminded me that the Sherpas had helped a lot with carrying and leading lately and wanted to go with the first team.

"I haven't completely ruled out the possibility of one Sherpa going with the team if conditions are bad," I told her. "It would be better, though, if we could keep it an all-woman ascent.

"Besides," I continued, "Chewang and Ang are both feeling ill. If there aren't four Sherpas to carry loads to Camp V, there won't be oxygen for the second team."

The wind howled all that night, threatening to blow our tents off the rib, and everyone at Camp III spent an uncomfortable night. I awoke at 3:00 A.M., needing to go out but dreading the agony of leaving my warm sleeping bag for the freezing night. Postponing it as long as possible, I lay there listening to the gusts of wind shaking the tent, and hoping that the anchors were secure. By 4:00 A.M. I couldn't wait any longer. I carefully squeezed through the small tunnel door, afraid that if I pushed too hard the momentum might send me right over the cliff. Once outside, I glanced at the brilliant display of stars, completed my task while hanging on tightly to the fixed line, and returned, relieved, to my warm bag.

In the morning my eyes were bloodshot, and there was a

film on my tongue. My mouth felt like a furry teacup and my head as though it had been split with an axe. I wondered if these symptoms were due to improper diet, nerves, or maladjustment to altitude. I hoped they did not presage anything more serious.

Vera Watson was also feeling poorly. The day before she had been too slow to reach Camp IV with the load she was carrying. Two-thirds of the way up she met Annie, Vera K., and Alison coming down; as it was near dusk, they persuaded her, though with some difficulty, to leave her load there and return to Camp III with them. Vera W.'s will remained strong, but she was unhappy about her slow pace. I suggested that she go down to Camp II for a rest and then come back up to join the second summit team, but she chose to stay at III instead. Chewang and Ang were casualties, too—Ang said he was altitude sick and went down to Base, and Chewang took the day off to rest.

Margi, Mingma, and Lakpa were going to Camp IV today; tomorrow they would continue up to put in Camp V. I got up early to organize the loads, but could barely see through the blowing snow and ice. By the time the three climbers had put on their crampons and were ready to leave, the wind was gusting with gale force. It was blowing snow so hard into our faces that we couldn't keep our eyes open.

"We don't climb today, memsahib. Too much wind. Too much snow. Very bad day," Mingma and Lakpa announced.

Margi tried to urge them on. "Come on, guys, let's try. Maybe there'll be less wind higher up. I'm psyched and I want to go now."

"No, memsahib. Today is a bad day. Sherpas take rest day. Tomorrow we climb."

Disappointed, Margi and I scrunched back into the tent and started cooking breakfast.

"If we didn't have to depend on these bloody Sherpas, we could have gone up today and gotten the damn thing over with," Alison said.

"I know," Margi said. "If this were a lower mountain, we wouldn't need them. The six Japanese just climbed Nilgiri themselves. I wish we were on our own."

I sat down to rework our logistics plan once again. We could still try for the summit on October 15, but there would be no oxygen for the second team. As I worked, breakfast was served, and it continued until noon. Strawberries, hash brown potatoes, bacon, cereal, assorted candy bars, salami. Lower down I would have loved this food, but up here I had to force myself to eat.

"This rest day isn't so bad," I tried to console Margi. "You and the Sherpas can get well fed and rested before going up tomorrow."

But after the stoves were turned off, I listened to the rat-a-tat-tat of the wind beating on the tent and began to worry. The gap of good weather between the end of the monsoon and the beginning of the fierce winter storms was closing fast. Even in clear sunshine the days were colder, and we could see windy plumes streaming off the summit. Were we too late? Would the wind ever stop, or would it keep blowing day after day? Was this the jet stream?

Suddenly I heard a new sound, a distant, low-pitched hum above the wind. Margi, Vera W., Alison, and I poked our heads outside the tent to investigate, and everyone started talking at once.

"What's that?"

"Look up. Do you see those black spots above the summit? What are they?"

"It's geese. Migrating geese."

"What are they doing here?"

"I guess they're flying from Tibet down to India, but what a route!"

These geese, the first animals we had seen in weeks, filled us with wonder. I couldn't understand why they chose to fly across the tops of the world's highest mountains. Why didn't they take the easy way across the low passes and through the valleys, where they could find food and water? Imprisoned on our tiny block of ice, we gazed up at the flying geese with some envy, realizing that in a few days they would reach the hot plains of India.

The wind whipped fiercely through the camp all the next day, but Margi, Mingma, and Chewang did move to Camp IV, and Irene and Piro came up to join Vera K. here at III. Piro was cheerful, but Irene looked small and tired, as close to frail as I've

Irene reaches Camp III on the first summit attempt.
Arlene Blum.

Two climbers heading towards Camp IV. Irene Miller.

ever seen her. Not surprising, as she had taken only one rest day in the last ten. After her hard work leading the ice step with Piro, she had gone all the way back down to Base Camp to greet a group of our supporters who had trekked into the camp and then had come straight back up to Camp III.

The first summit team was now together and eager to begin their attempt. The next morning, October 13, Piro, Irene, and Vera K. set out for Camp IV, the first leg of the final push. I went along to see them off and perhaps, finally, to catch a glimpse of the brown hills of Tibet.

Immediately above the camp we encountered the broken 400-foot ice wall Piro and Irene had led just after the storm. No steps had been chopped, and the climbing required concentration. Above, I could see the snow streaming off the top of the ice step in the wind. I struggled up the last hard-ice pitch and came out on the edge of the gently sloping plateau. The bitter wind was creating a ground blizzard there, driving a six-inch layer of blowing ice crystals along the surface. For the next few hundred feet travel was treacherous, with no fixed line and only occasional wands to mark the way. As I sat on the edge of the plateau, reluctant to unclip from the last fixed line and venture unroped through the stinging snow, Vera K. came up and marched by me resolutely. I followed slowly.

As the wind gusted even more savagely, the snow stung my face and hid the wands. I concentrated on wiggling my toes and thought of Fred Ayres, a professor of chemistry at Reed College and one of my early climbing mentors. Fred had made numerous first ascents in the Canadian Rockies and the Peruvian Andes wearing army surplus boots.

"The trick is to wiggle your toes on every step," he would

tell me. The cold was so intense here that even with double boots and insulated overboots it was pertinent advice.

"The bear went over the mountain," wiggle-two-three; "The bear went over the mountain," wiggle-two-three; "to see what he could see," wiggle-two-three. Reciting this children's song like a mantra to remind myself to wiggle my toes, I made slow upward progress against the gale. The slope became steeper and more slippery, and occasionally I would slip down a few feet, feel a surge of adrenalin, and stop myself. I tried not to think about avalanches. If one were to come down I could easily be swept off the edge of the plateau.

Finally I reached security at the next set of fixed lines where the slope steepened once again. I sat down to wait for Piro and Irene, who fought their way up leaning into the wind.

"I'm not going any farther," I told them. "It's getting late, and I don't want to go down these slopes by myself unroped."

"Yeah, this wind really takes it out of you." Irene looked discouraged from fighting the wind and deep snow, and she sighed deeply. "I've left some letters at Camp II for my friends in case I don't come back. Will you make sure they get them?"

"Oh, Irene, you'll be all right. But of course I will, if it comes to that." As Piro set off up the fixed line, I offered Irene some chocolate fudge and tried to find something encouraging to say.

"You've done really well so far—it's going to be beautiful up there—it looks like you'll have a full moon if you have to come down in the dark—I think the weather's going to be good for the next couple of days."

Irene, however, was not cheered. In fact, she looked as though she wished she were anywhere else. At this moment I didn't envy her position on the first summit team.

"Listen, Irene, if this wind and deep snow don't let up, you can take one Sherpa along with you to the top. They've helped a lot lately, and they deserve it."

She looked a little more hopeful and said, "That's a good idea. But we won't take a Sherpa unless we really feel it's necessary." Then she clipped into the fixed line and began to struggle slowly up under her heavy burden.

I turned my back on Piro and Irene and began my return journey down the mountain to Camp III. As I took the first steps down, I knew this was as high as I would get on Annapurna. Perhaps it was 22,000 feet; I'd been higher than this on several other mountains. I still hadn't seen the hills of Tibet, but it no longer mattered to me how high I got. All that mattered was that some of us get up this mountain and all of us get off it alive.

The snow was like little ball bearings sliding under my crampons. I would dig my axe in deeply, take two steps downhill, and move my axe. When walking on these slippery pellets of snow became too nerve-racking, I moved farther to the right and descended on old avalanche debris. The footing was more

Piro and Irene on their way to Camp IV, at the start of their summit attempt. Arlene Blum.

secure, but I was even more anxious here about avalanche danger. Then a cloud came in, and I could no longer see the wands. To calm my anxieties I thought about climbing back home in the High Sierra of California: hot granite, warm sun, quiet satisfaction.

Blindly I kept heading down in the cloud and finally another wand came into sight. At last I reached the top of the fixed line and clipped in with gratitude. I felt safer—if an avalanche were to come down, the ropes should hold me. Clouds covered the sun as I rappelled down toward Camp III, and soon I saw the camp silhouetted between two great ice cliffs.

Then I heard the now-familiar honking of the geese flying over the summit ridge at more than 25,000 feet. Heading straight toward their goal, most of them would cross the high peaks in a few days, though some of the weaker birds might not survive the rigors of the journey. Again I wondered why they chose this route. Perhaps it was because there were no distractions up here to tempt them from their destination. Whatever the reason, they chose the hard way.

In a sense we were like them. In this high, confined world, with no sound but the wind and our own voices; with no sights but the blue sky, white peaks, and bright colors of our tents and parkas; with no sensations but the cold of the ice and snow and the warmth of the sun, our sleeping bags, and stoves we had a chance to slow our world down, to examine ourselves and our purpose. An important question, as always, was why were we here? Answers came readily: to visit Asia, climb a mountain, test our limits, know ourselves. All these were true, yet they were not enough. Why would any woman risk her life to stand on the top of a mountain? The geese circled the summit once before resuming their flight south. Were they wheeling among the high peaks for the view? For the glory? I smiled and thought, "I bet they're doing it for the fun of it."

To the Top 14

October 14–15

I dreamed I was walking on the clouds among the highest Himalayan peaks. I jumped onto a cloud bank that led toward the top of Annapurna, but it raced by without quite reaching the summit. I jumped off this cloud bank onto the next, but that one didn't extend all the way to the tip of Annapurna either. The clouds kept moving by, and I kept jumping from one to the next, trying to find one that would take me where I wanted to go. Below on earth, my friends called to me, "Be careful! If you slip you'll fall to the ground." Until they said that, the thought of falling had not crossed my mind; I was totally intent on following the clouds to the summit. But as I listened, my concentration began to falter, and the clouds became thinner and less substantial, my footing more precarious. I began to slip and slide, falling to the earth.

I awoke. It was the day before our first summit attempt,

and the wind was blowing hard. The gale had not abated since I had returned to Camp III last night after seeing the first summit team off. When I got back, the large Sherpa tent was empty because all the Sherpas were either at Camp IV or down at Base, so I moved in by myself. Finally I had more than enough room, but it was very cold in the large tent alone. I slept in one heavy sleeping bag with another on top of me, wearing two wool hats, a wool scarf over my face, two sets of wool underwear, and a sweater. Still I shivered. The bottle of warm water I had put between the two sleeping bags was solid ice by morning. The temperature was less than 10°F. in the tent, and −20°F. outside.

Camp II reported via radio that winds had ripped the flies of the three tents down there, and the tents here at III had been straining in the wind all night. Conditions must have been even worse at Camp IV. I tried to call the summit climbers on the radio, but they didn't answer. Apparently they were asleep or their radio wasn't working.

We weren't the only ones having problems. Lopsang called from Base Camp to say that he'd heard on last night's news, broadcast from Kathmandu, that of the twenty-six expeditions currently climbing in Nepal, five had given up and gone home. Lopsang wanted to begin making arrangements for the evacuation of our Base Camp.

Lopsang (Base Camp): Avalanches are very bad this year all over Nepal. Most expeditions will not succeed. After one member, one Sherpa reach the top, we should go home. I will send for porters from Choya to come in one week. Over my signal.

At that moment Margi stumbled down from Camp IV looking exhausted and unhappy.

"What happened to you?" I asked.

"I froze my feet."

"Oh, no! How did it happen?"

The day before, Margi told me, she had started out with Mingma and Chewang about ten in the morning on the way to establish Camp V. At the steep ice wall above Camp IV, she had sat still in the bitter cold for thirty minutes, belaying Chewang as he led the step. Following him up, she noticed that one of her feet wasn't coordinated, and when she tried to wiggle her toes, they wouldn't move. "I yelled to the Sherpas, 'I'm going down. Feet frozen.' They waved, 'Bye bye, Miss Margi, bye bye.' So I went back to camp and melted a big pot of water and took off my boots. My right foot was white and frozen solid from the toes to the arch. When the pot of water was warm, I stuck my foot in it and thawed it out."

"Did it hurt much?" I asked.

"I don't know," she thought for a moment. "I can't even remember. I was there by myself all afternoon until the Sherpas came down after putting in Camp V. They told me they had pitched one small tent at 24,200 feet and that they had not used

Margi reaches Camp III after freezing her feet; Vera W. and Alison cook a meal in the foreground. Arlene Blum.

any more fixed rope beyond the step where I belayed Mingma —so the climbing must get easier up there.

"Vera K. came up soon afterwards and I had to go back out into the cold to set up another tent. It was hard work leveling the ice and putting up that tent. Irene and Piro got there just at dark, exhausted from the deep snow and wind.

"Irene said you told them they could take one Sherpa along to the summit. But one Sherpa wouldn't go by himself—they all wanted to go together. So they finally decided to include Mingma and Chewang in the summit team and take Lakpa along to carry loads."

"They what?" I exclaimed in dismay. With Lopsang and Ang sick at Base Camp and Wangel relatively inexperienced, no other strong Sherpas were left. "What about the second team? They won't have any Sherpas for support."

"I tried to tell them that," Margi said, "but they were awfully tired, and I don't think they were thinking too clearly up there. Besides, the Sherpas insisted they wanted to go with the first team."

"Yes, I know that. The Sherpas have wanted to go with the first summit team all along. But what about the second summit team?"

"I don't know. Piro told me I can't be on any summit team, that I'd risk losing my toes. I'm sorry not to get a chance for the summit, but on the other hand, I feel like Liz, relieved to get out of here alive." Margi looked pensive. "But if I drop out, that'll leave the second summit team pretty weak."

"I know. Wangel's up here to support them, but he's not as experienced as the other Sherpas."

"Maybe the second summit team shouldn't go," Margi suggested. "Vera W. has been awfully slow lately, and their Sherpa support will be Wangel and Lakpa at best. Who knows how strong Lakpa will be after a couple of carries to Camp V?"

"It doesn't sound too good," I agreed, "but Vera and Alison are determined to try. I've been trying to call the first summit team on the radio, but I can't get any answer from them. Do you know what's wrong with the radios?"

"Oh, it was a real screw-up," Margi said. "The first radio they took up there turned out not to be a radio at all. It was three batteries in a box that was supposed to contain a radio. Then I brought up another radio, and it stopped transmitting, though it still receives."

"Did they take that radio along to Camp V?"

"No. They left it, since it couldn't transmit."

"Damn, it's frustrating," I sighed. "I wish I could talk to them about taking all the Sherpas."

The radio problem was annoying, but it was not a serious problem for the climbers on their way from Camp IV to Camp V. They would probably be better off putting all their energy into the task at hand and not having to bother with reports over the radio. And, of course, the film crew would be watching the summit team through their long-range lenses from Camp I and could keep us informed of their progress.

Annie came out of her tent and hugged Margi.

"Hi, kid, good to see you. How are your feet?"

"Would you take a look at them, please, Annie? I don't feel much in my toes."

"Okay, sit down and take off your boots." Annie prodded at Margi's feet. "Not too much sensation right now, is there? They'll get better if you keep them warm."

Annie looked reflective. "I don't feel very good about the second summit team with you dropping out, Margi. If the Sherpas won't stay up there, that leaves just me, Alison, and Vera W.—that's not a very strong a team."

"You're right. There's a hell of a lot of mountain left to

Annie examines Margi's frostbitten feet. Arlene Blum.

climb, and I can tell you it's tougher up there than it looks from here," Margi said. "Going up to Camp IV day before yesterday I was breathing at least twice per step. I'd walk for twenty steps and then stop, lean over my axe, and gasp for a while. My feet were so heavy with ten pounds of boots, crampons, and over-boots on them that by the time I got to Camp IV, I was practi-cally lying face down in the snow at anchor points to change my jumar from one rope to the next.

"The altitude really affected me at Camp IV, though I don't notice it much here. I was irritable and didn't feel like cooking this morning. I just wanted everyone to get out of the tent so I could come down. It's only 2,000 feet higher up there, but it feels totally different."

"How were the summit climbers when you left this morn-ing?" I asked.

"Well, they weren't exactly feeling on top of the world. In fact, they said they'd rather go back to bed than leave for Camp V this morning. You wouldn't think it's something they had planned for two years. Their attitude seems to be, 'well, if we get up this damned thing, then at least we can come down.' "

An hour later, Marie radioed to us that the three Sherpas had left Camp IV about 10:30 in the morning and the three members somewhat later. All six made steady progress to the tiny red tent pitched just below the summit plateau at 24,000 feet. The Sherpas arrived in midafternoon and the members just at dusk. The last member to get there moved extremely slowly and didn't make it to Camp V until after dark. We speculated about whether it was Irene and whether she might be ill, but without the radio there was no way of knowing.

October 15

Summit morning was blessedly calm. At 7:30 Marie called from Camp I to tell us that four climbers had just left Camp V for the top. They were moving steadily, and conditions on the higher slopes looked excellent. Four climbers—I wondered who had not gone along and why. Was it the climber who had gotten to camp last yesterday? Perhaps she was now ill in the tent. But if the illness were serious, I assumed the others would not have headed for the top. I again cursed the loss of the radios but resigned myself to the fact that, for better or worse, the first team was on their own. We would have to wait at least until tomorrow to find out who the four on their way to the summit were.

Meanwhile, the second summit team—now minus Margi —was here at Camp III, ready to take their turn. Vera W. and Alison were eager to follow right behind the first team and take advantage of the good weather. But Annie had been having serious misgivings.

Vera W. popped cheerily into the tent. "Good morning. I'm so excited about going to Camp IV today. Are you ready, Annie?"

Looking very worried, Annie said slowly, "I've been thinking about it all night. I just don't feel our team is strong enough for a second summit attempt. It doesn't really seem safe to me."

"What do you mean?" Vera W. looked crushed, like a child whose most wonderful toy was being trampled in the mud.

"I'm sorry, but I don't feel good about going up under these circumstances," Annie stated quietly but firmly. As Vera was trying to absorb this news, Alison joined us in the tent, and Vera told her unhappily, "Annie doesn't want to come with us."

Alison looked startled. "Don't be silly, Annie. Come with us. We can do it, I know we can."

"I'm not being silly, Alison. I've thought about it hard all night and talked it over with Arlene and Margi this morning. I feel strong enough to get to the summit myself, but Vera W. hasn't been moving very fast. And now that the Sherpas are all going with the first team, I don't feel like there's enough support left for us."

"That's not true, Annie. Vera W. may be slow but she's steady. Wangel is going with us, and he'll stay at Camp V to help in case there's any problem. I think Lakpa's also going to stay and help us."

"Well, if the Sherpas really stayed, it would be safer," Annie said. "But will you promise me that if the Sherpas decide they're going back that you'll turn around too?"

"We can't do that now," Alison responded firmly. "We can't decide what we're going to do until we get up there and see what the conditions are like."

"I'm sorry," Annie repeated. "I'm not going. I think you and Vera W. would want to go ahead where I would want to

Annie explaining to Vera W. and Alison why she doesn't want to continue on the second summit attempt. Arlene Blum.

turn back. I'm not willing to take any more risks to get up this mountain. The weather could change in a few hours, and then where would we be?"

"When you came along on this expedition, you made a decision to take risks. Every time you crossed that avalanche slope, your life was in danger. This risk isn't any larger, and the reward could be so much greater. Come with us, please, Annie," Alison urged her again.

"This is different. When I crossed that avalanche slope, I thought, fuck it—if I die, I die. I had to do it. But this is a decision to take an additional risk. I can't make that decision and feel good about it. Without oxygen or support from Sherpas or members, I don't feel safe."

"Sherpas aren't much support anyway. We can do it ourselves," Alison insisted.

"It was very hard for me to make this decision, and I'm going to stick to it." Annie was positive.

I listened with increasing frustration until I couldn't help interjecting. "Alison, Annie has to make her own decisions. You can't talk someone into taking that kind of a risk. And I'm uncomfortable with the sparse support left for your attempt, too—I think you should give it up if the Sherpas all go down."

But Alison was determined. "I'm sure that Vera and I can make it ourselves. You've got to remember that this attempt is what our expedition is all about—a real all-women team. No Sherpas, little oxygen."

She turned to Vera W. "Well, now that there are just two of us, I think we should try for the center summit, not the main summit."

"Yes, let's. I've dreamed of you and I climbing the second summit together for a long time," Vera W. agreed. "It's not as high and it's closer, so it should be an easier climb."

"And it's never been climbed before." Alison began to look enthusiastic again. "What a coup that would be—the two of us doing a first ascent of a 26,000-foot peak. That would make the climbing world sit up and take notice, wouldn't it?"

On the trek when Vera W. had originally brought up the idea that she and Alison attempt the center peak, I had been skeptical. I hadn't wanted our resources split between two different objectives. But now that the first team seemed likely to succeed, Vera's and Alison's plan of climbing the middle peak sounded reasonable, as long as there was some support left for the attempt.

"What about the center peak, Arlene?" Alison continued. "How high is it? Is it legal for us to attempt it?"

"Yes," I said. "I checked with Mr. Gurung when you brought the possibility up on the trek. It's just over 8,000 meters, and it's legal for us to try it. But if you climb straight up from Camp V, it looks like there's some hard rockclimbing. It might be best to follow the first team's route to the saddle between the main peak and the middle peak and then climb up from there."

"The route straight up from camp is the most aesthetic line," Alison said. "I'd rather go that way. If two of us could climb that hard rock together, it would be more of an achievement than my Gasherbrum climb."

As Vera W. and Alison continued to talk excitedly about the possibility of the center peak, I understood better why Alison had been so discontented during much of the climb. Her climb of Gasherbrum III had been accomplished without oxygen, and with two women leading a significant portion of the difficult slopes. The nature of our climb—using both Sherpas and oxygen—made it seem a lesser accomplishment to Alison; it would not rival Gasherbrum unless she could climb a new route or try a different summit. I had to admire Alison's single-minded dedication—not just to climbing the mountain but to doing it with a certain style.

Camp I came in again on the radio to report the progress of the summit team.

Marie (Camp I): They're doing it! I just know they're going to make it. Four hours more to the top. It's so beautiful to watch. Deep blue sky, a plume of snow blowing off the top, and our friends way up there. A great day. Over and out.

Christy (Camp II): I'm worried about that plume. It means high winds on the summit ridge. They're stopping now. God, it's a long time. I wish they would start again. I guess they're putting on their oxygen, but I wish they would get moving. I can't stand all this waiting. Oh, they're moving again. It looks painfully slow from down here, but they're getting there.

Comrades on and off a rope, Vera W. and Alison take a break during a hard carry. Marie Ashton, © 1979 by the National Geographic Society.

As I listened, I could feel the excitement running through all the camps like an electric current. It did seem that we were very close to success at last. Here at Camp III, though, our most immediate concern was the second summit team. The plan, if the weather stayed good, was for Wangel to go to Camp V and wait in support while Vera and Alison made their attempt on the center summit.

Since they would take along the two remaining radios from Camp III, I decided to go down to Camp II where I could stay in touch with everyone except the first team. Margi and Annie wanted to remain at Camp III to greet the returning summit climbers. Alison and Vera W. packed and repacked, and finally at 11:30 in the morning, they were ready to leave for Camp IV. (Wangel had left a few minutes earlier.)

"Be careful. Don't take any risks," I told them as they left. "Remember, if you don't feel strong or the weather looks like it's changing, don't go any higher. If Wangel turns back, you should consider turning back too."

"Don't worry so much," Alison smiled brightly. "We'll be fine."

Vera W.'s early enthusiasm had waned during the morning's long discussions and delays. "All I want," she stated now,

"is to climb to a higher altitude than I ever have before. That's just a few hundred meters above Camp IV. I'm sure we can make it that high."

I waved goodbye to them and said a silent prayer for their safety as they shouldered their packs and set off for Camp IV. Although tents, sleeping bags, food, and oxygen as well as all the other necessary equipment were in place for them at Camps IV and V, and they had a radio with them, they were on their own now.

After seeing them off I crawled back into the tent where Margi and Annie were melting snow and getting our gear organized to go down. The atmosphere was gloomy. Without the radio that had been my constant companion for weeks, I felt cut off from all the summit-day activity. Margi confessed that she was very worried about her frozen feet, and Annie was disappointed because she had wholeheartedly hoped to climb Annapurna herself. We were all concerned about Vera W. and Alison and the possible lack of support for their summit attempt.

The three of us started washing the half dozen pots, with their burned and frozen remnants of old dinners, that had been left in the tents. Then I had a better idea. Looking at the ice chutes on either side of our camp, I suggested, "I'll throw these pots down the ice chutes and see where they land. If it's back on our trail, that might be a quick way to clear the gear from the camp."

"It's worth a try," Annie said. "But try not to litter the mountain too much."

I threw a pot of frozen shrimp creole down the Bobsled on my left and a pot of frozen macaroni and cheese down the gully on my right. "It's a scientific experiment. If I find macaroni and cheese, I'll know the right gully works. If it's shrimp creole, the left gully. If I don't find either, I'll know this is not a good way to get our loads down the mountain."

"Okay, keep doing your science," Annie chuckled.

After lunch I set off with my backpack stuffed full and a foam pad and sleeping bag dangling awkwardly on the outside. I was not happy about going down the narrow ridge to Camp IIIa by myself. Descending the ridge was much harder than going up had been. Originally there had been a few inches of raised snow on either side of our footprints along the crest, giving some feeling of security. However, the snow had blown away in the wind, and now our footprints were actually raised platforms, their sides dropping off a thousand feet. I walked down backwards, keeping the ropes taut and trying not to look at the sheer dropoff on either side. Occasionally I glanced back over my shoulder to see if I was anywhere near the end of the ridge, but it stretched on and on, a sinuous white tightrope

Descending the Dutch Rib. Alison Chadwick.

of snow. I longed for the warm sun of Camp IIIa and the world far below.

My pack kept pulling me off balance, and a couple of times I stepped off into the steep powder dropping away on either side of the narrow track. About a third of the way down to Camp IIIa, I said to myself, "What's a nice girl from the Midwest doing up here all alone, teetering along backwards on a narrow ridge at 21,000 feet in the Himalaya?" If I were to fall off this ridge, no one would know for a long time. Indeed, halfway down an anchor did pop out as I put my weight on it. The rope gave way, I lurched several feet, and almost fell off the edge. Only a second anchor in the same place had saved me from a serious fall. Terrified, I climbed back up to the anchor and pounded it in as soundly as I could. I thought about the climbers who would be coming down with heavy packs in the next few days. If the anchors were to start melting out, could they get down safely?

Descending Liz's ice pitch, the last climbing above Camp IIIa, I landed waist deep in a crevasse full of powder snow at the bottom. I felt like crying. Afraid of falling even deeper and not being able to get back out, I clipped my jumar to the rope and fought my way up to the surface. Finally, I stumbled into the site of IIIa and collapsed. After catching my breath, I switched on a tape recording of the Fourth Brandenberg Concerto and sat there in the warm sun for half an hour listening to Bach, eating glucose, and nerving myself for the final stage of my descent.

Continuing down I found that conditions on the steep face had deteriorated in the week I had been up at Camp III, making the overhanging rappel through the icicles extremely hazardous. I was concentrating on rappelling without touching any of the icicles when the tape recorder clicked back on with a continuous loud buzz a few inches from my ear. I couldn't stop to take off the pack and turn it off, so I kept going down with that annoying buzz in my ear. At the bottom the red rope was tangled, and I couldn't get enough slack to lean down and clip onto the yellow one. Perched insecurely on a couple of crampon points, I finally managed to untangle the ropes.

When at long last I reached the bottom of the rib and gratefully turned off the tape recorder, I found that things here had changed too; what had been solid snow was now an enormous crevasse. I was so preoccupied with getting out of there fast that I forgot to look for the dirty pots I had thrown down the couloirs. I would never know the results of that experiment.

The slopes below the Dutch Rib were icy in some places where the avalanches had scoured away the surface snow. In other places I had to pick my way across mounds of new debris. I hurried across that dangerous stretch for the last time. Finally I spotted a tiny speck off in the distance—Christy was waiting for me.

With safety in sight, my thoughts returned to the people still above me, particularly the first summit team. Were they all right? Had they made it to the top?

A Woman's Place 15

You never conquer a mountain.
You stand on the summit a few moments,
Then the wind blows your footprints away.

From the diary of Piro Kramar:

Intense craving for a huge sandwich—thick slices of dark German bread, sweet creamy butter, and hunks of salami. What we got was noodles. After dinner Vera K., Irene, and I crowded into the small two-person tent, thus assuring ourselves of a warm night. The tent platform, chopped into a steep slope, was not quite flat, so we tended to roll downhill all night. We used oxygen intermittently, which allowed us to sleep well in spite of the discomfort and our presummit worries. Vera K. woke us at 3:00 A.M., but it took four hours for all five of us to get ready.

Jockeying for position on a tiny ledge outside the tent, grappling with crampons, harness, and pack, I reached out and grabbed my camera to get it out of the way. There was a vague sensation of burning in my right index finger as it touched the bare metal. My mind was oblivious; I must have thought, this is a good glove, ignore that signal. Several minutes later, as I was buckling on my crampons, I looked down and saw that my finger looked like Swiss cheese sticking out through a hole in the liner glove. I took off the glove and the whole finger was white and wouldn't move. The dread of mutilation sent me leaping back into the tent, crampons and all. First I put my finger in my mouth and then on my belly. I lay down on two sleeping bags, put the third one on top of me, and slept for about ten hours that day, still wearing my crampons, the summit forgotten.

From Vera Komarkova's diary:

Chewang, Mingma, Irene and I started to climb shortly before 7:00 A.M. Fortunately, the weather was good for a summit day: cloudless skies and no wind. At this time of year, after the retreat of the monsoon, strong winter gales can prevent climbing at high altitudes. Although the winter winds had already started this year, they would also stop for whole days—and fortunately this was one of those days.

The terrain was steep and icy for a few hundred feet. Then the angle lessened and the ice disappeared. In some places the snow allowed easy cramponing; in others we broke through a crust of harder snow into the powder beneath.

Mingma and Irene move slowly and steadily toward the summit.
Vera Komarkova.

At 25,300 feet, after three and a half hours of climbing, I remarked, "I can feel my brains going!" Irene and I started using oxygen. By that point our pace had slowed considerably, and it seemed that the remaining 1200 feet might prove to be too much without oxygen. Perhaps if Camp V had been placed higher, we could have made the summit without it. After a few minutes to put on and adjust the apparatus, we continued.

The features which had been always present above us for so long kept changing their familiar shapes and sinking below the horizon. To our right, the upper part of the Sickle came level with us and then disappeared slowly below, as did the still unclimbed middle peak and finally the east peak. Only Dhaulagiri I and a very few other peaks still towered above. We had dispensed with words a long time ago; the only sounds were those of our crampons scratching the snow. The rubber balloon of the oxygen apparatus pulsed rhythmically with the efforts of our legs and lungs.

Near the saddle between the middle and main peaks, just before we reached the summit pyramid, our pace slowed even more. The snow was almost thigh deep. At one point, Chewang—an optimist from the start—sat down in the tracks he was breaking and announced, "Maybe no success." Chewang had reached this altitude on an earlier Japanese expedition but was prevented from reaching the summit by bad weather. I offered him my oxygen or to take over the trail breaking, and that was enough to make him jump up and almost run for a few steps.

Our route circumvented the steepest part of the summit pyramid. From below the saddle, we angled gradually toward the summit ridge over several patches of protruding rock and joined the ridge only after a long traverse below its crest. The snow was much less consolidated here, and traversing required care. For at least an hour after we finally gained the windy crest, we kept climbing over and around a succession of cornices and bumps in the summit ridge, unable to decide which was the real summit.

From Irene Miller's diary:

At 6:00 A.M. we pile out of the tents and start the difficult process of putting our crampons on. Mine don't fit. My good pair were lost in the avalanched cache. I hope these won't come off. It's a good day for the summit, almost no wind, cold and clear. We wear everything we have. I have seven layers on top and four on the bottom, plus a wool hat inside a balaclava inside my hood. And it's still cold.

Suddenly Piro dives cursing into the tent. She has frozen her right index finger while putting on her crampons. The decision not to go on and so jeopardize her career as an eye surgeon is easy for Piro, though Vera K. and I hate to see her miss the summit attempt.

Vera Komarkova and I and the Sherpas Mingma Tsering and Chewang Rinjing, rope together and start off shortly before 7:00 A.M. Not much to carry—two oxygen cylinders and masks, a little food, cameras, some emergency equipment, and a canteen of water. Right above camp there is a small crevasse and several hundred feet of steep going. The slope eases off as we come over the last bulge and onto the upper plateau. We are even with the bottom of a rock rib leading to the middle peak between Annapurna I and its east peak. Soon we become aware of the summit pyramid in the distance. I recognize it from all the books, and there it is at long last—the final pyramid, always in sight and unbelievably getting closer. I can gauge my progress by glancing to the left and seeing just how close I am to it, but don't let myself do that too often, as the distance doesn't seem to change very fast.

Snow conditions vary from hard cramponing snow to an awful combination of breakable crust and knee-deep marshmallow snow. Mingma goes first to break trail. I'm behind him, following his footsteps, but in that crust, being second is just as hard. Each time the crust gives way I fall back to exactly where I started.

I desperately want a short rest, but Chewang encourages me: "Slowly going, no stopping, I think success." I try to regulate the pace so I am breathing six times for each step, and I try not to slip back in the unstable footsteps. Our oxygen tanks are only good for six hours; we must get as high as possible before starting to use them.

After climbing steadily for two and a half hours, we slow to a crawl. Time for oxygen, Vera K. and I agree. We put on the masks, and I feel better momentarily. But soon I'm back to six breaths per step. I finally realize the bladder on my mask isn't moving the way Vera's is. "My oxygen's not working," I announce. Chewang and I fiddle with the end of the connector. All of a sudden I hear a gentle hissing as the oxygen begins to flow, and then I can manage on four breaths per step.

We don't talk as we climb higher. All our energy and concentration go into the steady, monotonous plod that is taking us toward our goal. There is still no wind, but we can see plumes of snow blowing off the summit in the winter gale. I think of my family and friends. Their love is a steadying force, easing my way up the mountain.

Just below the summit pyramid the snow is again very deep, and our pace drags. But soon there is less snow, and the walking gets easier. The bands of rock below the summit that I had worried about for months turn out to be no problem. We walk right over them, our crampons grating on the sandstone, and we gain the crest of the windy, corniced summit ridge. But where is the summit? Chewang gets summit fever and starts racing along the ridge trying to determine the highest point. We traverse three or four bumps, and finally there we are.

The summit of Annapurna I at last! At 3:30 P.M. on October 15, 1978, we are at 26,504 feet on top of the world's tenth highest mountain—on top of the world.

We have brought an assortment of summit flags: the Nepalese and American flags and one bearing the legend "A Woman's Place Is On Top," all held together with a Save-the-Whales pin. Chewang has had them tied to his axe and ready for some time. We try to get the flags to stand up properly for the summit photo, but the wind whips them around the ice axe. Vera K. takes photos as I pose between Chewang and Mingma.

How do I feel? Partly an incredible sense of relief because I don't have to walk uphill anymore. And a sense of accomplishment for myself and the whole team. We've done what we set out to do—there's no point higher. But mostly, I know that it's 3:30 in the afternoon, and we're going to have to make tracks to get down before dark.

Vera K.'s diary records other impressions of the summit:

The view was deeply fulfilling. White-capped massifs of the few higher mountains rose from a sea of brown, red, and blue hills and merged on the horizon with the deep blue of the sky. Impossible to identify any peaks except Dhaulagiri, just across the Kali Gandaki Valley. The steep south face of Annapurna could be seen below us when the swirling clouds occasionally cleared.

As Irene, Chewang, and Mingma posed for Vera K.'s camera, the watchers at Camps I and II all began shouting into their radios at once, and a great whoop resounded from camp to camp, up and down the mountain.

Ironically, the people closest to the top were unaware that the summit had been attained. At Camp V Piro and Lakpa were tucked into their sleeping bags, dreaming the day away with no radio to rouse them from their high-altitude lethargy. Annie and

Chewang, Irene, and Mingma on the top at 3:29 P.M., October 15. Vera K., who took the picture, can be seen reflected in Mingma's sunglasses.
Vera Komarkova, © 1979 by the National Geographic Society.

Margi at Camp III were also without a radio and did not know that we had succeeded. Margi's feet were hurting intensely; she spent the afternoon rummaging through the food stock at the camp and cooking up her favorites—trying to build up her strength for the descent. Annie had a stomachache and found Margi's cooking efforts unappetizing. Both of them were impatiently waiting for dusk, when I had promised I would send off some flares from Camp II to signal that the summit had been reached.

Vera W. and Alison, making their labored way from Camp III to Camp IV, did not turn their radio on until they reached Camp IV at dusk and so learned the news only then.

But at the lower camps, where there was a clear view of the summit, excitement had been building throughout the day. Christy said later she had felt as if a great vice was getting tighter and tighter around her chest as the day wore on. When the four tiny figures finally stepped onto the summit, Christy and Joan hugged each other and danced around shrieking, "Incredible, marvelous, fantastic!"

The film crew at Camp I was also terribly excited. When the climbers reached the top, Dyanna broke into a sweat but continued to film.

> Closer, closer still. My camera whirs as it takes in footage of the four climbers reaching the highest point. Suddenly they stop and move no further. They are there. The top! What they must see! A most fantastic thing from more than 2 miles below to watch these small figures on the summit with only windblown snow and sky above them.

The summit climbers: Vera K., Mingma, Chewang, and Irene.
Arlene Blum.

Dyanna stopped just long enough to hug Marie, scream, and jump up and down, then she went back to filming them putting the flags up. "It was beautiful—backlit figures with puffs of cloud."

As all this was happening, I was coming down the Dutch Rib for the last time. Christy had walked up from Camp II to bring me the news and spot me through the avalanche slope; she saw me step off the trail and fall into thigh-deep snow. As I struggled back out, I yelled at her, "Did they make it?" She nodded her head yes, and I sat down in the track and cried. It was a mixture of triumph for the summit, relief at having made it across the avalanche slope for the last time, exhaustion from the tension of the descent, and, most of all, joy in knowing that a woman's place was indeed on top—after all the years of planning and preparation, we had climbed Annapurna.

Christy came up and gave me a hug as I sat sobbing in the snow. Then she took my pack, something I don't usually let people do; but I was grateful this time as I walked slowly behind her down to Camp II.

Once there, I first talked to Mr. Gurung, who was calling from Base Camp, eager to know who had reached the summit so that he could send a message to the Tourist Ministry. I said we did not yet know the identity of the four summit climbers and asked him to announce simply that four members and Sherpas had reached the top of Annapurna. Of course, their identities would be known soon, but I thought it fitting, since the entire team had contributed to the success, that the first announcement give credit generally.

In the morning Mr. Gurung would send a runner to Jomoson, where the news could be cabled to Kathmandu. In two days from now, the word would be out, and the world would know that the first Americans and the first women had climbed Annapurna. The thousands of people who had supported us, bought T-shirts, worked with us—they would all know soon. I only hoped that they would realize how much their caring and energy had meant to us. The climbers at the summit could see the whole world at their feet, and much of the world would soon share the knowledge and joy of their success.

Meanwhile, the climbers were hurrying down from the summit. Their long slog was interrupted three times: once for food and twice when Vera K.'s and Irene's oxygen ran out. Vera K. had not realized it at first and struggled on for some time until it finally dawned on her that she was becoming anoxic. She stopped to take the oxygen bottle out to lighten her pack. Relieved of this weight, she made good time back down.

Irene's strength was dwindling rapidly. After her oxygen gave out, she dumped the bottle and continued on almost as if in a dream. She tried to move as fast as possible, but she would frequently slip on the broken snowcrust and have to struggle to regain her feet.

> Twenty feet above Camp V I am backing over the steep slope in the dark, step down somewhere I can't see, and fall six feet into a crevasse. I end up on my back with my feet sticking up in the air, laughing like crazy. I know it's perfectly safe because I am roped. Mingma pulls me out, and we continue. All the way down there is a gradually increasing sense that I have climbed Annapurna and survived. I can never be sure that I will live until I get back down to Camp II, but every step I believe it a bit more.

Piro was waiting for them at Camp V:

> At 6:30 in the evening I start getting bombarded by chunks of ice hurtling down, hitting the tent from above. The returning summit climbers are kicking them off the slopes as they descend. They finally arrive, giggling, then all pile into the Sherpa tent for dinner. I leave my tent to join them, and someone calls out, "There's no more room in here!" This is the first and last time I feel a pang of regret, or call it envy, that I didn't join them for the summit that morning. I don't want to go back to my empty tent all alone so I just stand there in the moonlight between the two tents, not knowing what to do. Then Vera K. calls out, "Okay, there's room now, come on in for some hot soup."

Just as the climbers reached the tents at Camp V, two red flares shot up into the sky above Camp II. They were meant to signal the success to Margi and Annie at Camp III, but the summit climbers saw them, too, and were warmed by the knowledge that their teammates all down the mountain were celebrating with them.

16 Other Summits

One by one, three tiny figures slowly make their way up the ice wall above Camp IV. At the top of the steep step, the slope eases off and the dotlike figures move together, stop, and are joined by three more dots descending from Camp V.

From Camp I and Camp II we followed the action far above through binoculars and telephoto lenses. At that distance we could not identify the six climbers above Camp IV, but we knew that the three going up were Vera W., Alison, and Wangel on their way to Camp V for the second summit attempt, and we assumed the three coming down were Chewang, Mingma, and Lakpa, who had presumably left Camp V earlier than Piro, Irene, and Vera K. The radio soon confirmed our assumption.

Vera W. (plateau above Camp IV): We've just met the Sherpas coming down, and they're in sad shape. All three are very tired, and Mingma says his feet are frozen. We asked Lakpa if he would go back with us to Camp V or whether he and Chewang would stay at Camp IV in support. But they said that they were going down and suggested that we go with them.

Arlene (Camp II): Well, how about it, Vera? You're at about 23,300 feet up there, so you've bettered your old altitude record.

Vera W.: No, we at least want to go to Camp V and bring down the gear from there. There's another slight problem. The Sherpas say there's not much food and fuel up there—we counted on those supplies. What do you think we should do?

Arlene: If you insist on going to Camp V, you should probably go back to IV and get more food and gas cartridges right away. Maybe one of the Sherpas would bring them up to save you the effort.

Vera W.: The Sherpas are too tired, and if we go down and come back, we might not make it to Camp V until after dark tonight. We'd like to go back to Camp IV now and get an early start tomorrow morning. Is that all right with you?

Arlene: That sounds fine, except that Irene, Piro, and Vera K. haven't left Camp V yet, and if they don't leave soon, they may not get down to Camp III tonight. Then you'd be awfully crowded at Camp IV.

Vera W.: Oh, they'll manage to get down. I think it's safer for us to spend one more night at Camp IV and then go up early tomorrow. Oh, by the way, it was Irene, Vera K., Mingma, and Chewang who made the summit. Piro had something wrong with her finger.

The Sherpas head down from Camp V to Camp II. Vera Komarkova.

Arlene: Irene! That's great. And good for Vera K. too. But what happened to Piro?

Vera W.: Her finger got frostbitten, so she turned back. The tip was hard and white and now it's all bloated, but she's pretty sure it'll be okay. One more thing. The route to the main peak looks awfully long. Alison and I have definitely decided to try the middle peak instead. The Sherpas say it's shorter. There are several books about Annapurna in the blue tent—could you see if any of them have a photo showing the route on the middle peak? Let us know anything you can find out. Over and out from the plateau above Camp IV.

I signed off, amazed by our conversation. We had been so preoccupied with the problem of food and fuel for the second team that the identity of the first summit climbers had been almost an afterthought. And thanks to the wonders of radio, the climbers could request a literature search at 23,000 feet.

I went to the blue tent and found a book with a good photo of the middle peak. I called back up to describe the routes to Vera W. and Alison, who by now were back at Camp IV.

Arlene (Camp II): It looks like there's some exposed rock and hard climbing up there on the middle peak. Seems risky for a party of two.

Alison (Camp IV): We at least want to go up and take a look.

Arlene: All right. But if the weather shows any sign of deteriorating, you should come down immediately. Do you agree?

Alison: Yes, we agree, but we're both quite strong at this point. Do you want to talk to the summit climbers? They've just arrived.

Christy gives Annie the welcome news that the summit has been reached.
Arlene Blum, © 1979 by the National Geographic Society.

Arlene: Yes. Congratulations, Irene and Vera K. We're so happy you made it. Everyone's just delighted down here.

Vera K.: Thanks a lot. We're happy too.

Arlene: How are you feeling?

Irene: Getting to Camp V and the summit was the hardest thing I've ever done in my life. Something extra carried me through on the summit day. I'm happy, but now I'm so exhausted, it's going to take me a long time yet to get off this mountain. Over.

Marie, Dyanna, and Christy chimed in from the lower camps with loud cheers.

Christy (Camp II): I want you to know I was standing here and had the pleasure of watching you make the summit. There was a plume of white snow blowing behind you against the deep blue sky. We saw the four of you in silhouette, and Marie and Dyanna were running the movie camera like mad.

Irene: Thanks to all of you. But listen, the way to the summit was paved with all your efforts, and you know that. It's a victory for the whole team, and we all worked for it.

Arlene (Camp II): But you worked especially hard for years and you deserved it. And that's why we're all so happy. Are you coming down to Camp III tonight? Over.

Irene: No. It's late and we're tired, so we're going to stay the night with Vera and Alison. Over.

Arlene: It's going to be crowded up there. You all deserve a good night's sleep, and I hope you can get it. Over and out.

Margi and Annie got back to Camp II just before dark after a harrowing descent from Camp III down the narrow ridge. Both were laden with huge, heavy packs, and at one point Margi took a 20-foot fall off the ridge but managed to jumar back up. They had not seen the signal flares the evening before, so they didn't know about our success. Christy and I told them the news, and we all rejoiced together.

Just then the three Sherpas straggled in from Camp V. Mingma was limping on partially frozen feet, and Chewang's feet were very cold. All three were exhausted after their extraordinary effort climbing and carrying loads high on the mountain, then descending all the way from Camp V to Camp II in one day. We hurried to undo their boots and crampons and fix some hot tea.

"Very good to be at Camp II," Mingma said. "Hard work going to summit. Now every day colder, more wind. Everyone should leave the mountain now. Let's go to Kathmandu and have a party."

"Yes, it's getting colder," I agreed, "but before we leave the second summit team has to have their chance."

"Coming down today was awful," Margi said. "With my feet in this shape, I couldn't go back up there for anything. I sure hope Vera W. and Alison can manage on their own."

Meanwhile, Alison, Vera W., Vera K., Irene, Piro, and Wangel were trying to make the best of a crowded night. Wangel moved into the two-person tent with one of the three sleeping bags. The five women wanted to talk and exchange information about the summit, so they all crowded into the three-person tent. The other two sleeping bags were given to Alison and Vera W., who would need as much rest as possible to continue up the mountain tomorrow. Irene, Vera K., and Piro would have to spend the night without bags, since theirs had been left up at Camp V for the second team to use; they would make do with their down clothing. As they melted snow and cooked in the cramped tent, Vera W. and Alison asked about details of the route, the difficulties of the main peak, and the possibilities for the center peak.

Vera K. cautioned them, "The two of you may have a hard time up there without oxygen. We were breathing at least five times per step before we turned on our tanks. I don't know if we'd have made it without the oxygen."

"Remember," Piro interrupted, "there's a half tank up there for sleeping and a full tank for Vera W. to use on the last stretch. Maybe Alison can take up another tank and then you'll all have oxygen."

"I've climbed higher than the center peak before without using oxygen," Alison said. "Since Vera W. moves a little more slowly than I do, her having oxygen should even things out."

That was reasonable. Alison had led severe technical rock at nearly 26,000 feet on Gasherbrum without oxygen. She had joked that she had a most peculiar physiology: at the beginning of an expedition she was usually slow compared to the men with whom she was climbing; but as she went higher, her slow steady pace didn't change, while the faster men would falter and sometimes stop. At very high altitudes she was stronger than most.

Irene was slumped in the corner of the tent, quiet and exhausted. "It's incredibly tough up there," she finally said. "The steps we kicked yesterday have probably filled with blowing snow by now. Are the two of you sure you want to go up? We could all go down together tomorrow morning."

"We're sure," Alison said. "We have to go up and carry the gear down in any case. There are three sleeping bags, two tents, a movie camera up there—thousands of dollars worth of gear. We'll decide what we're going to do when we see what the conditions are like at Camp V. If the wind is blowing hard, we'll just pick up the gear, turn around, and come back down. If conditions are good and we feel strong, we'd like to try the center peak. Could you tell us what it looked like from the summit?"

Vera K. made a sketch of the center peak, and she and Alison studied it carefully. There were several possible ways up the middle peak: among them a long easy route that followed the path of the summit climbers to the saddle between the peaks and a much harder line straight up the rocks of the center peak. Alison still favored the more aesthetic line straight up the rock.

"That route sure looks tough," Vera K. said. "It might take you more than one day. Maybe as long as three days."

"We'll take a bivvy sack, stove, and extra food just in case," Alison said. "I wouldn't like to bivouac up there, but there's a full moon. Maybe we can just keep climbing all night. Do you want to come with us and have another go at the top, Piro?"

"Sorry," Piro responded, "my finger would never stand for it. And I'm exhausted. I'm going down. But I'll tell you what —we'll stay at Camp III until you and Vera W. are back."

"Thanks, Piro." Alison perked up. "That makes me feel better. Moral support, if nothing else."

Sleeping five in the tent was warm but cramped. Vera K. took some sleeping pills, fell sound asleep on her back with her legs stretched out, and slept comfortably all night. Vera W. and

Alison each had a sleeping bag and slept on the outside, relatively uncrowded, positions in the tent. Irene slept the sleep of the exhausted. The night was hardest for Piro, who valued both space and solitude.

In the morning everyone felt reasonably fit and able to go on her way, either up or down the mountain. Wangel, who should have had a good night with a tent and sleeping bag all to himself, announced that he was too ill to stay high and had to go down to Camp II at once. When I learned that there was now no Sherpa support at all for Vera and Alison, I decided to make a last attempt to talk them out of continuing.

Arlene (Camp II): I'd rather you wouldn't go up there without Sherpa support. You've done a great job already, and you can come down now. The gear at Camp V isn't that important —it can be left there.

Vera W. (Camp V): We want to at least go up and take a look at the center peak. Maybe we'll just bring down the loads. It would be awful to leave all that gear up there, and we want a chance for the center peak if things look good.

Arlene: Okay, Vera. Go ahead to Camp V, and we'll talk again about your going higher after you see the conditions there. Try to get an early start.

Vera W.: We will, but it's impossible to find anything in this tent. They're always three extra bodies in front of what you're looking for or sitting on top of it.

Arlene: Well, do the best you can. Try to persuade Wangel to stay up if you can. Over and out from Camp II.

Joan (Camp I): Good luck to you. But do be careful going up, Alison and Vera. Take your time and be sure to get started soon.

Marie: I'm really proud of you, Vera and Alison. I never cease to be amazed at the things you've done, and I know you can do it. We'll be filming you all day. Over and out from Camp I.

As the five climbers in the shadow of the ice wall readied themselves for their respective journeys, my anxiety about the second summit team continued to grow. I didn't question the concept of a two-woman attempt or Vera's and Alison's ability to pull it off. After all, Vera W. had climbed solo to the 22,800-foot summit of Aconcagua and Alison had climbed to 26,000 feet on Gasherbrum III, but the lack of support worried me more and more.

By this time all the climbers except Vera W. and Alison had already been to the summit or for various reasons, had made the decision not to attempt it. Of those of us remaining below, Annie and I were still fit, and if Vera or Alison were to become ill high on the mountain, we would of course go back up to help them. But we two were not strong enough to carry a sick or disabled climber down by ourselves, which was why I had insisted on hiring Sherpas. At this point, however, we could not expect much help from them: Ang and Lopsang were ill at Base Camp; Wangel, who claimed to be ill, was going down; and Mingma, Chewang, and Lakpa had been to the summit or Camp V and did not want to go back up again.

On many Himalayan expeditions, after one team successfully reaches the summit, the momentum is all downward. The rest of the team is tired, the danger suddenly seems unjustifiably great, and everyone wants to go back and have a party, as the Sherpas had suggested. Vera W.'s dream during the storm had anticipated this mood, and Alison had several times told me that she was very concerned we would pack it in after one team reached the top. I did want to give Vera W. and Alison the chance that they so much desired, and I admired their perseverance—indeed their heroism in going up without support. But I couldn't help worrying about the risk.

Again I called Camp IV to reiterate my concerns and reassure Vera and Alison that the gear at Camp V could be abandoned. Vera K. answered the radio; she told me they were ready to set off at once and didn't want to stop to talk about it now. They would call tonight from Camp V.

So I got out my binoculars and watched the two small figures move slowly and steadily up over the ice step and toward Camp V. The film crew, who were also watching them from Camp I, reported that they were making more rapid progress than the first summit team, who had been burdened with much heavier loads. Since the first team had also left in the late morning and reached Camp V about 5:00 P.M., we were confident that Vera W. and Alison would finish the trip before dark. I was relieved that they were climbing well after their crowded night at Camp IV.

Piro, Irene, and Vera K. didn't begin their slow descent from Camp IV until several hours later. Irene's ill-fitting crampons made it particularly difficult for her; on a steep ice slope one came off and she fell, just managing to stop herself on the edge of a dropoff. It was nearly dark by the time all three arrived back at Camp III.

The film crew again reported that Vera W. and Alison were making good progress toward Camp V. By dinner time the face was too heavily shadowed for filming, so Marie and Dyanna stopped watching and went into the mess tent for dinner. On their last call of the day, they estimated that Vera W. and Alison were twenty minutes below Camp V and moving well.

I left my radio on, expecting to hear from Camp V shortly. But Vera and Alison did not call. After dinner I began to call Camp V on the radio, but there was no response. I was worried about them, but finally I had to assume that their radio was broken like that of the first summit team. I slept fitfully that night, awoke early, and resumed my efforts to contact them.

Arlene (Camp II): This is Camp II calling Vera and Alison

Arlene calls Vera W. and Alison again and again on the radio.
Christy Tews.

at Camp V. Come in. Camp II calling Camp V.

No response. I tried again and again.

Arlene: Camp II calling Camp V. Please come in. Camp V, if you can hear me but cannot transmit, send off a flare to indicate you're okay.

No response. No flare. Nothing.

So I sat at Camp II on that calm, windless, perfect day, scouring the slopes above Camp V with binoculars and constantly calling the other camps on the radio. Instead of feeling triumphant that we had climbed the mountain, I was becoming increasingly agitated. Presumably Vera and Alison had made it to Camp V last night and were in the tent. But the film crew had been watching the whole slope with their telephoto lenses constantly since dawn this morning. They said that if anyone had come out of the tent at Camp V, even for a moment to go to the bathroom, they would have seen her, and they'd seen nothing.

As I called Camp V over and over, I began to consider the possibilities. First, the radio up there was broken, and Vera and Alison were taking a rest day. This was possible because they said they would not climb if the winds were high, and I could see a great snow plume blowing off the summit and swirling down the upper plateau. Second, still assuming a broken radio, they might have made an early start for the center peak and gotten out of sight before we started to watch. In that case we might see them coming down soon. Or, third, something could have happened to them. And it was this last, almost unthinkable, possibility that frightened me so much.

Throughout that interminable day I continued to scan the slopes with binoculars and call Camp V. I also called the other camps frequently. At Camp III no one was particularly worried about Vera and Alison. Piro, Vera K., and Irene had been with them only twenty-four hours before and assured us that they were strong, determined, and in good spirits when they had left for Camp V. I was the only member here at Camp II since Christy and Annie had carried a load down to Camp I and decided to spend the night there. At Camp I the film crew, Joan, Christy, and Annie were becoming increasingly anxious but didn't seem to want to discuss the worst possibility. Margi at Base Camp was extremely concerned and suggested trying to send some Sherpas up at once to see if anything was the matter.

That night at dinner I talked with the Sherpas about going up the mountain in the morning to see if Vera and Alison needed help.

"We think memsahibs are fine," Mingma said. "On summit day Dr. Piro and Lakpa slept in tent all day at Camp V. Alison and Mummie [as the Sherpas had taken to calling Vera W.] are probably sleeping all day today at Camp V. They will come down tomorrow. Do not worry, bara memsahib."

"I hope you're right," I said, "but what about the radio?"

"Radio broken," Chewang said. "Do not worry, bara memsahib, if no radio and Mummie and Alison not back tomorrow, we will go up and look. But we are very tired. We must rest one more day before we can make a safe trip back up mountain."

"Thanks, Chewang. I know you are very tired, but if there's no word, you must go up and look."

I went back to my tent and called again on the radio.

Arlene (Camp II): Camp II calling Camp V. Camp II calling Camp V. Please make some signal, any signal. Please. Please.

But only Camp I came on to tell me again that they hadn't seen anything all day. They would start watching again at dawn the next day.

I spent a sleepless night alone in the tent at Camp II—one of the most agonized in my life. I could not give up hope but I feared the worst. If something was wrong up there, our strength for a rescue was minimal. Although the three women of the first summit team had stayed at Camp III, their support was mostly moral, for they were too exhausted to climb up again.

If there were still no sign of movement in the morning, I would have to send the Sherpas back up. Despite their fatigue, they could still go from Camp II to Camp IV in one day and give us a report from Camp V by noon of the following day; and in an emergency they could probably carry a climber down. Their

Christie and Marie scan the slopes from Camp I for a sign of the missing climbers. Dyanna Taylor.

strength would be crucial to any rescue attempt.

I spoke to the Sherpas again the morning. "There is still no movement at Camp V. You must go up and look for Vera and Alison right now."

"No," Mingma stated flatly. "Our feet are still frozen. We're too tired. We cannot go up today."

"Somebody must go up to Camp V at once to see if Vera and Alison are sick in the tent," I said again more firmly. "You're much faster than we are; you will get up there tomorrow if you leave now, and it would take us three days."

"We're sure Mummie and Alison are okay," Mingma said. "But if they don't come down tomorrow, we will go up. Today our feet are too cold and we are too weak."

Indeed, the Sherpas did look haggard. They had spent the previous day lying in the sun trying to regain some warmth and strength, and they were doing the same today. I had to agree that another day of rest would make their trip faster and safer, and I couldn't force them to go up the mountain in this condition, so I consented on their firm commitment that they would leave early the next morning.

As we spent another endless day waiting and watching, I couldn't help thinking how wonderful it would be if we could all be at Base Camp celebrating instead of enduring this agony of suspense. Every time I heard an avalanche, I felt it down in my soul. Annapurna had given us the summit, but would it take away our lives?

"Please," I prayed over and over, "let us see them coming out of their tent. Please, that's all I want in the world."

At three in the afternoon Annie and Christy came back up

from Camp I very downcast. They, too, had spent the morning watching the face and calling on the radio, and they reported the mood at Camp I as tense and gloomy. "We can't imagine what's happened to them," Christy said. But we could imagine only too well.

At four snow began to fall heavily. Piro and Vera K. were staying at Camp III in case of a possible rescue, Irene was on her way down from Camp III by herself. She was still so exhausted that there was no point in her staying up there any longer. If the snowfall were to continue, her trip would be very hazardous, and Piro and Vera K. could be stranded at Camp III. Worse still, the storm would be even more severe up higher where Vera and Alison were, wherever that was.

Just before dinner Irene arrived from Camp III. I asked her again about Vera's and Alison's mood before they left Camp IV and about their final summit plans.

"They were feeling pretty feisty when they left," she told me. "They wanted to try the center peak and took along a stove and a bivvy sack in case they had to be gone two or three days."

"A bivouac? At those altitudes? At this time of year? They didn't mention a word about that to me." I was astonished.

"It does seem insane to me now down here," Irene agreed, "but at the time it seemed reasonable."

With a great sigh, I finally voiced my worst fears. "I'm afraid they may have slipped below Camp V."

"It's possible," Irene said slowly. "It's steep right below Camp V. There are two pitches of hard snow, almost ice. But I don't think they'd have any trouble climbing it."

"Is there any place to belay?"

"Yes. A narrow crevasse you can just put your axe in—it's in the middle of the slope, right between the two pitches."

"Is it possible that they could have missed the crevasse? Or could they have gotten off route?"

"Yes, it's possible. But the film crew said they were right on route and had plenty of time to reach Camp V before dark. Piro thinks they're doing a two- or three-day bivouac climb and are just out of sight. That's why we haven't seen any movement up there all day."

"I hope Piro's right." But I didn't believe that explanation. "You look really wiped, Irene. How are you feeling?"

"I'm going to live, but lately I've been feeling betrayed by my body," Irene admitted. "When I crawled into the tent at Camp III my head was down low, and I sort of fell forward and landed on the stove. I didn't realize I had a burn until several days later when I found myself touching the burn scab."

"It doesn't look too bad," I said.

"And then coming down the red rope today I overshot and fetched up astride with all my weight on the tangles at the end of the rope. I spun around and was facing outside, dangling and bouncing up and down with my full weight on that red rope. I had a panicked moment when it seemed like I would be there for the rest of my short life—but the tangle turned out to be something I could undo with one hand. Then just as I was about to cross the avalanche chute for the last time, a pretty good avalanche came down off the Sickle. But it missed me, and here I am. I guess I've survived."

I hugged Irene and together we walked in to dinner. After dinner Christy, Irene, and I were lying in our sleeping bags trying to stop worrying and go to sleep when suddenly we heard a yell from outside.

"Lights. Lights! We see lights! Memsahibs coming down to Camp IV!"

It was nine o'clock in the evening and the moon was full. Without bothering to dress, we ran out into the freezing night and eagerly scanned the slopes. None of us could see any lights. The Sherpas repeated that they had seen lights descending to Camp IV, which could only be Vera and Alison. The idea that they would come down in the dark made little sense, but we didn't think of that at the time. We so desperately wanted to believe it was them that we somewhat convinced ourselves the lights were real. We managed to sleep soundly that night for the first time since Vera and Alison had left Camp IV.

The next morning, after two hours with no sign of motion on the face, we were forced to admit that the lights must have been reflections of the full moon and that Vera and Alison were still missing. The Sherpas were getting ready to go up and look for them; today they would go directly to Camp IV and tomorrow on to Camp V. We waved goodbye to the Sherpas with a mixture of anxiety and relief—at least we would have some definite information soon. Then Annie, Irene, Christy, and I began to plan what we would do, depending on what the Sherpas found out.

"First, if the Sherpas find Vera or Alison ill or exhausted at Camp IV or Camp V, what should we do?" I asked.

"We still have some reserves left," Christy said. "We could get Ang and Lopsang and maybe even Wangel to come back up."

"I suppose so," I agreed. "And whether or not the Sherpas are well enough to come up, Piro, Vera K., Annie, you, and I could try it. I expect we could manage.

"The second possibility is that we won't find the climbers at either camp. If there's any sign, of course, the Sherpas will look further. If there's no sign, what do you think we should do? You know the terrain, Irene."

"The Sherpas should at least go up the steep slope just above Camp V and take a look at the summit plateau for signs of them," Irene suggested. "I don't think we could manage a search all the way to the summit, but we could look as far as the beginning of the plateau."

"Yes, that's a good idea. Then . . ." I hesitated, and forced myself to continue, "what if there are bodies at Camp V?"

"I guess we'd have to bury them in a crevasse. We couldn't carry them down, that's for sure," Christy said realistically.

I had to agree. "Considering the terrain up there, it would be dangerous to bring them down and risk people's lives for bodies."

Leaving that subject with relief, we went back to what we would do if they were ill or injured. A mail runner at Base Camp could be sent to Jomosom for reinforcements. In a few days fresh Sherpas could be helicoptered in to help with the evacuation.

"God, I hope it's just that someone's ill up there," Christy looked near tears.

"I just don't know," Irene shook her head. "They've been up an awfully long time. You can't believe how cold it is up there. The cold and the wind really take it out of you." She looked grim.

"Let's try not to think about it. We'll know something soon." Annie was trying to comfort everybody.

Yes, we would know soon. These days of waiting were becoming unbearable. I could hear my heart thumping, and the words kept playing over and over in my head: We'd know soon.

And then the radio came on—hysterical Sherpa voices.

"Yeshi, could you come translate?"

Yeshi hurried over from the cook tent and took the radio. "Mingma and Lakpa see a red jacket by Camp IV," he said excitedly. "They think it's Alison's jacket."

I couldn't breathe. It meant the worst.

"Red jacket near big crevasse across from Camp IV. They will go look."

I wasn't surprised, but I wasn't ready to believe it. Annie and Christy were hugging and trying to comfort each other, tears running down their faces. No one said anything.

Ten minutes later the Sherpas came on the radio again, their voices frantic. Even before Yeshi translated we knew what they were saying.

"Mingma and Lakpa, they say they see Alison. She is still tied to a rope and that rope leads into a crevasse where Mummie is."

I took the binoculars and looked to the left of Camp IV. Knowing exactly where to look now, I could just make out a vague red blur—Alison's jacket. And I saw the dots that were the Sherpas approach the spot, then stop and descend rapidly. We later learned that when the two Sherpas got to within 50 yards of the body, their progress was stopped by a large crevasse. They turned and ran down the mountain as though chased by evil spirits.

Apparently Vera and Alison had never reached Camp V that night. They must have fallen on the steep ice below the camp or been knocked off the slope by ice or rock fall. They fell nearly a thousand feet until they were stopped to the left of

Alison Chadwick-Onyszkiewicz. Irene Miller.   *Vera Watson.* Piro Kramar.

Camp IV when Vera slid into a crevasse.

Although the news was not unexpected, we were totally stunned. It couldn't be true. Vera and Alison—so alive, so full of energy and enthusiasm, loved by so many people. As I sat numbly in the snow, unaware of what was happening around me, disconnected images of Vera and Alison ran through my mind. I thought of Vera in her sunny kitchen, preparing a wonderful meal for us, or dancing up a rock face, every move made with style and grace. And Alison—I saw her at Noshaq base camp arm in arm with Janusz, or playing with the children on the trail to Annapurna.

Between them, Alison and Vera had climbed hundreds of mountains, and they knew that a fall on a steep slope can happen to any climber at any time. One foot placed insecurely just a fraction of an inch from safety, a shift of weight, a slip, a fall —the infinite difference between life and death. But why did it have to happen to them? Why could they not have put that foot just a little to the left or the right in a more secure place?

Slowly I began to collect myself and think about what had to be done now. Some of us—probably Piro and Vera K., since they were still at Camp III—should go up the next day to see if there was any evidence of what had caused the fall, or how they had died. We would try to find out all we could.

After all my worrying about the lack of Sherpa support for Vera's and Alison's summit attempt, the presence of Sherpas wouldn't have made any difference in this case. Because the Sherpas were faster, they usually climbed on their own rope, separate from the members. Indeed, the Sherpas accompanying the first team had reached Camp V several hours ahead of the members.

That night I dreamed I was with Vera and Alison, and that I was falling. I imagined kicking my foot into the snow, stepping up, then, as the step crumbled away, losing my balance, slipping and starting to fall, trying to arrest myself, but tumbling head over heels down the ice slope. Or I dreamed I felt a tug from behind, was pulled out of my steps, tried but failed to hold on with my ice axe—falling, over and over. Sometimes I dreamed of an avalanche falling on us all. I woke up sobbing and cried for the rest of the night.

I kept wanting to play the record backwards—to change the summit teams, the lead climbers, the mountain; to change ever having wanted to climb an 8,000-meter peak. But the record would not reverse. The reality was that we were alive and Vera and Alison were not. And in the midst of all this, I also felt some anger toward them for leaving us and for making it impossible to rejoice in the summit. Then immediately I felt guilty about being angry. As I learned later, this resentment and guilt were shared by others on the team.

Everyone else spent a wretched night too. Christy didn't sleep at all, and Marie threw up in the middle of the night. For Vera K. and Piro, sharing one sleeping bag at Camp III, it was the worst of all; they stayed awake all night, dreading the prospect of going up to the bodies. I had assumed that because Piro was a doctor it would be easier for her. But she said not.

"I hated the idea of going up there," she told me later. "I've never seen a person I've known dead. If you go into ophthalmology, you don't have that much to do with death."

Morning came, as it always does eventually. At Camp II Annie, Christy, and I lay in our sleeping bags as if drugged, while Vera K. and Piro started out to climb up to the bodies. The face was still in shadow, and it was very cold; they had climbed only a few hundred feet above Camp III when I heard from them on the radio.

Piro (above Camp III): This is Piro and Vera K. on the ice step calling Arlene at Camp II.

Arlene (Camp II): This is Camp II. Go ahead.

Piro: My finger is freezing again. I can't go on without the risk of damaging it severely. Vera K. and I want to turn back. We don't feel that it's that important to look at the bodies.

Arlene: I was hoping you would be able to bury the bodies.

Piro: I'm fairly certain my finger would be severely frostbitten if I went up.

For a surgeon, a right index finger is vital. Piro had not hesitated to give up the summit; I couldn't ask her to continue now and risk losing its use.

Arlene: Okay, come down. And be careful.

Piro: We'll see you later this afternoon. Over and out.

So we were never to know exactly what had happened to Vera W. and Alison. As Piro and Vera K. turned their backs on the mountain and faced down toward the world of living things, the life and energy we had brought to the top of this frozen place began to recede farther and farther from Vera and Alison. We didn't want to leave our friends up there, but the time had come to clear the mountain. There was nothing more we could do for them.

The pyramid of people and supplies we had so laboriously constructed would now be dismantled, but a vital part had broken off and would remain on Annapurna. The rest of us would go back down to the Base Camp and try to accept what had happened, to understand and respect the choice Vera and Alison had made and not to feel bitter. They were two strong women who loved the mountains and cared deeply about climbing. Still, it was hard to accept the terrible blow that the mountain gods had dealt. If only one foot had been placed a little farther to the right. . . .

The Memorial 17

October 21–22

The time had come to take down the colorful tents at Camp II that had sheltered us over these past weeks. Was it only weeks? It seemed as if we had lived up here for a very long time. Christy and I packed up huge loads—at least 70 pounds—and stumbled down the glacier in the hot sun. Now that the climb was over, the air was calm and the mountain looked sunny and benign. I could not help glancing up from time to time to the serac near Camp IV where I knew Alison and Vera were.

When we reached Camp I, we looked at the face through a 500-millimeter lens and could unmistakably see the red of Alison's jacket. This clear sight hit me hard, and I sat down heavily on a rock, full of grief. The Sherpas believe in reincarnation and have had much experience with death in the mountains, but they, too, were severely shaken by the tragedy. Lopsang sat near me, looking at the serac with binoculars and shaking his head. Then he came over, patted me on the shoulder and said, "Let them go. You have to let them go."

The mist came up from the Miristi Khola as we packed up what was left of Camp I and began to walk down toward Base Camp for the last time. Each step into the gray, muffling fog took us farther from Annapurna, from Vera and Alison. Each step brought us closer to the reality that they were not coming with us. Occasionally I felt waves of elation that we had actually succeeded, had reached the top of Annapurna, but mostly I was filled with despair. We stumbled through the moraine rocks and for the last time labored up the steep, rocky slope leading to the first grass. The green grass and the tiny flowers made me feel like crying, and I lay down in the meadow to rest. The slender grass blades were like velvet on my skin after all these weeks of ice and snow.

Down at Base, our friends gathered around, and tears ran down my face as I hugged Margi, Christy, and Irene. Margi, hobbling around in huge ensolite booties to protect her tender feet, tried to cheer me up.

Christy carries an 80-pound load from Camp II down to Base.
Arlene Blum.

Lopsang, Christy, and Marie descend to Base Camp in the mist.
Arlene Blum.

"You did a good job, Arlene," she said. "You did a great job. Don't worry. You couldn't have done anything any differently."

I was grateful to her—truly, I felt close to all of these women. During the last months we had experienced so much together. Our hearts were full now, but there was very little to say.

"Have a bath," Irene suggested practically. "The one I had yesterday was wonderful. And the food down here is pretty good."

The bath *was* wonderful. Now that it was fall, the air was chill and the stream was smaller, as the glaciers that fed it were no longer melting. There was neither enough water to get totally immersed nor any desire to do so. I sat next to the stream, washing myself bit by bit; it was almost a surprise to see my body emerge from the layers of down, sweat, and salt that had encased it.

The porters Lopsang had sent for arrived from Choya to carry our gear down, and I dressed hurriedly. It would still take an enormous amount of organization and hard work to get us and our gear back to Kathmandu. I was grateful now for the need to make lists; it was much better to keep busy than to think about what had happened. I went through the motions of dealing with the porters and Sherpas and making our plans like an automaton.

Throughout the day the rest of the team members and Sherpas straggled down to Base Camp with enormous packs. Piro arrived with her finger still heavily bandaged, but she was confident it would heal and that she could continue to perform surgery. What an enormous difference such a small thing as a tear in a glove can make. Had it not been for that small hole, Piro would certainly have made the summit.

Joan came down last, after thoroughly cleaning up the Camp I site. I told her how much I appreciated her hard work for the expedition even though she had not been able to climb high; she responded by praising the job I had done leading the climb, saying she could not have done so well herself.

Soon the team was together again at Base Camp. Looking up at the remote summit, it was hard to believe that any of us had ever stood there, even harder to comprehend the great loss that accompanied our achievement. But we had gained something more than the summit. The years of planning and the months of climbing together had changed and strengthened us. We had survived the hardest physical and psychological stresses and found that as a team we could do great things. Each woman had contributed her abilities and effort in full measure, and each was rewarded with the knowledge that her contribution had helped us attain our goal. In addition, we had gained the friendship and warmth that now united us. The long-standing conflict between Joan and me had been amicably resolved, and no other lasting antagonisms had developed during the past stress-filled months. For me, this was as important as having reached the summit.

That evening I wrote letters to Alison's parents and husband, to Vera's husband and friends, and to Liz, whose skills had so aided the climb and who cared so much about all of us. I wrote them the factual details of the last days and tried to find words of comfort, which always ended up sounding like platitudes: "She died doing what she loved best . . . Annapurna is a fitting place for them to rest . . . It was a quick and painless death." The words brought little comfort to me as I wrote them, and I doubted whether they would help Vera's and Alison's families and friends. But what else could I write? That they should be here with us still—that it wasn't fair the mountain had extracted so terrible a price?

Vera and Alison, like all high-altitude climbers, had taken risks in the mountains before. Vera had told us many stories of her solo climb of Aconcagua: of severe storms, hallucinations, the horror of finding a boot with a human leg bone in it. Still she had persevered, climbing all the way to the top and back down by herself. And Alison, while climbing Noshaq in 1972, had been part of a team that elected to continue onto the top in the late afternoon, even though they knew that the descent would be hazardous in the dark. Coming down, Alison lost her crampon, fell, and stopped herself just in time above a cliff. But this time neither she nor Vera had been so fortunate.

As I struggled with those letters, I heard the sounds of the Sherpas dancing and singing around the campfire near the kitchen. The other members were gathered around the fire watching them dance, but I stayed in the mess tent, feeling close to Vera and Alison and the people who loved them.

Arlene chips the names of Vera and Alison onto the memorial stone.
Marie Ashton.

Early the next morning I walked over to the stone on which are engraved the names of seven other climbers who died on this side of Annapurna. Marie had lettered Vera's and Alison's names on a blank side of the rock facing the mountain. The sun had not risen, and the morning was chill as I began to chip out the letters on the stone, using a hammer and screwdriver. Their names in the rock would stay here forever, looking toward the summit they had so hoped to reach.

October 17, 1978
Vera Watson
Alison Chadwick

Suddenly I heard a clattering noise in the distance. "A helicopter," someone yelled.

"It must be Marquita!" I exclaimed. Marquita Maytag had been a friend since my 1976 trip to Everest, when she was the American ambassador to Nepal. She had told me that if we reached the summit of Annapurna, she would come to Base Camp to congratulate us, and apparently she was keeping her word.

As the helicopter approached, everyone rushed around the camp to secure things against the downblast from its rotors. The porters, many of whom had never seen a helicopter before, were astounded at this creature from the sky. Even we were shocked at this sudden apparition from the mechanized world after our months of isolation.

Marquita got out and formally congratulated us. "What a wonderful thing you have done for yourselves and for the women of the world."

I introduced her to the team. She looked around and asked, "Is this everyone?"

"No," I said. "The second summit team did not come back."

"What!"

"Vera Watson and Alison Chadwick fell to their deaths while making their summit attempt."

"Oh, no!" Marquita's face crumpled. "I can't believe it. How horrible."

I tried to comfort her. She had to face all at once the terrible fact that we had lived with for the last three days.

"Is there anything I can do? Should I get more Sherpas by helicopter to bring down the bodies?" she asked.

"No. It's no use. The bodies couldn't be brought down without risking many lives. Thank you, Marquita, but there's nothing anyone can do."

"What happened?"

"They fell a thousand feet from just below Camp V. Either one of them slipped, or they were swept down by a small avalanche or rockfall. The Sherpas said the bodies were separated. If either had been alive, she would probably have gone over to the other, so they were presumably dead when they landed."

Marquita is a strong woman. She composed herself and went on with her congratulations, if somewhat mechanically.

Joan, Irene, and Marquita discuss the climb. Sandy Formoso.

The team celebrates our victory with champagne and fried chicken.
Arlene Blum.

She had brought us fried chicken, sandwiches, a case of California wine, and, best of all, our mail. As we sat in the warm sun, reading our letters and feasting on the first fresh food and wine we had tasted in weeks, Marquita told us the welcome news that Wanda Rutkiewicz had just climbed to the top of Everest, making the summit in one eight-hour push all the way from the South Col—a remarkable achievement. Alison would have been happy to hear that.

During the course of the day we all took turns chipping the letters of Vera's and Alison's names in the memorial stone. We had planned to hold a memorial service that afternoon, but kept putting it off, fearing the finality of it. At last, when it was almost dark and the summit shrouded in fog, we could wait no longer; we would be breaking camp early the next day. We walked over to the rock in the somber twilight and stood there silently. Our minds and hearts were filled with thoughts of Vera and Alison, but we could not say anything.

Finally Christy started the service. "We are gathered to pay tribute to Vera and Alison, our dear friends. Does anyone have a memento of them to leave here?"

Christy held out a box that contained photos and mementos of the other climbers who had died on Annapurna. It had been placed in a hollow on top of the memorial stone. We added pictures of Vera and Alison, a rock from the summit of Annapurna, and I left a prayer scarf that had been given me by a monk from the monastery at Thyangboche. I had worn it on Everest to protect me from avalanches.

"I hope this will help keep their souls safe here on Annapurna," I murmured. Then Christy put the box back on the stone, and we piled heavy rocks on top of the monument to rebury the box.

"I miss Vera and Alison so much," Christy said. "I miss Vera's warmth and enthusiasm and how much she cared about all of us and this climb."

"Without Vera's drive from the beginning, we would have given up and never gotten approval for the expedition," I said. "When things looked bad, Vera Watson persevered, and so we were able to come here."

"I miss Alison's concern and her integrity and her idealism," Marie said. "She really believed in women's climbing and what women could attain."

We all locked arms and sang the old Quaker song, " 'Tis the gift to be simple, 'tis the gift to be free, 'tis the gift to come down where we ought to be. . . ." Then the Sherpas began to chant, "*Om mani padme hum, om mani padme hum* . . . The jewel is in the lotus, the spirit of humanity is in the universe" —the spirits of Vera and Alison stay with Annapurna. Members and Sherpas chanted together with arms linked.

The mountain did not reappear as we trooped back in the heavy fog to dinner. After dinner everyone went over to the campfire to dance and be together on our last night. I looked around at the faces, golden in the flickering light, thinking about what we had all shared and wondering what effects this experience would have on our lives.

Annie and Yeshi were sitting comfortably with their arms around each other. Annie would be staying in Nepal for a month, and the two planned to go trekking. Joan, Margi, and Vera K. also had plans to stay and trek in Nepal. Watching Vera K. dancing energetically with the Sherpas, you could not tell she had just climbed a high mountain. She looked strong and full of enthusiasm—indeed, she was already thinking of organizing an expedition to climb Dhaulagiri. Christy would be going out early the next morning with Marquita's helicopter to telephone the tragic news to Vera's and Alison's families and friends.

The isolation and sensory deprivation that we had lived with so long was ending. As we descended the next day, we would first encounter shrubs, then trees, finally forests. We would see animals and meet local people. Only too soon our tight group—united by both our shared victory and our shared sorrow—would be intruded upon by the tourists from all over the world who trek up the Kali Gandaki in November. Then we would meet our friends and the press back in Kathmandu. Finally, we would all separate and try to resume our normal lives. But for the moment we simply relaxed and watched the Sherpas dancing.

The bonfire at Base on departure day. Arlene Blum.

When I had crossed the avalanche slope for the last time, I felt myself on a distinct edge: on one side was the abyss of falling snow, burial, death; on the other side was life and a renewed appreciation of its value. Those weeks spent under the threat of imminent death—followed by the loss of Vera and Alison—had taught us to see the important things, to focus on essentials. We had risked our lives, and our reward was in part a reaffirmation of life.

The next morning we had to clean up the camp and burn the garbage. We made a huge bonfire of all the boxes. A kind of madness seized the Sherpas and porters, and they began throwing things helter-skelter into the fire. Aerosol cans exploded, bottles broke, even leftover food was thrown in. It was an amazing scene in a country where every conceivably useful item is valued and saved. Perhaps this frenzy of burning was some sort of exorcism. I watched with a fascination that verged on horror.

When everyone else had left, I went and sat by the memorial stone a last time. I touched Vera's and Alison's names and tried to focus on the happier times of the last months. I remembered Vera playing with the puppy on the trek, Alison's and Liz's delight when they established Camp I, the joy of the summit, the ethereal beauty of this world of rock, ice, and snow. And then I thought of the migrating geese, which had been flying back and forth between Tibet and India since before the Himalaya had been uplifted and would continue to do so long after we were all forgotten.

I stood up. My feet moved automatically, step by step, carrying me away from Annapurna.

Epilogue

An excerpt from the final entry in Annie Whitehouse's diary reads:

> Flying back home over a blanket of clouds, the sun setting behind us leaving a rim of colors: pink, orange, yellow, fading into the deep blue sky. The expedition is over, and my life in Nepal is turning to memories. . . . The end of my climbing with my dear companion, Vera Watson, but she will live forever in my mind. The end of my life as it was, as a result of my commitment to Yeshi. . . . The clouds along the horizon have erupted into brilliant orange. It is good to know that every end is also a beginning. The end of this long day is the first flickering light of a star. One by one, the stars will show their light, glow brightly, then fade into the light of the rising sun.

There have been other endings and beginnings for the Annapurna team members since our return from Nepal. On February 16, 1980, Joan Firey died in Seattle, Washington, of a rare bone marrow disease. In her last months, she continued to inspire those who knew her with her courage, vitality, and warmth. We all will miss her.

For the rest of the Annapurna team the future holds plans for more climbs. In fall, 1980, Vera Komarkova will lead a women's team up "The Pear" on Dhaulagiri I, a technically demanding route that has been attempted many times but never successfully climbed. Alison would have been delighted.

"Cloudwalking" to Dhaulagiri. Arlene Blum.

Annie and Yeshi. Vera Komarkova.

Liz Klobusicky continues to do hard climbs in Europe with her husband, Nicko. Annie Whitehouse has a permit for 1982 to climb Ama Dablam in Nepal, which she and many others regard as the most beautiful mountain in the world. That team includes Vera K., Piro, and Annie's husband, Yeshi Tenzing (they were married in Wyoming in 1979). Both Annie and Margi Rusmore have been invited to go on a proposed expedition to Tibet in 1981.

Irene Miller (now going by her maiden name, Beardsley) and her daughter Teresa will trek together in Nepal during the summer of 1980. At about the same time, I will be leading a small Indian-American women's expedition to Brigupanth, a beautiful, unclimbed 22,000-foot ice peak on the Gangotri Glacier in the Indian Himalaya. Piro and Christy will be on the team, as will several young women who I hope will be able to use this experience to organize their own expeditions in the future.

Change is coming slowly, however. Besides the climbs just mentioned, very few women are included in the dozens of other expeditions approved by the AAC for the next few years.

We have established a memorial fund in Vera's and Alison's names to provide support for women's high-altitude climbing. When we first proposed the fund, we met resistance. "You've got to give money to men climbers too. There are just not that many women who climb," one venerable AAC member assured me. I protested that the money had been raised on the premise that it would go for women's climbing and should not be used for anything else. The response was that "women are good at things like raising money and supporting climbing. But if you're going to have a substantial fund, you should give a share of the money to the real climbers, to the men."

And that, unfortunately, is still the attitude of some in the "high and serene circles" of the climbing establishment. Nevertheless, our fund *was* established through the AAC to support women's expeditionary mountaineering, and Alison's family and friends have set up a similar fund in Britain. Last summer we sponsored the first of what has become an annual climbing meet in the Tetons to teach women climbers about expeditionary planning. Some forty women and men participated.

Annapurna itself remains unchanged—still beautiful, remote, indifferent to human concerns. A year after our climb an American eight-man expedition attempting to repeat the Dutch Route without Sherpas or oxygen was making excellent progress until the wind coming from an enormous avalanche down the Bobsled blew Camp III and its three occupants off the Dutch Rib.

Recently a Swedish team wrote to me for advice about their scheduled 1981 attempt on the north side of Annapurna. In my reply I warned that the mountain was extremely avalanche prone but did not try to discourage them. I could not tell them the risk was too great; they would have to make that decision for themselves. In mountaineering, the truism holds: the greatest rewards come only from the greatest commitment.

On Annapurna our entire team took the risk, made the commitment. Only time will reveal its full consequences. As Maurice Herzog declares at the end of his book: "There are other Annapurnas in the lives of men."

And in the lives of women as well.

Irene on the way to Annapurna with Dhaulagiri in the background.
Arlene Blum.

Afterword to the New Edition

In recent years, more and more women have been finding high adventure and quiet satisfaction in the mountains: backpacking, skiing, rock climbing, and mountaineering. The presence of women in rock climbing is especially evident, with many women skillfully leading the hardest routes in Yosemite, the Tetons, and other technical rock areas.

Progress in expeditionary climbing has been slower. Of twenty-nine Himalayan climbs endorsed by the American Alpine Club in 1981 and 1982, only ten teams had any women climbers, and just four included more than two women in the party. However, some important accomplishments should be noted. The Vera Watson–Alison Chadwick-Onyszkiewicz Memorial Fund for Women's Climbing has helped support three climbing meets, a French–American women's climbing exchange, and expeditions around the world in which more than forty women have participated. These include the 1980 women's attempt on Dhauligiri I, led by Vera Komarkova; the first ascent by an American woman of Mount Kennedy, in the Yukon; a climb of Cassin Ridge on Mount McKinley; a two-person, alpine-style ascent to the 26,000-foot level of Yalung Kang (a summit of the Kanchenjunga massif); a difficult alpine traverse in the Peruvian Andes; and other expeditions to the Himalaya, the Karakoram, the Andes, Canada, Greenland, and Alaska. The American Women's Himalayan Expeditions (P.O. Box 5455, Berkeley, CA 94705) is still selling Annapurna T-shirts to benefit the memorial fund.

In 1980 I led the Indian–American Bhrigupanth Expedition, which succeeded in making the first ascent of this difficult 22,300-foot peak. The team consisted of Piro Kramar, Christy Tews, two Indian women, and three young American women who reached the summit on their first trip to the Himalaya. And in April of 1982, all eight members of the American Women's Ama Dablam Expedition made a successful ascent of this striking mountain. On both of these expeditions, Sherpas did not carry loads above base camp; the climbers did all the leading, made all the decisions, and reached their summits safely and successfully.

In the fall of 1983, Annie Whitehouse will join four of the women who climbed Ama Dablam and five men to attempt the difficult west-ridge route on Mount Everest; this will be the first major American expedition to be composed equally of men and women climbers. The Indians are ahead in this respect. In the fall of 1982, an Indian team of half men and half women climbed Nanda Devi, India's highest mountain.

My most recent expedition and my greatest dream after Annapurna was a 2,000-mile trek across the Himalayan regions of Bhutan, Nepal, and India. My partner for this nine-month walk, completed in June 1982, was Hugh Swift, a writer and veteran Himalayan trekker from Berkeley, California.

On expeditions such as Annapurna, Bhrigupanth, and Ama Dablam, women have gained confidence, technical ability, and leadership skills. Now the time has come for people to be accepted on expeditions not as men or women but as climbers. Women and men have complementary abilities, and they can and should climb their "Annapurnas" as equals, with mutual respect.

Arlene Blum
April 1983

Bibliography

This listing includes both works referred to in the text and a selection of books about mountaineering and exploration by women.

Anderson, John R. L. *The Ulysses Factor*. New York: Harcourt Brace Jovanovich, 1970.

> Study of mankind's urge to explore, including a chapter on women explorers.

Another Ascent of the World's Highest Peak—Qomolangma. Anon. Peking: Foreign Language Press, 1975.

> A colorfully illustrated account of the 1975 Chinese ascent of Mount Everest on which sixteen women climbed above 25,000 feet. Includes a chapter entitled "Women Do an Equal Share with Men."

Barrett, Katherine and Robert Le Moyne. *The Himalayan Letters of Gypsy Davy and Lady Ba*. Cambridge, England: W. Heffer & Sons Ltd., 1927.

> Poetic and picturesque journal of an eccentric British couple's travels in Ladakh and Baltistan.

Bell, Gertrude, *The Letters of Gertrude Bell*. 2 vols. London and New York: Bell, Ernest & Benn Ltd., 1927

> Fascinating letters of this brilliant scholar, archaeologist, and Arabist. Includes accounts of several difficult Alpine climbs.

Bishop, Isabella L. Bird. *Among the Tibetans*. New York: Fleming H. Revell Co., 1894.

———. *A Lady's Life in the Rocky Mountains*. Norman, Okla.: University of Oklahoma Press, 1960.

> Two of the ten delightful adventure books written by this perceptive traveler.

Blum, Arlene, Irene Miller, and Vera Komarkova. "Triumph and Tragedy on Annapurna." *National Geographic* 155, 3 (March 1979): 295–311.

> First published account of the 1978 Annapurna climb.

Cannan, Joanna. *Ithuriel's Hour*. London: Hodder and Stoughton. 1931.

> A novel of personal conflict and deception on a Himalayan expedition.

Clark, Ronald. *The Victorian Mountaineers*. London: Batesford, 1953.

A well-written chronicle of some of the earliest climbers in the Alps, including a chapter on "The Women."

―――. *An Eccentric in the Alps: The Story of Reverend W. A. B. Coolidge*. London: Musem Press, 1959.

Coolidge's Aunt "Meta" (Marguerite Brevoort) and his dog Tschingel were companions on hundreds of Alpine climbs, including many first women's ascents.

Cole, Mrs. *A Lady's Tour Round Monte Rosa*. London: Longman, Green, Longman and Roberts, 1859.

A quaint account of early Alpine excursions from 1850 to 1858.

Cumming, C. I. Gordon. *Granite Crags of California*. Edinburgh and London: William Blackwood & Sons, 1886.

Travels in California's Yosemite Valley in 1878; like many female authors of her time, Cumming used only the initials of her name.

David-Neel, Alexandra. *Tibetan Journey*. London: John Lane, The Bodley Head, 1936.

Compelling tales of the author's explorations in forbidden Tibet.

―――. *My Journey to Lhasa: The Personal Story of the Only White Woman Who Succeeded in Entering the Forbidden City*. New York: Harper & Bros., 1927.

Classic account of a 2,000-mile walk across Tibet by a 56-year-old Tibetan scholar disguised as a beggar woman.

Deacock, Antonia. *No Purdah in Padam: The Story of the Women's Overland Himalayan Expedition, 1958*. London: George G. Harrap and Co., 1960.

Three British women travel overland to India, trek three hundred miles from Manali to Ladakh, and make the first ascent of Biwi Giri (18,700 feet), which they named Wives' Peak.

Dingle, Graeme. *Two Against the Alps*. Christchurch, New Zealand: Whitcombe and Tombs, 1972.

The first winter traverse of the rugged New Zealand Alps by the author and Jill Tremain.

DuFarr, Freda. *The Conquest of Mount Cook and Other Climbs*. London: George Allen and Unwin, 1915.

Excellent account of an Australian woman's climbs in the Southern Alps of New Zealand, including the first ascent of Mount Cook by a woman.

Duncan, Jane E. *A Summer Ride Through Western Tibet*. London: Smith, Elder & Co., 1906.

Fascinating account of the first Western woman to visit parts of Ladakh and Baltistan.

Dunsheath, Joyce; Eileen Gregory; Hilda Reid; Frances Delany. *Mountains and Memsahibs*. London: Constable and Co., 1958.

Climbs in the Kulu-Spiti-Lahul areas of the Indian Himalaya, including Deo Tibba (20,000 feet).

Dunsheath, Joyce. *Guest of the Soviets*. London: Constable and Co., 1959.

Experiences of the first woman to climb the Caucasus Mountains of the USSR.

————. "Mrigthuni, Garhwal." Expeditions and Climbs section. *American Alpine Journal* 14, 2 (1965):472.

Ascent of this 22,490-foot peak by an Indian women's expedition led by the author.

Dunsheath, Joyce, and Eleanor Baillie. *Afghan Quest: The Story of the Abinger Afghanistan Expedition, 1960*. London: George G. Harrap and Co., 1961.

The adventurous journey of two British women to Afghanistan where they made a good attempt to climb Mir Samir (19,880 feet).

Dyhrenfurth, Hettie. *Memsahib in Himalaya*. Leipzig: Verlag Deutsche Buchwerkstätten, 1931.

The author's experiences while accompanying the 1930 Kanchenjunga Expedition to India and Nepal.

Edwards, Amelia B. *Untrodden Peaks and Unfrequented Valleys: A Midsummer Ramble in the Dolomites*. London: George Routledge and Sons, 1873.

Classic account of early climbs in the Italian Alps.

Engel, Claire Elaine. *They Came to the Hills*. London: George Allen and Unwin, 1952.

Entertaining profiles of leading British climbers, including Lucy Walker and Mrs. Aubrey LeBlond.

————. *Mount Blanc*. London: George Allen and Unwin, 1965.

An outstanding anthology about Europe's highest peak.

————. *Mountaineering in the Alps*. London: George Allen and Unwin, 1971.

A well-written historical survey by this eloquent Alpine scholar.

Fortescue, Winifred. *Mountain Madness*. Edinburgh and London: William Blackwood and Sons, 1943.

Alpine holidays among the aristocrats.

Freshfield, Mrs. Henry. *A Summer Tour in the Grisons and the Italian Valley of the Bernina*. London: Longman, Green, Longman and Roberts, 1862.

————. [By a Lady]. *Alpine Byways*. London: Longman, Green, Longman and Roberts, 1861.

Both of the above are charming reminiscences of Alpine tours and scrambles, the second published anonymously.

Gribble, Francis. *The Early Mountaineers*. London: T. Fisher Unwin, 1899.

Includes a chapter on the "First Lady Mountaineers."

Hamilton, Helen. *Mountain Madness*. London: Wm. Collins and Son, 1922.

Novel set in the Alps.

Herzog, Maurice. *Annapurna*. Translated by Nea Morin and Janet Adam Smith. New York: E. P. Dutton and Co., 1953.

His classic account of the first ascent of an 8,000-meter peak.

Hillary, Sir Edmund. *From the Ocean to the Sky*. New York: Viking Press, 1979.

A 1,500-mile journey up the Ganges from the Bay of Bengal to its source in the Himalaya.

Irwin, Robert William. *Challenge: An Anthology of the Literature of Mountaineering*. New York: Columbia University Press, 1950.

Contains a chapter on Gertrude Bell (see listing under Bell).

Jackson, Monica, and Elizabeth Stark. *Tents in the Clouds: The First Women's Himalayan Expedition*. London: The Travel Book Club, 1957.

Three British women explore the Jugal Himal of Nepal in 1955. First ascent of Gyalgen (22,000 feet plus) and an attempt on Dorje Lakpa.

Knowlton, Elizabeth. *The Naked Mountain*. New York: G. P. Putnam's Sons, 1935.

A well-written account of the 1933 German-American expedition to Nanga Parbat. This was the first time a woman was included in an attempt on an 8,000-meter peak.

Kogan, Georges, and Nicole Leininger. *The Ascent of Alpamayo*. Translated by Peter E. Thompson. London: George G. Harrap, and Co., 1954.

An account of the Franco-Belgian expedition, which made the first ascent of Alpamayo in the Cordillera Blanca of Peru. Claude Kogan and Nicole Leininger climbed Quitaraju—the first time a peak over 20,000 feet was climbed by an all-woman team.

Lambert, Raymond, and Claude Kogan. *White Fury*. Translated by Showell Styles. London: Hurst and Blackett, 1956.

Dramatic narrative of pioneering attempts on Gaurisankar (23,440) and Cho Oyu (26,750) in Nepal by the two authors. Kogan established a world altitude record for women on Cho Oyu.

LeBlond, Mrs. Aubrey. *Mountaineering in the Land of the Midnight Sun*. London: T. Fisher Unwin, 1908.

Tales of climbing and exploration in Norway.

———. *True Tales of Mountain Adventure for Non-Climbers, Young and Old*. London: T. Fisher Unwin, 1903.

Accounts of Alpine climbing, including several involving women.

———. *Adventures on the Roof of the World*. London: T. Fisher Unwin, 1907.

Further dramatic tales of Alpine adventure.

Lunn, Arnold. *Matterhorn Centenary*. London: George Allen and Unwin, 1965.

Contains a chapter on "The First Ascent by a Woman," about Lucy Walker's ascent of the Matterhorn.

Maillart, Ella K. *Forbidden Journey—From Peking to Kashmir*. Translated by Thomas McGeevy. London: William Heinemann, 1937.

Adventurous travels of a Frenchwoman across China and Kashmir in the 1930s.

———. *The Land of the Sherpas*. London: Hodder and Stoughton, 1955.

Excellent photographic record of a trip to the Khumbu region of Nepal in 1950.

Mazuchelli, Elizabeth Sarah. *The Indian Alps and How We Crossed Them*. London, 1876.

Account of two years' residence in the eastern Himalaya and a two-month journey into the Kanchenjunga region.

Merrick, Henrietta Sands. *In the World's Attic*. New York and London: G. P. Putnam's Sons, 1931.

Travel in Kashmir and Ladakh.

Messner, Reinhold. *Everest: Expedition to the Ultimate*. Translated by Audrey Salkeld. London: Kay and Ward, 1979.

The first ascent of Mount Everest without oxygen. Includes a description of 1975 Japanese women's and Chinese expeditions.

Middleton, Dorothy. *Victorian Lady Travellers*. London: Routledge and Kegan Paul, 1965.

This author was the first to recognize and applaud the achievements of Isabella Bishop and Annie Taylor.

Miller, Luree. *On Top of the World: Five Women Explorers in Tibet*. London and New York: Paddington Press, 1976.

An inspiring and well-researched account of the adventures of five remarkable women who explored the Himalaya and Tibet during the late nineteenth and early twentieth centuries.

Milne, Malcolm, ed., *The Book of Modern Mountaineering*. New York: G. P. Putnam's Sons, 1968.

Includes an insightful chapter by Monica Jackson on "The Woman Climber."

Moffat, Gwen. *Space Below My Feet*. London: Hodder and Stoughton, 1961.

The frank biography of the first woman to become a certified climbing guide in Britain.

———. *Two Star Red*. London: Hodder and Stoughton, 1964.

Account of the author's work in mountain rescue with the Royal Air Force.

———. *On My Home Ground*. London: Hodder and Stoughton, 1968.

The entertaining life and times of a professional writer-climber.

Mons, Barbara. *High Road to Hunza*. New York: Faber and Faber, 1958.

Description of travels in Hunza in 1956 by the author and her husband.

Morin, Nea. *Woman's Reach. Mountaineering Memoirs*. London: Spottiswoode, 1968.

Memoirs of a long and notable career in the Alps, Britain, and the 1959 Ama Dablam expedition. Includes a listing of many first women's ascents.

Murphy, Dervla. *Tibetan Foothold*. London: John Murray, 1966.

A sensitive and lively story of the author's work with Tibetan refugees in India following a bicycle journey from Ireland to India.

———. *The Waiting Land: A Spell in Nepal*. London: John Murray, 1968.

Vivid impressions of travels in Nepal.

Nicolson, Marjorie. *Mountain Gloom and Mountain Glory: The Development of the Aesthetics of the Infinite*. Ithaca, New York: Cornell Press, 1959.

Scholarly study of mountains in Western literature.

Pares, Bip. *Himalayan Honeymoon*. London: Hodder & Stoughton, 1940.

Interesting descriptions of Sikkim and the author's meeting with 1938 British Everest team.

Peck, Annie S. *A Search for the Apex of America*. New York: Dodd, Mead, and Co., 1911. Published in England under the title *High Mountain Climbing in Peru and Bolivia* (T. Fisher Unwin, 1912.)

Classic narrative of expeditions in Peru and Bolivia, including the first ascent of the north peak of Huascaran by this adventurous New England professor.

———. *The South American Tour*. New York: Doran, 1913.

More travels in South America, including an attempt on Illampu in Bolivia.

The People's Physical Culture Publishing House. *Mountaineering in China*. Peking: Foreign Language Press, 1965.

Well-illustrated record of ascents by Chinese mountaineers, including a number of women climbers.

Petzoldt, Patricia. *On Top of the World. My Adventures with My Mountain-Climbing Husband.* New York: Thomas Y. Crowell and Co., 1953.

Warm account of her climbs with Paul Petzoldt, including the east ridge and north face of the Grand Teton and the 1938 K2 expedition.

Pierre, Bernard. *La Conquête du Salcantay.* Paris: Dumont, 1953.

Climbs of a French-American team, including Claude Kogan, in the Cordillera Blanca in Peru.

———. *A Mountain Called Nun Kun.* Translated by Nea Morin and Janet Adam Smith. London: Hodder and Stoughton, 1955.

An enthusiastic story of the first ascent of Nun Kun (23,410 feet) in Kashmir by Claude Kogan and Bernard Pierre.

Pigeon, Anna, and Ellen Abbot. *Peaks and Passes.* London: Griffith Fanne, Okeden and Welsh, 1885.

The author's climbs included the steep southeast precipices of Monte Rosa, characterized as the first great climbing feat by a woman.

Pilley, Dorothy. *Climbing Days.* 2d ed. New York: Harcourt, Brace and Co., 1953.

Vivid reminiscences of a woman who made many guided first ascents in the Alps and Britain in the 1920s. An excellent chapter on the early history of women's climbing.

Plunket, Honorable Frederica. *Here and There Among the Alps.* London: Longmans, Green and Co., 1875.

Vivid account of early alpine journeys motivated "by the wish to persuade other ladies . . . to pass the snow-marked boundaries of the Alpine world."

Reclus, Elisée. *The History of a Mountain.* Translated by Bertha Ness and John Lillie. New York: Harper & Brothers, 1881.

A poetic dissertation on mountains and their inhabitants.

Richard, Collete. *Climbing Blind.* Translated by Norman Dall. New York: E. P. Dutton and Co., 1967.

Inspiring story of a young blind woman who is both a mountaineer and a cave explorer.

Ridgeway, Rick. *The Last Step: The American Ascent of K2.* Seattle: The Mountaineers, 1980.

Account of the successful 1978 American K2 Expedition that included three women climbers: Cherie Bech, Dianne Roberts, and Dianna Jagersky. Bech and Roberts carried loads above 25,000 feet without using oxygen.

Scarr, Josephine. *Four Miles High.* London: Victor Gollancz, 1966.

Story of the Women's Kulu Expedition which made the first ascents of three 20,000-foot-plus peaks in India in 1961 and the Women's Jagdula Expedition to the Kanjiroba range of Nepal in 1962.

Schaffer, Mary T. S. *A Hunter of Peace: Old Indian Trails of the Canadian Rockies*. Banff: The White Foundation, 1980.

Exploration of the Canadian Rockies by a remarkable woman guide and pioneer.

Seghers II, Carroll. *The Peak Experience: Hiking and Climbing for Women*. Indianapolis and New York: The Bobbs-Merrill Co., 1979.

A rather misguided book by a man who shows little knowledge of either women or climbing.

Sharma, Man Mohan. *Of Gods and Glaciers on and Around Mt. Rataban*. New Delhi: Vision Books, 1979.

Story of the first Indian ascent of Mount Rataban in the Zanskar Range of Ladakh by an all-woman team.

Shipton, Diana. *The Antique Land*. London: Hodder and Stoughton, 1950.

Engrossing story of life in the Chinese province of Sinkiang by the wife of the noted British mountaineer Eric Shipton.

Shor, Jean Bowie. *After You, Marco Polo*. New York: McGraw-Hill Book Company, Inc., 1955.

Account of an adventurous attempt to retrace Marco Polo's route.

Smith, Janet Adam. *Mountain Holidays*. London: J. M. Dent and Sons, 1946.

A pleasant account of climbing holidays in the British Highlands and the Alps.

Sykes, Ella. *Through the Deserts and Oases of Central Asia*. London: Macmillan and Co., 1920.

Travel through Chinese Turkestan.

Thompson, Dorothy E. *Climbing with Joseph Georges*. London: Titus Wilson, 1962.

The author's climbs with the guide Joseph Georges from 1923 to 1933 in the Alps.

Ullyot, Joan. *Women's Running*. Mountain View, California: World Publications, 1976.

First and best of many current books on this subject.

Underhill, Miriam. *Give Me the Hills*. London: Methuen and Co., 1956.

Delightful autobiography of a leading American climber including the first "manless" ascents of the Matterhorn and the Grépon.

Visser-Hooft, Jenny. *Among the Kara-Korum Glaciers in 1925*. London: Edward Arnold and Co., 1926.

Explorations of the Himalaya from Ladakh to Hunza.

Williams, Cicely. *Women on the Rope: The Feminine Share in Mountain Adventure.* London: George Allen and Unwin, 1973.

A ladylike history of women's mountaineering.

Workman, Fanny Bullock, and William Hunter Workman. *In the Ice World of the Himalaya: Among the Peaks and Passes of Ladakh, Nubra, Suru, and Baltistan.* London: T. Fisher Unwin, 1900.

————. *Through Town and Jungle: Fourteen Thousand Miles A-Wheel Among the Temples and People of the Indian Plain.* London: T. Fisher Unwin, 1904.

————. *Ice-Bound Heights of the Mustagh: An Account of Two Seasons of Pioneer Exploration and High Climbing in the Baltistan Himalaya.* London: Constable and Co., 1908.

————. *Peaks and Glaciers of Nun Kun: A Record of Pioneer Exploration and Mountaineering in the Punjab Himalaya.* London: Constable and Co., 1909.

————. *The Call of the Snowy Hispar: A Narrative of Exploration and Mountaineering on the Northern Frontier of India.* London: Constable and Co., 1910.

————. *Two Summers in the Ice-Wilds of the Eastern Karakoram: The Exploration of Nineteen Hundred Square Miles of Mountains and Glaciers.* London: T. Fisher Unwin, 1917.

Classic accounts of exploration and mountaineering by this indefatigable Massachusetts couple.

Young, Eleanor Winthrop. *In Praise of Mountains, An Anthology for Friends.* London: F. Muller, 1948.

A study of mountains in literature.

Index